TO
EGYPT
WITH LOVE

MEMORIES OF A BYGONE WORLD

For my children, Ilana and Daniel,
and grandson Theo, with love

To my husband Mike and sister Nicole,
who listened and encouraged me

In memory of my parents, Jacques and
Linda, and my sister Claudine

Contents

TO
EGYPT
WITH LOVE

MEMORIES OF A BYGONE WORLD

Introduction

When Covid-19 happened suddenly and unexpectedly, life as we knew it stopped virtually overnight. We were forced to go into total lockdown for 12 weeks from March 23rd 2020 and each one of us had to find ways to cope and manage the isolation. Until then, I had enjoyed a very active life, volunteering for charities dedicated to helping refugees and asylum seekers, picking up my grandson from school, and baking as often as I could. I knew that the pandemic would change my social life and, in all probability, because of my age and vulnerability, I would not be able to carry on with what I had enjoyed doing, not for a while at least.

The weather was exceptionally good during the initial three months of lockdown and this made things easier. I was able to exercise every day and we even managed to have three short breaks in the UK. However, with autumn fast approaching, it became clear that the virus was still out there and showing no sign of disappearing. Most of us had known this all along, although we had been reluctant to acknowledge it. We were facing the prospect of more waves of the pandemic and frequent lockdowns, this time without the morale boost of warm days and the anticipation of summer. The thought was daunting and it slowly dawned on me that I would have to find something to replace my previous active life. One of the consequences of this pandemic was that I also became more aware of my own mortality and increasingly felt the need to leave something behind for my children and grandson.

I decided to write some of my story, so that my heritage, along with that of many Egyptian Jews, is not forgotten. We had a unique culture, but I fear that with the passage of time and new generations, this will disappear. Every individual story written about our lost world is important and will hopefully provide an insight into our rich, unique and diverse customs and traditions. As people die and memories fade, it will become much harder to learn about our community. Perhaps one day my children, like me, will want to know about their roots and some of their family history, and I hope that this short account of part of my life helps and leaves a small legacy for the next generation.

Writing about growing up in Cairo has been a healing process. My experience may be slightly different from other Jews living in Egypt at the time, depending on their social status and the circumstances in which they left, or were forced to leave. Nevertheless, throughout all our stories and memories, there is a shared common thread – the acknowledgment that, while it lasted, life in Egypt was good, as well as the sense of loss and trauma at being uprooted.

Each story reflects a profound love and nostalgia for what we have lost, while at the same time accepting, albeit with a sense of pain and bewilderment, that a country we had thought of as our own no longer wanted us. This did not happen overnight, but in stages – first complacency, ignorance and disbelief, eventually followed by fear and, in some cases, terror. My story is not unique. It is the story of all the Jewish migrants who had to leave the land of their birth and learn to make a new life in another country. In the case of my parents and others of their generation, it is a story of resilience and survival.

There is an old prophecy in Chapter 15 of the Book of Genesis, where the Lord tells the Patriarch Abraham precisely what is going to happen to his offspring in Egypt – 'your offspring shall be a stranger in a land that is not theirs and shall serve the people there who will afflict them for four hundred years … and afterwards they will leave'. The very same set of events that happened three thousand years ago was repeated in the twentieth century, when once again the Jews were forced out of Egypt.

I would like to quote a passage from a book by Avraham Bar-Av (Bentata), called 17 Sheikh Hamza Street, Cairo. It offers an interesting interpretation – and a sense of inevitability – as to why the Jews were eventually forced to leave Egypt:

'We lived our lives in Egypt like a grafted limb. We were never part of the amazing entity called Egypt. We were members of a rootless elite that managed to bloom in the fissure between a rotting, corrupt regime and the dying British Empire. We ignored the domestic and regional changes that spelled the end of our days in Egypt. It looks as if we had built our cosy little homes on the back of a dormant crocodile. The moment it started to show signs of waking up, the walls of our existence in Egypt began to crack. The more the national aspirations intensified, both our own and those of Egypt, the more the repelling forces became brutal and unbridgeable until the final expulsion'.

Whilst the author makes a valid point, I do not entirely agree with it. There is no doubt that the Jews also contributed greatly to the development of modern Egypt and left behind an important legacy. Jews have always adapted wherever they have ended up living and, in many instances, have flourished. They did this partly out of gratitude for the country that had welcomed them, but also to improve their lives and that of their community. This was certainly the case with the Jews of Egypt. On the whole, and at least until 1948, they got on well with their Arab neighbours and enabled the country to prosper.

However, in most cases, they lived on the fringe of the real Egyptian society, happy to remain within the confines of their own immediate circle. My parents, their families and friends certainly never made the effort to socialise with Egyptian people, even with the wealthier middle class ones. I don't think the possibility ever occurred to them. Theirs was a narrow-minded way of life, where work, family and socialising were important, but there was little else beyond that. Whilst I wish they had made the effort to look beyond their own community, I accept that I am looking at things with the eyes of a 21st century Western European, where the thought of anything that resembles colonialism is uncomfortable.

I was nearly 14 when we left Egypt and the more I remember about my childhood, the more I realise I had been kept in a bubble. I had taken everything I had for granted and hadn't given it any thought. Yet, whilst I had been enjoying the privileges of what had amounted to a colonial style upbringing, the real Egyptians, the ones to whom Egypt belonged, were not having such an easy time. Like any third world country, there was poverty and the economy relied heavily on the Europeans and their expertise. Avraham Bar-Av is in a way correct: the Egyptian revolution of 1952 was inevitable and a natural development waiting to happen; but this does not make it less painful to accept.

Jewish tradition is built on a foundation of memory, zakar or zakhor. Judaism invokes the faithful to carry in their hearts the commandment to remember, thus ensuring continuity throughout the ages. During the Passover Seder, in remembering and recounting the exodus from Egypt, Jews see themselves as the people who have come forth from Egypt, out of Egypt, to freedom. Though we were not enslaved, our Jewish community was once upon a time an integral part of Egypt's story. Sadly, 1956 saw the end of 2600 years of Jewish life in Egypt.

Like most children, I had no interest whatsoever in my family history when I was growing up and I didn't ask any questions when I had the opportunity. It's too late now, as the people who had the answers are no longer here and I am left trying hard to put the little I know into something coherent. I have read most of the books that Egyptian Jews have written about their family and what they remember of their life growing up in Egypt. They have been able to put family trees together and could only have done this with some assistance. Perhaps they were lucky enough to find documents or heard stories from their elders. For my part, I do not know enough to build a family tree which would go back a few generations, nor am I in contact with anyone who could help. Therefore, what I have managed to write about my family is relatively short and only covers my parents' generations. I have also had to rely on memories and conjectures.

Some family history

My mother's family – The Gubbays

My maternal grandparents were born and lived in Aleppo. The name derives from the Arabic word *haleb*, meaning milk. It is an old belief that when the patriarch Abraham wandered into Syria, he fed the poor with milk that he had taken from his sheep near Aleppo. I have found a document stating that my grandfather, Mourad Gubbay, was born in approximately in 1875. My grandmother's name was Mazal, which means lucky. Unfortunately, she did not live up to her name and had a hard life.

I do not know whether my grandparents were wealthy or poor. In Abraham Levy's book The Sephardim, there is a photograph of a gentleman called Ezra Ruben Gubbay. He was born in 1845 so was older than my grandfather. He is described as 'a merchant of British nationality, whose family had originated from Baghdad and come to Aleppo via Calcutta in British India'. It's quite possible that he was related.

My grandfather's family also originated from Calcutta and held a British passport, which they had probably acquired in recognition of services rendered. The Jews from India were able to rely on the consuls of their country of origin for protection and some 'native' ones had also managed to acquire a foreign nationality, one way or another. It must have meant that, at the very least, they would have enjoyed the status of foreign subjects and been free from the whims of the local Turkish governors (Aleppo had become part of the Ottoman Empire in 1516).

In The Book of Jewish Food, Claudia Roden describes what life was like in the 1900s. Until 1905, they all lived within the old city walls in the Jewish quarter, close to their synagogue. They were observant, answered to their Hakham (Rabbi) and got on well with the Muslim population, who treated them with respect. They wore Arab clothes and European ones only for special occasions. They all spoke Arabic – in fact, that was the only language my grandmother spoke and she could not read or write.

The rabbis did not allow girls to have an education. They learnt all they needed to know about housekeeping from their mothers and got married at an early age. Extended families lived together in the same house, which was built around an inner courtyard. Women were married by arrangement, sometimes as young as 13 and often to men who were much older. The same custom exists with Muslim families all over the Middle East.

In those days, marriages were a negotiation and often a way to tighten the tribal knot and keep resources within the family. They were arranged according to circumstance and not compatibility, and they always lasted. Husbands and wives knew their roles and duties, and did not expect any of the other stuff which would make them seek the help of a therapist. The man was the breadwinner, and the woman took care of the home and the children. The only problem, and a big one, was that the husband often died young, leaving behind a widow. This is what happened to my grandparents.

Aleppo was once a great city and one of the key centres along the legendary Silk Road. A main caravan route linked it to Baghdad and Basra and goods from the East passed through its markets, on their way to the Mediterranean coast and Europe. Many businesses thrived. They specialised in importing and exporting goods from the Far East, such as spices, dried fruits and silk, which were highly prized at the time. The community included poor people as well as prosperous bankers, merchants and shopkeepers. I have tried to imagine where my grandparents fitted in and have concluded that they were not well off, although I understand that another branch of the family was.

The social centre for the women and young unmarried girls was the *hamam* (*b*ath house) where they met on a Friday afternoon, after they had finished their preparations for the Shabbat. They gossiped and showed off their fine clothes, whilst having a bath and a massage. It was also there that mothers selected suitable brides for their sons. Before her wedding, it was traditional for the bride to go to a *mikve* – the Jewish ritual bath. She was accompanied for good luck by a woman from the community who had borne many healthy children. There were also her mother and sisters, the groom's mother, an elderly aunt and other friends. After she had submerged herself three times and said the ritual blessings, she came out and food was served.

The formal visiting of older relatives by various members of their respective families on the afternoons of Jewish holidays was an important custom in Jewish Aleppo. It is a custom which survived in Egypt and later in the various countries of the Diaspora when the Jews were forced to leave. The visit could only be terminated after the sipping of a cup of Turkish coffee served by the host. In Egypt, it was the opposite – this, along with various pastries, was the first thing that was served to guests.

Sephardic Jews are often subdivided into Sephardim, from Spain and Portugal, and Mizrahim, from North Africa and the Middle East. The word *mizrahi* comes from the Hebrew word for eastern and there is much overlap between the two. When the Jews were expelled from Spain in 1492, many of them were absorbed into existing communities in Northern Africa and the Middle East. Strictly speaking, my mother's family were Mizrahim, but there are no clear-cut lines. My uncle Leon's surname was Mizrahi, yet he was from pure Spanish descent.

The importance of Aleppo diminished greatly with the opening of the Suez Canal in 1869, when it ceased to be the centre of the camel-caravan trade. The Suez Canal shortened the distance between Europe and the Far East, and the Silk Road lost its importance. All the commerce built around it went into complete decadence and many Jewish families became destitute.

The brainchild of Ferdinand de Lesseps, the Suez Canal took 15 years to build and was considered one of the engineering achievements of the century. It opened a

direct passage between the Mediterranean and the Indian
Ocean, and created a vital link between the Western World
and the riches of the Far East and India. The Khedive of
Egypt commissioned Verdi to write an opera to mark the
inauguration of the canal. Verdi produced the magnificent
opera Aida, but unfortunately it ran late, and the opening
night failed to coincide with the inauguration.

The new economic opportunities Egypt offered may
be one of the reasons why my grandparents decided to leave
Aleppo and settle there. It was seen as the new Eldorado and
Aleppian Jews had already begun to search for alternative
ways to conduct commerce. Many of them knew about
the opportunities in some destinations because of earlier
commercial ties and, in other cases, they were drawn to
localities by assessing the inherent trade potential.

My grandparents arrived in Cairo in 1910. Like all
the Jews of Aleppo, they were determined to remain loyal
to their roots and keep their *haleb* culture, which they
considered superior to the local one. They preserved their
original customs and their food, fragrant with pistachios,
almonds, apricots and rose water. There are still places where
this tradition has survived almost undiluted.

When they arrived in Egypt, my grandparents had
one child, my uncle Mayer who was three years old at the
time. They went on to have another four children in a short
period of eight years – Victor, Marie, Linda (my mother)
and Clement. Sadly, my grandfather died suddenly of a
heart attack very soon after Clement was born, leaving my
grandmother a widow with a boy of 11 and four children
under 10. My uncle Mayer had to leave school and go to

11

work to provide for the family. The little money he earned would not have been enough and life must have been hard. I can only guess how they managed. There was a free school for the Jewish community in Cairo called the Jewish Alliance school and this may be the school my mother and her siblings attended.

A few months ago, I came across a benevolent society called The Drop of Milk, still operating in Cairo. I remembered that for all the festivals my father went to the main synagogue called Ismailia (it is still there on Adly Street) whilst my mother and her sister went to a small one round the corner. It was situated in a basement and opened once a year for the High Holy Days. Its name was *La Goutte de Lait*, which is the French for The Drop of Milk. There had also been a school called *École de La Goutte de Lait* and, alternatively, this may have been the school my mother and her siblings attended.

In the absence of a government welfare system, the Jews of Egypt tended to take care of their own, with a large network of charitable organisations. These were set up to look after the orphans, the widows, the elderly, those who were destitute and the insane. There was even a pot of money for young girls who wished to marry, but their families couldn't t afford to give them a dowry. In the Jewish community, it was important for the bride-to-be to provide one.

The Drop of Milk was originally established in 1921 as a charitable NGO tasked with supporting the Jewish community's needy and disadvantaged. If this benevolent society had helped the family, my mother may have continued to attend their synagogue out of loyalty or habit. The organisation was recently revived in 2014 with the aim of preserving the country's Jewish heritage, as the community dwindles. It organises cultural events and distributes information, thereby seeking to make the public aware of a now obscure part of Egypt's legacy. It has been surprisingly successful and has been equally accepted by the very small Jewish community and Egyptian society as a whole. Thanks to its efforts, the main synagogue in Cairo, Shar Hashamayim (which was originally called the Ismailieh Temple), is now regularly open for prayer services and tours.

Impoverished young women were taught embroidery skills in Jewish schools. Bridal trousseaux, beautifully handmade table and bed linens and lingerie were regularly purchased from them. This may have been the way my mother and my aunt were able to supplement the family income. Whatever happened, the family managed to attend school and receive a good education. They spoke French amongst themselves and Arabic with my grandmother. Two of my great aunts, called Bahia and Emilie, lived in the same building and visited my grandmother daily. Bahia was a widow and had two sons; one of them, called André, was extremely good looking and had all the girls chasing after him. He had no airs and graces, despite his good looks and, at the sporting club we all frequented, I felt proud to be related to him.

Although I visited my grandmother's house almost daily, I remember very little about her. She was always in her bedroom and from time to time wandered off into the street, so she may have had early dementia. She was a heavy smoker and the smell of tobacco when you went into her room was strong. We called her *nonna* and my sister Nicole remembers that she used to ask her to climb into her bed. Her hair was white and always neatly pinned up. She lived with my aunt Marie and uncle Clement, who was still a bachelor. She always referred to her native city by its Arabic name of *Haleb*. In a strange way, although she did not participate in the day-to-day running of the house, she was very much the centre of it. She had been a wonderful cook and had taught my mother and aunt everything she knew. Egyptian Jews had a profound respect for their parents and were devoted to them, and my mother's family was no exception. Looking back, I wish I had got to know her better, as she was the only living grandparent I had.

Mayer was the oldest and the patriarch of the family. We respected him and were a little scared of him as he could take umbrage quite quickly – at least that is what my mother said. He married Iris and had two daughters, Doris and Monique. He died of a heart attack at the age of 82. Doris lives in London and Monique in Manchester.

Victor married into a 'good' family'. He and his wife Nina did not have any children. They are the uncle and aunt I remember most fondly. They were absolutely wonderful to me when I lived with my parents for two and a half years with two children under five. Things were difficult at times, and Victor and Nina were very kind. They invited me to tea with the children every Sunday afternoon and the time spent with them and their warm hospitality helped enormously. Victor was diagnosed with cancer but died of a heart attack while in hospital. Nina was totally dependent on him, but managed to carry on with much dignity. Sadly, she was brutally killed in a hit and run accident while crossing the road.

Marie was two years older than my mother and they were always very close. I was very attached to her when we lived in Cairo and I spent a lot of time in her house. She married someone called Isaac Hamaui. He was a gentle, mild mannered man who would not say boo to a goose. We called him Zaki. I can't remember what his job was, but he owned some land somewhere outside Cairo. The system at the time was for landowners to rent their land to peasants, who would work it and give the owner a portion of the profits. I don't think my uncle made much money from this.

My aunt fell pregnant soon after she got married but the baby was stillborn. She had to wait another 10 years to have another child and then had two children within a year of each other, Rony and Danièle, who both live in Milan. Rony was born by Caesarean section and when my aunt fell pregnant again within three months, the doctors advised her to have a termination. There were a lot of family discussions but in the end she decided to carry on. Fortunately, everything went well with the birth.

Clement was the youngest and seemed to have quite a liberal lifestyle. He used to travel abroad a lot, went to the races and nightclubs, and I believe had many affairs. He adored my grandmother and could not do enough for her. He was also very close to Marie. He was married twice, the first time to someone called Huguette. The marriage lasted less than a week, as it transpired that the young lady had only married my uncle hoping to make the man she actually loved jealous – which actually worked. A few years later Clement married Rita and they had two children, Dalia and Marc, who both live in Milan. Clement followed the same fate as his father and two brothers, and also died of a heart attack. He was only in his 50s.

The Aleppo culture had a strong influence on my mother and her siblings. It was a secretive one, where you never discussed your private life with anyone outside the family and tragedies or unpleasant events were not talked about. I used to think it was indifference, but now I understand it was the way a certain community behaved; if my mother appeared reserved and unemotional, it was probably as a result of her culture and upbringing. Money was very important, because Aleppian Jews were materialistic and wealth mattered.

My father's family – The Chouchans

My father's family originates from Toledo and are therefore the true Sephardim (Sepharad means Spain in Hebrew). They belong to a slowly disappearing culture and were expelled from their ancestral home in 1492 during the time of the infamous Inquisition, when an edict from Isabella of Castile and her husband Ferdinand of Aragon decreed that all Jews must leave, unless they agreed to convert to Christianity.

It must have been traumatic for the Jews to be forced to leave. They had considered themselves loyal Spaniards and were devastated by the Edict of Expulsion. Many had come to prominence as scholars, doctors and mathematicians, and had served as highly respected advisers or ministers to rulers, Muslim or Christian. Suddenly, they were reduced to the status of poor refugees, fleeing in fear of their lives and leaving behind their beloved country.

It is said that, when the Jews left Spain, they took with them the key to their house, perhaps in the hope that they would be allowed to return one day. This was passed on from generation to generation, usually on the eve of the marriage of the oldest child. There is a beautiful Ladino song called *Adio Querida,* which means Farewell my beloved. There are many interpretations, but my favourite one is that the beloved in question is Spain and the song is about the pain they felt when they left. History tends to repeat itself. The German Jews must have felt the same devastation when, after being such an integral part of their country's success, they began to be persecuted when the Nazis came to power. The Jews of all the Arab lands went through the same trauma.

My ancestors, like many others, travelled through the Mediterranean and eventually settled in Constantinople in the Ottoman Empire. They were welcomed by Sultan Bayazid II, who declared that Spain's loss of its Jews would be his own gain. In the 16th century, Constantinople (now Istanbul) became one of the leading Jewish centres of the world. Although my father told me that my grandparents had lived there, he sometimes spoke of Smyrna (now called Izmir) so there must be some family connection. I also heard the name Salonika mentioned – a port on the Aegean sea – and my father spoke some Greek, so I wonder whether some members had settled there.

In the Ottoman Empire, religious minorities were allowed to practise their religion and were offered a degree of protection under the system of *millet*, which had been developed to implement the status of non-Muslims under Islamic law. Christians and Jews were regarded as *dhimmis* and were viewed as second class citizens. They were to be kept separate and unequal, but at the same time protected. In return, they were required to pay a tax and pledge their allegiance to the Ottoman ruler. In this way, they were able to retain control over all their internal disputes and agreements, such as marriage, divorce and inheritance. After being the subject of persecutions in Spain and Portugal, they welcomed this protective system, as it allowed them to live in peace and govern themselves under Jewish law.

Although the Jews adapted to some Turkish customs, they remained Spaniards at heart and were nostalgic for the country of their forefathers, which they considered their true home. They kept the foods, customs and songs and continued to speak Spanish as it had been spoken in the fifteenth century, before the Castilian pronunciation came to the fore. They wrote in Spanish and Hebrew characters, and added some words from the places where they had subsequently lived. Their language became known as Ladino. Many of their songs were about their past which had been lost, others were about happier occasions. My father's family were proud of their heritage, as I am.

In my grandparents' days, there were 60,000 Jews and as many as 40 synagogues in Istanbul. They played an important part in Istanbul's economic and cultural life and practised all kinds of professions, from doctors and bankers to street vendors, jewellers and printers. Some wealthier families lived in the affluent parts of the city, but most knew only insalubrious and overcrowded quarters. They were very observant and celebrated Shabbat and all the festivals. I suspect my grandparents were not very wealthy and lived in the poorer area of the city, though of course I can't be sure.

As with the Jews of Aleppo, the gradual collapse of the Ottoman Empire left them struggling financially, and many chose to leave and seek their fortune somewhere else. My grandparents left Constantinople for Egypt around 1908. They had one son, David, who must have been in his early teens. My father, Jacques Albert, was born in Cairo in 1910. A girl called Marie followed shortly after.

My grandmother died and my grandfather Abraham married a lady called Berta, who was also from Constantinople. They had five children together, four girls and one boy – Sophie, Suzanne, Esther, Salomon and Mathilde, all very close in age apart from Mathilde, who was always considered the baby of the family. Berta treated the children from the first marriage as her own and my father loved her. They were by all accounts a very united family, apart from David, as there seem to be a rift there.

My father's family spoke Ladino amongst themselves, especially when they did not want the children to understand what they were saying. They would converse in French for a while, then eventually slip into Ladino. There are many aphorisms, sayings and proverbs in Ladino which they often quoted. A favourite one was '*kada kola en su luge y todo se topará*' which means, 'everything in its place and everything will be found'. At home, I remember that if something got lost or misplaced, you tied a knot in a handkerchief, in the firm belief that by dint of this simple expedient, the missing object would be found. Funnily enough, more often than not, it was.

Ladino is a mixture of medieval Spanish, Hebrew and French words with Spanish endings. It was widely spoken in families originating from Spain, but unfortunately, because only a handful of people know it nowadays, it is a dying language. My generation is the last to have lived amongst people who spoke Ladino as their mother tongue and whose lives were shaped by the Judeo Spanish culture. It makes me sad that their language and characteristics are coming to the end of their historical lives; the new generation is not interested and yet my family, along with the many Jews originating from Spain, has ancestors going back 500 years or more. They were part of a thriving and powerful Sephardic civilisation which spanned the Ottoman Empire, stretched to Europe and the New World, and produced writers, poets, dramatists, intellectuals and great sages.

Until recently, little attention has been paid to the Jews of Spanish origin, yet their civilisation is a treasure for the entire Jewish people. It's good to know that lately there has been a resurgence of interest in Ladino folk songs. There are chat rooms on the internet and more scholarly attention is being given to the literature of the Sephardim of the Ottoman Empire. I taught myself Ladino a while ago, for no other reason than my love for the language of my ancestors. I was fairly successful, as my knowledge of French and Spanish helped a great deal. Unfortunately, there was no one left I could speak or practise with, so I soon forgot what I had learnt.

My father had a cousin called Esther who left for Israel with her mother in 1948. She often came to stay with us when we moved to London and knew a lot about my father's family, having done a lot of research. Some of her knowledge was factual and some anecdotal. Needless to say, it never occurred to me to ask questions or try to find out a little more and I am sure she would have filled some of the gaps. She was the other Esther of the family and, to distinguish her from my father's sister, who had the same name, she was known as 'Esther de la tante' – which translates as 'the aunt's Esther'!

My aunt Mathilde – we call her Matty – has told me a little about the family. Marie died from typhoid when she was 21. My grandfather worked in leather goods, but had to give up work when he fell ill; I think it was a mental illness, perhaps depression and a few family members have suffered from this. Money must have been tight, but my father had a good job and was able to support his family. I have vague memories of the block of flats where they lived, which was very modest and had no lift. I don't remember much about my grandfather. His name was Abraham, but we called him *papou,* and he died when I was young, about eight or nine. My father took us to say goodbye and all I can recollect is that he was lying on his bed, all dressed in white.

I don't know much about my uncle David, as he was never around and seemed to fall out with my father and the rest of the family regularly. He was much older anyway and his children were only a little younger than my aunts. He had four children, but I only remember the name of two, Moise and Sarah, who emigrated to Israel in 1948. David and his wife Louise joined them a few years later. The Jews of Spain like giving a Spanish flavour to their children's names, so Moise was called Moisico and Sarah was known as Sarika.

Although David was much older, it was my father who became the head of the family from a young age, even while my grandfather was still alive. Life must have been hard. They lived in a small apartment and had to share bedrooms. My grandfather was a very religious man and a student of the Torah. I don't think he was a good businessman and he never earned much money. When he became ill, my father had to support the family. He made sure that his brother and sisters continued to attend school and paid for their education, which may be the reason why his sisters remained devoted to him throughout their lives. He was very strict with them, as strict as he would be with me later, but his siblings respected him and accepted this, apart from Matty who, by all accounts, was a tearaway.

As a teenager, Matty had been the black sheep of the family, constantly clashing with my father and rebelling against him. They constantly clashed because they were both very stubborn and strong willed. She has told me a few stories about how she used to escape, even when she was locked in her room. She had found a job at the British Officers' club and mixed with them socially, something my father strongly disapproved of. She was only 16 at the time.

She married a Jewish man, but my father was not happy about her choice. They eventually fell out, or rather my father fell out with her. I don't know when this happened, but they never saw each other again and she moved to the US after leaving Egypt. My father never mentioned her and changed the subject when I asked him why. I always thought that something really dramatic must have happened, but it seems it hadn't; perhaps he had been too stubborn to try and build bridges.

Sophie married Leon whom she met at her place of work, John Dickinson & Co, a leading British stationery company. My father also worked there and had risen to the rank of Managing Director after starting at the bottom. Sophie and her husband were my favourite aunt and uncle when I got to know them well years later. They lived in a suburb of Paris and I used to visit them regularly. Sophie was a wonderful cook and pastry maker, and the kindest, most generous person I have met. She adored my father and then me by extension. Leon had a great and very dry sense of humour. They had one daughter, Esther, who lives in Paris.

Suzanne, Esther and Salomon all left Egypt for Israel in 1948, just after the establishment of the State. They were amongst the 20,000 Jews who left between 1948 and 1949. Some were inspired by the idea of a homeland, the poorer ones went seeking economic opportunities in Israel. The departure of my aunts and uncle left a huge gap, and my father's family was never the same.

Although he did not talk about them, my father must have missed his family. It was forbidden to communicate directly with the people who lived in Israel. The only way one could get news was through someone in Europe, and even then, the information had to be guarded and coded in order to avoid being accused of communicating with 'the enemy'. All the letters which came from abroad were first passed through a censor. In fact, we were not even supposed to say 'Israel' as we feared the servants would hear us and denounce us. So, when we wanted to refer to it, we would always say *chez nous* which means 'in our home'.

Suzanne married in Israel to Benjo and they had three sons, Fiko, Avram and David. Fiko lives on a kibbutz near the Gaza border with all his family. Avram and David both live in the suburbs of Tel Aviv. Esther had three daughters, Malka, Yaffe and Bettie. They all live in Haifa. By some strange coincidence, Salomon, who was Sophie's brother, married Gilda, who was her husband's Leon's sister. It's called keeping it in the family. They had two girls, Bettie and Carla. They live in Israel in Holon.

In contrast to my mother's family, where no one raised their voices, my father's was noisy and excitable. They sometimes quarrelled, but made up almost immediately. They were warm and generous, had a modest way of life and were happy with it. They did not socialise much and if they did, it was with other members of the family. I empathise with their idiosyncrasies, their warmth and their outlook on life, and I have a favourite phrase which I share with my cousin Esther, Sophie's daughter. She lives in Paris and we have long chats on the phone. When we refer to a certain member of the family we often say '*il /elle est typiquement Chouchan*' meaning he/she either looks or behaves like a Chouchan. I did not see my aunts Suzanne and Esther after they left Egypt for Israel, yet I recognise them instantly in a photo.

My mother's family did not have a typical look, but had a family resemblance. They were ambitious, pragmatic, I would say phlegmatic, and not given to shows of emotions. I didn't get hugs from my mother or Aunt Marie, just a peck on the cheek. They were very private and my mother never discussed anything personal with her friends, no matter how close they were. When asked, she always said that everything was fine. I am a mixture of both families – emotional, anxious and superstitious like my father, but not given to shows of affection, probably following in my mother's footsteps.

My mother was always polite and friendly with my father's family, but there was no real warmth between them or any close relationships. Years later, my aunt Sophie commented that she had always found my mother and her sister rather 'cold'. The two families may have been Jewish, born and brought up in Egypt, but they came from different cultures and so behaved accordingly. They were both shaped by their upbringing, when money was tight and were generally intent on improving their financial circumstances. They had very little interest in politics and only to the extent that it affected their lives. I can't remember anyone taking part in demonstrations or openly discussing politics.

Cairo

Cairo in World War II

My parents met in Groppi, the legendary tearoom and pastry shop in downtown Cairo. It was not an arranged meeting and they were introduced to each other casually by one of my uncles or by mutual friends. My mother was 25, which was considered old in those days. She was very attractive, tall and slim, and I believe my father was very taken by her and did all the chasing. She had no dowry, which was an important part of the marriage negotiations in Jewish families, but that did not bother him. After their wedding, my parents left for their honeymoon in Alexandria. However, my father got scared when, nearing Alexandria, they heard the sound of bombs, so he turned the car around and they went back to Cairo. It was the time of the First Battle of Alamein during WW2.

When my parents married on 28 June 1942, the war was ravaging Europe and the Nazis were at the height of their territorial expansion. However, British troops stationed in Egypt continued to behave as if they were on vacation. They had an enviable social life and there were plenty of opportunities for entertainment, with none of the shortages in the European continent. Two big hotels in Cairo, the Shepheard's and the Semiramis, were frequented by British soldiers. Their attitude was arrogant, especially towards the native population and they behaved like occupants.

The British had come to Egypt in hordes, attracted by the colonial lifestyles and easy pickings. They considered themselves as the upper crust of white masters and it is no wonder that the Egyptian population hated them. The British and other Europeans in Egypt continued to enjoy the good life, while Europe and other parts of the world fell in ruins. The Mena House hotel in Giza was another perfect place for information and rumours, for instance about Rommel conquering Libya and soon reaching El Alamein.

In the autumn of 1940, the half million strong population of Cairo had been increased by only a few thousand British and Empire troops; by the following spring, these numbered 35,000. The Cairo traffic, which included creaking wheelbarrows piled high with vegetables and the small Fiats and Austin Sevens of the European community, now had to share the streets with an ever-increasing number of staff cars, motorbikes and military trucks. In the large department stores like Cicurel, Chemla or Le Salon Vert, business carried on as usual, with lavish displays of glass, fabrics and cosmetics. Groppi, the most famous cafe in Cairo, was still serving magnificent pastries and, in the Shepheard's hotel, the stock of decent champagne did not run out until 1943. Even then, there was no shortage of Algerian, South African or Palestinian wine.

Rationing had been in force for nine months in

England, but the Greek groceries of Cairo were still packed with butter, sugar, eggs and paraffin. Many varieties of fruit, such as oranges and dates, were piled high into round baskets in the greengrocers, as were great mounds of vegetables produced in the warm soil of the Delta. The British officers newly arriving in Cairo were told not to mention the blitz in London, as the fear was that it would create a bad impression locally. The British occupation was not popular, and if it became known how weak Britain was, Egypt might show herself reluctant to provide the labour and facilities on which the British war machine in the Middle East was to depend.

On June 13, 1942, the army of Rommel was less than one hundred kilometres from Alexandria. The Germans had managed to establish a network of espionage in Egypt. They were helped by the Muslim Brotherhood and a group of Egyptian army officers, amongst them Gamal Abdel Nasser and Anwar Al Sadat, who both subsequently became leaders of the revolution which would overthrow the monarchy. Luckily, the British managed to dismantle the German network of espionage and arrested the spies.

In July 1942, their troops were pushed back to Alexandria, but in November Field Marshal Montgomery and his Eighth Army won the second battle of Alamein against Rommel. The danger to Egypt and the Jewish community had thankfully passed.

The Nazi ideology held great attraction for many, as did Italian fascism, probably because Germany was the only European power that was not considered as 'colonialist'. They felt kinship with the anti-Jewish propaganda articulated by the Nazis and many anti-semitic incidents took place in Cairo. There is no doubt that, if the Germans had succeeded at Alamein and entered Alexandria, the Jews would have been left to their fate.

One of the reasons why this pro-Nazi sentiment existed was that Egypt was under British control. The local population hated the British, so they applied the old adage 'the enemy of my enemy is my friend'. They thought they could rid themselves of the British should the Nazis win. Some Jews panicked and left – for the Sudan, the Belgian Congo, Rhodesia and South Africa. Others waited until the last minute before taking any action.

I dread to think what could have happened if the Germans had won. They would have quickly occupied the whole of Egypt and either killed the Jews or sent them to concentration camps. Many in the Jewish community were optimistic or barely realised the danger until Rommel was a few kilometres from Alexandria. They were also in total ignorance of what was happening to the Jews under Nazi rule, as no one knew about the Holocaust at the time. I have been told that my father was in Greece when WWII broke out and that he just managed to catch the last ship sailing to Alexandria. That does not surprise me – he was always late and insisted on leaving everything to the very last minute.

As a centre of international politics and administration, the great days of wartime Cairo came after Alamein. The Minister of State's office was the focus for all British diplomatic missions in the Near and Middle East and every nationality in occupied Europe had its national branch of the Red Cross and its military office in the city. Although the war's progress westwards eventually called for other headquarters, most notably the Allied Forces Headquarters in Algiers, GHQ Cairo retained its significance as a supply base, as well as the pivot for coordinating operations in the Middle East, the Mediterranean and North Africa.

In November 1943, Chiang Kai-shek, the leader of the Republic of China, Roosevelt and Churchill gathered in Egypt for the Cairo conference and agreed that Japan would be forced to give up China and surrender unconditionally. Operation Overlord, the invasion of Europe, had to be discussed. The Mena House Hotel in Giza, a few kilometres from Cairo, became the conference's headquarters and the venue of all the British and American chiefs of staff. The hotel was protected by 500 anti-aircraft weapons. An RAF observation post was even installed on top of the Great Pyramid of Cheops.

Compared to London or Paris, Cairo underwent little change during or after the war. The Anglo-Egyptian upper crust and the European community carried on as they always had and the British still sipped their gin slings on the terrace of the Shepheard's hotel. Some were in uniform, as the British continued to maintain a force of 80,000 in Egypt, largely in the Suez Canal zone. However, the majority were in linen suits, with the women in straw hats and cotton frocks. There was still polo and racing at the Gezira Club, and dancing at the Auberge des Pyramides. It was not until Saturday, 26 January 1952, that Cairo went through one of the most extraordinary upheavals in its long history. The city that the British had known and loved virtually vanished overnight – this pivotal event will be explained in more detail later.

The birth of modern Egypt

Egypt was still an Ottoman province when Napoleon landed in Alexandria in 1798. By then, it had dwindled into a provincial backwater of the Ottoman Empire. The Egyptians had known taxation and oppression, droughts and plagues without end. The magnificent medieval city of Cairo was falling to pieces and all that remained from her former glory was the University of el Azhar, the oldest and most respected centre of Islamic study.

Napoleon brought with him the ideas embodied in the French revolution – Liberty, Equality and Fraternity. This was a shock to the Ottomans because it underlined the extent to which Europe had advanced, whereas it had languished and declined. Muhammad Ali, an Albanian commander in the Ottoman army, was sent to Egypt to fight the French. He succeeded and was in turn rewarded by the Sultan, who appointed him Viceroy of Egypt. The history of Egypt under the Muhammad Ali dynasty (1805 - 1953) spans the later period of Ottoman Egypt, the Khedivate of Egypt under British patronage and the nominally independent Sultanate of Egypt and Kingdom of Egypt, ending with the Revolution of 1952 and the formation of the Republic.

Although he lacked a formal education, Muhammad Ali was a man of great ability and vision, who wanted to bring Egypt back to its past glory. He encouraged foreign entrepreneurs to come and assist in developing the country, which thus became a beacon of hope for those who wanted to escape oppressive regimes or countries in decline. In the years following the departure of the French in 1801, the Egyptians found a leader in Muhammad Ali. He opened Egypt to the world, pulling it out of centuries of stagnation. He brought in engineers and scientists to modernise the country.

Europeans started to arrive, not only British and French, but also Italian, Greek and Maltese. They worked as merchants, dealers, teachers, doctors, lawyers and financial and technical consultants. Under an Ottoman system known as Capitulations, they paid no taxes and could only be tried in their own courts, which put them beyond the reach of Egyptian law.

Muhammad Ali and his successors were responsible for turning Cairo into a European-style city with wide boulevards and public squares, parks and gardens. Two vast squares were built in the new city – Soliman Pasha Square, which was the centre of the residential area and Ismailia Square, the centre of the business area. In the late 1880s, more squares were added to reflect the European-ness of the city.

In the early 1900s, two upper class neighbourhoods were built – Maadi and Zamalek on the island of Gezira, where the wealthy could escape the crowded city. Maadi was paralleled by the waterfront promenade known as the Nile Corniche. At that time, it was a small residential village on the banks of the Nile, about 15 kilometres south of Cairo. It has now changed beyond recognition and has become part of the giant metropolis that is Cairo. The gardens and villas have been replaced by high rise buildings and apartment blocks.

Heliopolis, meaning City of the Sun in Greek, was the first satellite city to be built around Cairo. This was in the desert, six miles to the northeast of the city and connected to Cairo by tram. Back then, it was very picturesque as it combined the most diverse architectural styles. It was advertised as having *ni poussière, ni moustiques* – no dust or mosquitoes. Most of the wealthy people from Cairo moved there to create a beautiful suburb, with luscious parks, charming villas, grandiose apartments and hotels in a unique architectural style, a mixture of Byzantium and Egyptian. Heliopolis smelled of jasmine, because of all the jasmine plants in the villas along the streets. My father's sister, Aunt Sophie, lived in Heliopolis for a short while after her marriage. We often used to visit her and I remember the wide avenues and trams.

Ferdinand de Lesseps was a French diplomat and administrator who was responsible for the construction of the Suez Canal. De Lesseps had been inspired by reading about Napoleon's abandoned plans for a canal that would allow large ships wishing to sail to the east to go directly from the Mediterranean to the Red Sea, thus cutting out the long sea journey around Africa. The first work on the Suez Canal started in 1859 under Muhammad Ali's son, Mohamed Said. Construction began at the most Northern part of the Canal in Port Said.

The excavation took 10 years and an estimated 1.5 million people worked on the project. Unfortunately, in spite of the objections of many British, French and American investors in the project, many of these were poor labourers and it is believed that tens of thousands died while working on the Canal, from cholera and other causes. Political turmoil in the region negatively impacted the construction of the canal. Egypt was ruled by Britain and France at the time and there were several rebellions against colonial rule. An Egyptian, looking at his country in the late nineteenth century did not have to be a passionate nationalist to reach the conclusion that it was being run by, and for, foreigners.

Muhammad Ali's grandson, the Khedive Ismail – also known as Ismail the Magnificent – carried on his work. Wide boulevards and streets were laid out on his orders, along the lines of the Paris of Baron Haussmann and the architecture of many buildings was reminiscent of the French capital in the 1870s. Under him, Egypt increased its production of cotton, which fetched very high prices because of its excellent quality. As a consequence of the American Civil War, it became the biggest exporter of cotton. Rice was the second most important agricultural export and the third was onions.

There were three distinct classes of people in Egypt: the very wealthy upper class, which included Muslim landowners, Europeans, Armenians and Jewish merchants and traders; the middle class, composed of all Europeans, almost no Muslims, who worked in offices, stores and schools; and the lower class, made up of the Egyptian fellahin (the uneducated peasants), the servants and the street vendors.

By the time I was born, my family fitted in somewhere in the middle class. My father and maternal uncles all had good positions and earned a good salary, especially by Egyptian standards. Rents were cheap and food plentiful.

The Jewish community ranged from the extremely wealthy at the top to the much poorer ones, who sometimes found it difficult to make ends meet. We had a good standard of living – this assumption is supported by the fact that my parents went out almost every night to the best restaurants and night clubs Cairo had to offer; they were members of a sports club, and my sisters and I went to a private school. Of course, we were not sent to boarding schools abroad, like the children of the rich families, nor did we go to Europe for our summer holidays. The reason for the latter may not have necessarily been financial, as my father was terrified of flying and my mother would have had no interest in visiting any city in Europe, even Paris. She preferred holidays by the seaside in Egypt, where she could be with her family and friends.

Egypt was a melting pot of cultures and communities, and it's difficult to determine why they had ended up there. Descendants of the Jews from the Iberian Peninsula had come to Egypt in the sixteenth century and again in the nineteenth. They came from Salonika, Smyrna, Istanbul, the Balkans and North Africa. Immigrants from the Yemen and North Africa had started to come as far back as the Middle Ages.

This original community, which had been in Egypt for many generations, was joined by several waves of immigrants. Some historical facts may give an indication as to why this happened. There was a large Armenian community, and they may have sought refuge in Egypt after the Armenian genocide of 1895 in Turkey and again in 1915. The Greeks may have migrated to Egypt for economic reasons and to escape the poverty in their country. Many of them opened groceries or worked in the catering industry. The French had originally been attracted to Egypt by the then viceroy of Egypt, Muhammad Ali, who had promised them high salaries and many special favours. They contributed greatly to the modernisation of the country, were responsible for a new era of progress and civilisation, and had a huge cultural influence.

Egypt was a British Protectorate for more than 75 years and its presence was everywhere. WWII had affected Cairo by making it more cosmopolitan than ever. As the headquarters for the Allied Forces in North Africa, the city had been bursting with soldiers from dozens of nations, as well as European refugees and countless spies. Although I was very young at the time, I remember the British officers walking along the streets in their khaki Bermuda shorts. They were not used to the sun or the heat, so their faces were always red. Their preferred haunts in Cairo, apart from all the night spots, were the bars of the Shepheard's hotel and the Nile Hilton.

The opening of the Suez Canal attracted more economic migrants to Egypt – from Malta, Portugal, Spain, Belgium, Russia, Poland and many more. Some of them initially came to make money and return to their country, others stayed. What was fascinating about Egypt was that, whilst bringing their own culture, traditions and cuisine, all the communities lived peacefully side by side and respected each other. Cairo thus became a cluster of different communities – Muslims, Cops, Jews, Syro-Lebanese Christians, as well as French, Maltese, Cypriot and Greek expatriates. They all did business together over endless cups of Turkish coffee and glasses of syrupy tea. Life in Egypt was far better than in Europe – taxes were minimal, food was plentiful and cheap, and most households had more than one servant.

French came to Egypt by the sword in 1798, when Napoleon Bonaparte's army landed after its voyage across the Mediterranean. For the better part of two centuries, Egypt was a privileged land for the French language, despite only remaining under French control for a few years and being placed under English domination for more than 60 years. It even reached the statute of being the co-official language with Arabic. Until as recently as the presidency of Anwar Sadat, it was a marker of prestige and a common tongue among much of the Egyptian literary and political elite. In 1937 in Cairo, among a total of 65 foreign publications, five were published in English and 45 in French.

Furthermore, French was expanded in Egypt through education, with the establishment of Catholic missionary schools and the operations of the Paris based Alliance Israélite Universelle. In 1860, it embarked on a Jewish *mission civilisatrice* to uplift and modernise the Jews of the Middle East by imbuing them with French education and culture. The opposition to British imperial policy in Egypt throughout the nineteenth century allowed many Egyptians, not only Jews, to embrace French culture as an acceptable form of European modernity. By the late nineteenth century, French was the lingua franca of the entire business community. Knowledge of a European language was a requirement for a white-collar job in the private sector.

France's support for missionary activities resulted in the increased use of the language in Egypt. Eventually, the curriculum of French religious schools changed, pushing religion to one side and making exceptions to allow in Jews and Orthodox Christians. These religious schools had an excellent reputation and many Jewish families chose to send their children there.

Most Europeans were educated at the French, Italian and American mission schools, of which there were several. This was one area where the British lagged far behind. Apart from the Victoria College in Alexandria (known as the VC) and the Gezira Preparatory school in Cairo, the British had neglected education in Egypt. It was a policy started by Lord Cromer, who disapproved of education on the grounds that a little learning was a dangerous thing.

The Egyptian middle classes were closer in spirit to provincial France than to the tale of One Thousand and One Nights, and generally believed that a veneer of French culture was necessary for anyone aspiring to refinement. They favoured a foreign education and it was not unusual for Muslims to send their sons to the Catholic mission schools. The most gifted then went to the American University in Cairo or Fuad I University on the Giza side of the Nile. From there, the brightest ones followed their fathers into the business or became teachers, lawyers and government officials. However, the plum jobs still tended to go to the Europeans, thus encouraging many students to turn to politics, where they could vent their frustrations in nationalistic and anti-British demonstrations.

One observer of Cairene society once described the

wealthy upper class as *'la haute Juiverie, la haute Musulmanie et la haute Copterie du Caire'*. These people had French governesses and English nannies for their children. Their sons went on to Oxford or Cambridge and their daughters to finishing school in Switzerland. Children of the haute bourgeoisie, Muslims, Christians and Jews, were often educated in boarding schools in France or Switzerland. A few Anglophile elite families sent their sons to England or to Victoria College in Alexandria and it was not uncommon for the boys of very prominent Muslim families to be educated in such schools. Children of the Jewish lower middle class generally went to the schools of the Jewish community, where the language of instruction was French, but Hebrew and other Jewish subjects were part of the curriculum.

For the wealthy Jewish upper middle classes, time was divided between their villas in Alexandria and Cairo and the hottest months spent abroad, in Geneva or Paris. They spoke very little Arabic and only to communicate with the servants. Jean Naggar in her book, Sipping from the Nile, evokes her very privileged childhood and fairytale existence in a halcyon time in Egypt, before her family's expulsion in 1956 as a result of the Suez crisis.

Each community had its own clubs, theatres and cultural societies, but they also learnt from each other, thus making Egypt a true melting pot. All religions were respected, and in every town and city there were numerous mosques, churches and synagogues. Each religion had many sects. The Christians had Catholics, Protestants, Coptic, Anglican and Orthodox. There were Sunni and Shiite Muslims and the Jews had the Sephardi, Ashkenazi and Karaite. All these communities managed to exist peacefully side by side and respected each other's religion and celebrations.

A brief description of Cairo

In her book, Cairo in the War, Artemis Cooper gives an excellent description of the city in the 1940s. The social, commercial and political life took place within a mile radius of Midan Ismail Pasha (now Tahrir Square). The commercial centre of the town lay between Midan Ismail Pasha and the Ezbekieh Gardens – an area of broad streets lined with offices, apartment blocks and the occasional modern department store. The architectural style of these buildings was either Italian, Art Nouveau or Neo-Arab. The signs displayed on all the buildings were in French and Arabic.

The roads were busy, but traffic moved freely and there was no problem parking, as there were far fewer cars at the time. However, unless the owner of the car had a chauffeur, he parked at his own peril. All cars without chauffeurs were subject to the urchins of Cairo and, unless the owner was willing to have his car 'guarded', he might well return to find the air let out of his tyres. Most submitted to this small-time protection racket and, for those who did not have cars, both taxis and horse-drawn carriages were frequent and inexpensive.

Immediately south of the Ezbekieh Gardens was the immense palace of Abdeen, the chief residence of King Farouk, built by the Khedive Ismail in 1863. This was surrounded to the North and East by the offices of the Household, inspectorates and barracks for the Palace Guards. The rest of the Abdeen quarter was distinguished by a large number of mosques and schools.

Westwards towards the Nile were the Parliament buildings, surrounded by a constellation of ministries. Between them and the river was a fashionable quarter which took its name from the Midan Kasr El Dubbara. The richest Egyptians and members of the royal family lived in this area in large, imposing mansions. Just to the south lay the winding, tree-lined streets of Garden City. The houses there were closer together and intercepted with office and apartment blocks. The area was mainly favoured by middle class Egyptians, who liked the proximity to the centre of the town.

The British preferred the upmarket suburb of Zamalek – being on an island in the Nile, it had a fresher feel than Garden City. Zamalek was made up of long straight boulevards lined with plane trees, and its houses and apartments were simpler and airier than those on the east bank. The smart suburb of Heliopolis had been built to the north-east of the city and, a few miles to the south, lay Maadi, with its large villas set in spacious, luxuriant gardens.

Beyond these two suburbs and in between the central area, Cairo was a Muslim rather than a cosmopolitan city. Contact between the two worlds was restricted to commercial transactions, and neither the British nor the French and English speaking Egyptian upper classes had any social contact with the ordinary Arabic speaking people of Cairo. The main streets of the lower class area of the city were filled with prosperous little shops, cafes and businesses. This is where the visitor to Cairo could find the donkeys, street vendors, bazaars and cafes that make up the cacophony of Arab life. However, the area behind it was in stark contrast – dwellings of brick and mud were piled together without drainage or running water. The streets split into a labyrinth of narrow alleyways where children played in the dust. The men were willing to travel wherever there was work, but the women rarely went beyond the well where they fetched their water.

Nevertheless, there were landmarks in this lesser-known area. In the Mouski district, to the north-east, stood the tenth century mosque of el Azhar and the great courtyard of the Islamic University, where the students sat on the ground in small groups to listen to the discourses of their religious teachers. Just behind el Azhar was the famous Khan Khalili bazaar, where tourists and residents alike came to purchase beads, silver, alabaster, rugs, spices and perfumes.

The British garrison in Cairo was housed in the Citadel of Muhammad Ali, a vast complex which included married quarters, tennis courts, stables and training grounds. As well as being protected by this large garrison, the British way of life was enshrined in five magnificent institutions, two of which looked directly onto the Nile, the British Embassy in Garden City and the Cathedral of All Saints, Bulaq. Between the Cathedral and the Ezbekieh, in the area that could be described as Cairo's West End, was the Turf Club, an exclusively British, all male establishment at 32 Adly Pasha Street, which would not have looked out of place in St. James in London. A few minutes' walk from there was the Shepheard's hotel which, after the Pyramids, was the most famous landmark in Cairo.

The British officers had access to the most magnificent sports grounds ever seen in the heart of a capital city, the Gezira Sporting Club. It covered the entire Southern end of Gezira Island, with gardens, polo fields, a huge golf course, race course, cricket pitches, squash courts, croquet lawns and tennis courts, as well as a huge swimming pool surrounded by a terrace known at the Lido. The Sporting Club was not exclusively British, and members included the richest and most Westernised Egyptian families and wealthy Jewish families, although they were greatly outnumbered by British ones.

Cairo's memory lives largely in the names of its streets and squares, all of which have been changed. Ismailia Square, the business centre of Cairo, has always been an important landmark and the square has made history on many occasions. In the 1950s, mass protests became a feature of the square, which grew in significance over the decades. One of the most notable demonstrations was in 1951 against the British occupation. The British army barracks of Kasr-e-Nil were demolished eventually, and the square was renamed Horreya (Liberty) in 1952 and al-Tahrir (Liberation) in 1953. The events brought about by the revolution of 25 January 2011 catapulted Tahrir Square to International fame and it was on live news channels across the globe for weeks. Regardless of how events unfolded after the toppling of the Mubarak regime, Tahrir Square has now become one of the most famous in the world.

On the other side of Tahrir Square in downtown Cairo was Soliman Pacha Square, which we referred to by its Arabic name of Midan Soliman Pacha. It was an imposing square which enjoyed a commanding position at the intersection of three important avenues, with seven belle époque buildings overlooking it. This was the location of some of Cairo's most popular and successful shops and services. Groppi was situated at one corner and was once known as the 'most celebrated tearoom this side of the Mediterranean'. Café Riche, also situated in the square, was another hub of social activity. It was a popular venue for many rising performers, among them the celebrated and legendary singer Om Kalsoum.

The square was the heart of the residential area in downtown Cairo and had been named after General Jean Anthelme Seve, also known as Soliman Pacha Al Faransawi, Egypt's fabled French-born general. He had won many battles, proving that Muhammed Ali's arsenal was second to none. He converted to Islam and, in return for his dedication, was showered with medals and important positions.

The name was changed to Talaat Harb Square in February 1964, in honour of a leading Egyptian economist and founder of the Banque Misr. The statue of Soliman Pacha, which I remembered so well from my childhood days, was removed and replaced by a statue of Talaat Harb. The renaming was part of a sweeping effort by Egypt's President, Gamal Abdel Nasser, to rid the city of all reminders of Muhammed Ali's dynasty and the British occupation era. Despite this, the old name is still remembered, and even young taxi drivers will take you straight there if you ask for Sharia Soliman Pacha.

Kasr-el-Nil street in central downtown was Cairo's financial district. At the junction with Ash-Sharif street was the National Bank of Egypt and this was also where the Bourse – stock exchange – was situated. At the turn of the 20th century, the building designs were part of a plan to create a new international downtown district, linking Egypt's rich Islamic heritage and institutions with the many new foreign enterprises. Emad el Din Street was regarded as the vibrant centre of Cairo nightlife, where both sides of the street were packed with cinemas, theatres, nightclubs and bars.

The Shepheard's hotel on Ibrahim Pacha street was one of the most prestigious hotels in downtown Cairo and occupied the former palace where Napoleon had once established his headquarters. Many visiting dignitaries chose to stay there, which gave it its special cachet. This was where Winston Churchill had met in secret with President Roosevelt, and Rommel had also stayed there.

The hotel's celebrated terrace was guarded by two small sphinxes taken from a temple in Memphis. It was set with wicker chairs and tables and commanded a lofty and shaded view of Ibrahim Pacha Street. That was where the British officers liked to sit, always looking as though they were lording it over everybody. There was always a crowd at the foot of the terrace, mainly coach drivers and beggars of all descriptions. In stark contrast, Rolls-Royces used to pull up one after the other. Beyond the terrace was the Moorish Hall, where the ladies liked to congregate. It was dimly lit by a dome of coloured glass that hung above it. The huge ballroom featured lotus-topped pillars modelled on those of Karnak. The British liked the atmosphere of the Shepheard's, but some found it oppressive. One visitor wrote that it was like living in the British Museum.

The Long Bar of the Shepheard's Hotel was famous, probably because the Swiss barman called Joe was known to be one of the best-informed people in Cairo. During the Desert War, it was said that anyone who wanted to find out the Order of Battle for the next offensive only needed to sit in the Long Bar for a while, and keep his ears open. The hotel was one of the first buildings to be completely burnt down in 1952 during the riots of Black Saturday – for the Egyptians, it was the quintessential symbol of British colonialism.

Groppi was a legendary tearoom in Cairo and a favourite meeting place, where people regularly went to see and be seen. It was founded in 1909 by a Swiss pastry chef called Giacomo Groppi. It was very cosmopolitan and the centre of the Cairo social scene. As you entered the shop, the first thing you saw were counters full of the most delicious pastries, rivalling those found in patisseries in Paris. There were éclairs au chocolat, marrons glacés (caramelised chestnuts) and delicious millefeuilles. It was difficult to choose, but my favourite was a huge chocolate meringue with delicious Chantilly cream in the middle. Another specialty was their peach melba, an ice cream which came in a tall, fluted glass and was served with whipped Chantilly cream.

Groppi was also famous for its ice cream. It came in

candy striped cardboard cups, each bearing a different colour which reflected the individual flavours and I loved all of them, especially the hazelnut and the chocolate ones. It was always a dilemma having to choose between a cake and an ice cream. I could never decide and would have had both, but of course I wasn't allowed. Groppi was also famous for its chocolates, which were renowned worldwide. Apparently, King Farouk was so impressed with the excellence of its chocolates that, during World War II, he sent one hundred kilograms to King George as a present for his daughters, Princesses Elizabeth and Margaret.

Groppi's art deco interior was lovely, with its distinctive glass ceiling and Venetian mosaics. Beyond the counters there was a large tearoom, where people could sit, have a drink and socialise. It was very elegant, with high ceilings and beautiful chandeliers. There was also an outdoor garden, and mezze were always served with drinks. This tearoom symbolised cosmopolitan Cairo in the 1940s and 1950s and I was very disappointed to note how much it had declined when I visited in 1994. The beautiful front was still there, but gone were the magnificent cakes and pastries. Instead, all I could see were a few chocolates for sale. The good news is that there is currently a project to restore Groppi to its former glory.

No one could compete with the Jewish owned shops of downtown Cairo, where the employees were mostly European. There was Benzion, where you could buy yards of the softest cotton and the snobbish Grands Magazine Hannaux, which sold very expensive bags and accessories. Chemla was known for its wonderful fabrics, as was the

Salon Vert – that is where my mother bought the materials for her dresses, colourful fabrics in cotton, silk, lace and organdie. It was an expedition and a treat to go there and choose a fabric. The rolls would be laid out for the customer, who would drape a fabric on her shoulders and look in the gigantic mirror to see how it looked on her. There were no synthetic materials and everything was made of cotton or silk, as Egypt was one of the foremost cotton-exporting countries. We didn't have to worry whether a fabric would crease, since everything was sent to the ironer's shop, even if the item had only been worn once.

My mother also used to shop in smaller department stores such as Orosdi-Back, Chemla, Maison Gattegno or Sednaoui – all those names are evoked with a great deal of nostalgia. Sednaoui was the only department store in Cairo not owned by Jews. Interestingly, there are currently 80 Cicurel, Oreco and Hannaux stores in Egypt, all under state control and in a state of disrepair. The people who shop there now have no idea that once upon a time all these stores were owned by Jewish people.

The most upscale and biggest department store in Cairo was called Maison Cicurel. Their full name was Grands Magasins Cicurel et Oreco. The Cicurel branch developed into Egypt's largest and most fashionable department store. They specialised in ready-to-wear men's and women's clothes, shoes, handbags and houseware, much of which were imported from Europe. It had an excellent reputation for quality and was a purveyor to the Royal palace during the reigns of Kings Fuad and Farouk. The Oreco branch of the firm consisted of thrift stores serving the lower middle classes.

Many people in the Jewish community shopped in Cicurel. It was our equivalent of Selfridges in London, with floor after floor of French and Italian fashions where you were served by an army of overly deferential sales ladies, most of them Jewish. The Cicurel stores had a foreign cultural character due to their largely Jewish staff, their exclusive and largely imported merchandise and the use of French by employees and customers on the shop floor. It tended to employ only attractive young shop girls, who were paid a salary and a commission. Working there gave a young girl a certain cachet, especially as they had access to all the latest fashions.

Despite the emphasis on foreign goods and culture in their stores, the Cicurel family regarded themselves as Egyptians and saw their business activities as contributing to the national economy. Because it was favoured by the Royal family, unlike the other major Jewish-owned department stores, the Cicurel firm was not placed under government administration during the 1948 Arab-Israeli War. The main Cairo store was damaged by a bomb on July 19, 1948, most likely the work of the Muslim Brotherhood, but it soon reopened. The building was destroyed in the Cairo fires of January 26, 1952, another indication that militant nationalists regarded it as a foreign institution. It was quickly rebuilt with the support of General Muhammad Naguib after the military coup of July 23, 1952.

At that time, shopping in Cicurel was considered by the elite and the middle classes as part of the trappings of the European culture. There is no doubt that Cairo in the 1930s, 40s and early 50s was very glamorous, and the women were elegant and always fashionably dressed. They liked to show off, and shoes and handbags had to match to rest of their outfit. Egypt had good shoemaking and handbag factories and the quality of the leather was excellent. Fashion was important in Cairo. There was always much gossip about who was wearing what, how they walked or who they were with.

The influence of the Jewish community

The Jewish community in Egypt made significant contributions to culture, education, health, commerce, industry and many other areas of Egyptian society. Many families distinguished themselves and made their mark on the country. They had an impact on several spheres, including agriculture and finance. Some funded the education and training of gifted youths, others were associated with successful companies and were known philanthropists. They contributed to the development of cotton cultivation and its export and were instrumental in the booming of the Egyptian textile industry.

The *haute Juiverie,* the Cattauis, the Rolos, the Hararis and the Menasces, to name a few, were the financiers of Egypt. They moved in royal circles – Madame Cattaui Pasha and Valentine Rolo were both said to have been mistresses of King Fuad. Joseph Cattaui Pasha served as President of the Jewish Community from 1924 until his death in 1942. He co-founded the Banque Misr with Talaat Harb Pacha and Fuad Sultan Bey, and joined its board of directors. He also became an associate of the Suarez brothers and contributed to many of their projects. Sir Victor Harari Pasha was a brilliant financier who devoted his life to business and philanthropy. The Menasces family had been ennobled by the Emperor of Austria.

The upscale suburb of Smouha in Alexandria was the brainchild of Joseph Smouha, a British Jew living in Egypt. It had its own tennis courts, schools, hospitals, synagogues and churches. Two wealthy and prominent Jewish families founded the highly regarded academies called L'Ecole Cattaui, the private academy for boys, and Marie Suarez, its counterpart for girls. Members of both families had a significant influence on Egyptian cultural and economic developments, especially Moise Cattaui Pasha, who held an important position in the Egyptian government. The Jewish community subsidised both schools and the nominal tuition was based on a student's financial resources. Some others who had become quite wealthy joined forces and built Jewish hospitals in Cairo and in Alexandria.

The Suarez were a family of Egyptian bankers of Spanish descent. During the 1880s, several members joined forces to establish the Credit Foncier Egyptien, the leading mortgage lending institution. They also founded the Helwan and other railway constructions, the Cairo Omnibus Company and the Tanta Water Supply. The Suarez family, together with the Cattauis, established Egypt's first successful sugar refinery and contributed to the country's agricultural development.

Many Egyptian Jewish men were merchants. They

dealt in what is known as import/export, but the truth is they seldom exported anything. Lucette Lagnado, in her bestseller The Man in the White Sharkskin Suit, has described how her father did not have an office, but conducted his business from the bar of the Nile Hilton. Some men turned to manufacturing during World War II, as there was nothing to import. Some, like my uncle Zaki, Marie's husband, owned some land in a village outside Cairo. There were no contracts between individuals, everything was agreed verbally, and you relied on the other person's word. Of course, there were times when people did not pay on time, or did not pay at all.

There are also some big names among Egyptian Jews who left their mark in the fields of art, theatre, cinema and journalism.

Yaqub Sanua, known as the Egyptian Molière, launched his own theatre company in 1870 and presented around 26 plays. He believed that Egypt deserved its own culture, as Cairo's French Comedy Theatre, established in 1869, did not perform in Arabic. When invited to perform at Ismail Pasha's palace, Sanua staged three plays there, all in Arabic. These comedies included a moral and, between the lines, social criticism. He was promptly dubbed Egypt's Moliere. Sanua also founded a magazine called Abou Naddara, where his caricatures highlighted the hot topics in the early days of popular Arab journalism. However, his activities angered the Royal family, who ordered the closure of his magazine and exiled him to Paris. For many, Sanua remains the undisputed pioneer of the Egyptian stage.

Togo Mizrahi was born in Egypt in 1901 to a Jewish

family of Italian descent. He is viewed as one of the most important figures in the history of the Egyptian cinema and one of the most influential. Togo acted under the pseudonym Ahmed al-Meshriqi. He then revealed his true Jewish identity by making a series of movies where the main character was a Jewish Egyptian. The authorities accused him of cooperating with Zionist organisations in Palestine and he was exiled to Italy, as he refused to travel to Israel.

The Frankel brothers pioneered animated film in Egypt. The story of the family starts like many a tale of travels and immigration, so typical of Jews everywhere for most of the 20th century. Within just 50 years, this creative family passed through Rechytsa in Russia, Jaffa, Alexandria, Cairo and Paris. The turning point in their history took place in the late 1920s, when Walt Disney's Mickey Mouse was released. The brothers decided to introduce animation in the Arab World after watching the iconic Mickey. When they presented their film to one famous Egyptian producer, his reaction was *bokra fil mish mish*, which roughly translated means 'when hell freezes over', literally 'tomorrow in the apricot season'. As an homage to the producer who had rejected them, they named their first film *Mafish Faida* – 'it's no use'. They went further in mocking that sceptical guy by naming their animated hero Mish Mish Effendi.

Thus the Egyptian version of Mickey Mouse was born. Mish Mish Effendi was an eccentric, lanky fellow with a tarboosh, who always got into awkward situations, then got away with it, thanks to lots of funny gestures and loads of grace and humour. On 24 May 1935, one could read on the front page of the newspaper La Bourse Egyptienne 'Mickey

Mouse got an Egyptian brother – First Frenkel Brothers animated film'. The film was released in 1936 in cinemas in Cairo and Alexandria, and played for four consecutive weeks, winning everyone's admiration.

Mish Mish Efffendi became a national star. Egyptian companies hired the brothers to produce commercials with his character, the government used him for propaganda and the Ministry of Agriculture purchased a tutorial film in which Mish Mish teaches how to cope with cotton crop parasites. The Frenkel brothers were even awarded a national medal. After Israel's Declaration of Independence, they emigrated to France and continued to make films, but without the success they had enjoyed in Egypt.

Nijjma Ibrahim was born on 25 February 1914 as Polini Odeon. She was known for her tragic roles and played the role of Rayya in a famous film called Rayya and Sakina. She acted in more than 40 films and passed away on June 4, 1976. She is buried in Cairo.

Leila Mourad was one of Egypt's best-known actresses and a famed singer. She was born Liliane Mordechai on February 17, 1918 to a family of Jewish descent. Her father was Ibrahim Zaki Mordechai, a respected singer and musician. Mourad converted to Islam in 1946. In 1952, there were rumours that she was donating money to Israel; she denied those allegations and instead collected donations for the Egyptian army. She refused to submit to pressures to be sent away to Palestine and preferred to stay in Egypt until she died on November 21, 1996.

Dawood Hosni was a composer and musician born on February 16, 1870 to an Egyptian family. His real name was David Haim Levy. Famous Egyptian artists such as Om Kalsoum and Leila Mourad sang some of the songs composed by him. His works include some of the best-known folk songs which are now part of the Egyptian cultural heritage.

A few words about Egypt's film industry

The Arabic we knew was the one spoken in the streets – not the same as that of Syria, Sudan or Libya and completely different from the pure Arabic you hear on the news channels. However, this colloquial Arabic is understood throughout the Middle East because of Egypt's thriving film and TV industry. Egyptian cinema has long dominated the screens of the Arab world.

In 1935, a company called Talaat Harb founded Misr studios, which were on a par with any Hollywood film studio. Thus began the golden age of Egyptian cinema, which became the most lucrative industry after textiles. Misr studios exported its films throughout the Arab world, where they won immense popularity. The most popular genre was the musical comedy, thanks to singers-composers such as Farid-el-Atrach, and Abd-el-Wahab, and dancers such as Tahia Carioca and Samia Gamal. The films were escapist, light-hearted and fun. This genre became known and loved throughout the Maghreb and the Middle East.

Youssef Chahine, who was one of Egypt's most famous film directors, released his first film in 1950. It was called Papa Amine and was a frivolous musical comedy.

It was not until after the Nasser revolution that Chahine turned to the Neo realism for which he became famous. After 1952, laws were passed to protect the film industry and the abolition of the monarchy saw the beginning of a different film style, more patriotic and historical, and more concerned with social issues. Egypt is still prolific in its film industry and Egyptian films and TV series are watched by all Arab speakers.

One could write a social history of Egypt through their cinema. I have watched countless films and TV series and have learnt a lot through them. The film The Yacoubian Building (based on the book) merits a special mention. It is a scathing portrayal of modern Egyptian society since 1952 and is reported to be the highest-budgeted film in the history of its cinema. The setting is downtown Cairo and the actual building is a real one. It's instantly recognisable with its art deco and still stands in what used to be called Soliman Pacha Square.

Arab television drama is known as *musalsal* (plural *musalsalat*). They are a television form of melodramatic serialised fiction, similar in style to the Latin American telenovelas. The Egyptian series known as the Ramadan series (the Super Bowl of Egyptian television) are very popular. During the evenings of the month of Ramadan, after the Iftar meal is taken to break the day's fast, families across much of the Arab world gather to watch these special dramas on television. Most *musalsalat* are 30 episodes, or about one episode for each night of Ramadan. These series are an integral part of the Ramadan tradition.

A recent series which caused some controversy is

called Haret El Yahud (The Jewish Quarter). This was an area where once Jews, Muslims and Christians all lived peacefully side by side. In the opening scene of the first episode, people of the three faiths take shelter together in a synagogue during an Israeli air raid. The series mainly follows a Jewish family living in Haret El Yahud in 1948. It astonished Egyptians with its sympathetic treatment of Egypt's Jews and its depiction of their fierce anti-Zionism. The villains in the piece are in fact the Islamists of the Muslim Brotherhood. The love interest of the heroine, called Laila, is a Muslim military officer celebrated as a hero in the Jewish community. The series appears to be the first on Egyptian television in at least six decades to respectfully depict Jewish families at prayer in a synagogue or having a Shabbat dinner.

It has stirred a fierce debate, about both Jews and Egypt. Some have praised it for celebrating the pluralistic ethos that prevailed under the British-backed monarchy of King Farouk, a liberal culture that was destroyed by Nasser's 1952 coup. Others have criticised the series for 'making the Jews look better than the Egyptians', as one viewer complained on the Facebook page of the film makers. A few have expressed horror that a Muslim military officer might marry a Jew – they don't marry in the end, but the fate of their romance is part of the suspense throughout the 30 episodes of the series.

It was only many years after I left Egypt that I began to appreciate Egyptian music and films, such as the singers Om Kalsoum, Leila Mourad and Farid El Atrach and the films of Youssef Shahine. Om Kalsoum was not just a singer and an icon. She was, and still is, the greatest singer the country has ever known and is synonymous with Egypt. The daughter of a village sheikh, she had a cult following; the intellectual elite and the illiterate masses worshipped her equally and one of her greatest admirers was King Farouk.

Om Kalsoum, also known as the Nightingale of the Nile and the Star of the Orient, gave a live concert every first Thursday night of every month. The concerts began promptly at 9pm. They were mostly broadcast from a theatre in the Ezbekeya Gardens and on that night, the whole of Egypt, from pashas in their palaces to fellahin in their hovels, held its breath. People gathered round the radio to hear their idol and, in cafés, apartments and shops, they all stopped what they were doing for the duration of the concert. Her transcendent and evocative voice had everyone spellbound.

She was a cult figure and Egyptians venerated her. Whilst her voice had a stunning range and power, she also became the inspiration and interpreter of an authentic revival in Arabic song. She sang about unrequited love and the torments it brings. Her best-known song is called *Enta Omr*i – You are my life. Each of her songs could last half an hour or more and her concerts went on until past midnight. She was always backed by a full orchestra who played for more than ten minutes before she started singing. This was the case with all classical singers.

Belly dancing was an art form and some accomplished belly dancers went on to become stars in their own right. There was Tahia Karioka, a voluptuous brunette, whose skill and sensuality on the dance floor made her the single most respected belly dancer in the Middle East. Her rival, Samia Gamal, landed a role opposite Robert Taylor in the film Valley of the Kings and married a Texas millionaire. When the belly dancers swayed and gyrated on the dance floor, the audience held its breath, totally spellbound. A dance called the karaoke became very popular in Egypt in the 1950s.

Omar Sharif remains Egypt's greatest export, but he is also an example of the Egyptian regime's intolerance. He was born in Alexandria as Michel Demitri Shalhoub to a Christian family, which traced its roots back to Lebanon. He converted to Islam in his youth in order to be allowed to legally marry his fellow actress, Faten Hamama. She was much loved and, when he married her, their popularity knew no bounds and they quickly became the golden couple.

Sharif left for Europe a few years later, however, in a form of self-exile, after becoming disenchanted with the new military regime. His marriage consequently broke down and they divorced. In 1968, the Egyptian authorities turned him from hero to enemy of the state because of his Funny Girl 'onscreen' romance with Barbra Streisand, a Jew. Sadly, Omar Sharif started gambling and drinking heavily. He is now best known for his appearances in both British and American productions, rather than as an Egyptian actor. Uncle Clement met Sharif several times, as they were both horse racing enthusiasts and accomplished bridge players.

I have discovered many interesting facts through watching Egyptian TV series, things that I probably would not have necessarily known about when I lived in Egypt. First cousins are allowed to marry – in fact this is encouraged and seen as keeping the family ties. In the poorer classes, it is the man who divorces the wife and he is the only one who can instigate proceedings. This is similar to the *Get* in Jewish religious law, which only the husband can obtain. The middle classes would probably have recourse to a good lawyer. Men are still allowed to take more than one wife and, anecdotally, can even do so without the first wife's knowledge.

My families and their friends did not seem interested in Egyptian culture. They didn't listen to any of Om Kalsoum's concerts and didn't go and see any Egyptian films. This must have been noticed by the local population around us, since we lived in their country, but insisted on behaving in what must have appeared a superior way. However, most seemed to accept this and take it for granted, as they were easy going and good humoured on the whole. Whenever I watch old Egyptian films, I am reminded of their exceptional characteristics, their warmth and accommodating temper, their sense of humour and unfailing hospitality.

My childhood

The formative years

I was the firstborn, followed by my sisters Nicole and Claudine. Claudine sadly passed away in 2016 after what felt like a relatively short illness. The custom with Sephardic Jews was to give a child two names, the second one being a Hebrew name or the name of a living grandparent, which was considered an honour. However, my parents only gave me the one name and did the same with both my sisters. My mother was ill for a while, having developed an abscess, so she found it difficult to breastfeed me. Being the first child on both sides of the family, I received a lot of attention. I was a chubby baby and toddler, perhaps because I was very spoilt. I am told that, at a very young age, all I wanted to eat were *menenas* (our version of *ma'amoul*, the date-filled pastries) and bananas. I hated all vegetables. My father fussed a lot over me, but my mother was much more laid back. I had very frizzy hair which was combed in plaits when I got older. It was very difficult to put a comb through it and it was an ordeal which I dreaded every morning.

My father's sisters, Suzanne and Esther, doted on me

and often looked after me; they were very close in age and neither was married. They left Egypt for Israel in 1948, very soon after the creation of the State. I was only five at the time but I know it left a big gap in my life and a huge sense of loss, perhaps even trauma. One minute they were there every day, the next minute they had disappeared and no one had explained why. When my sister Nicole was born in 1946, I was no longer the only child or the centre of attention.

When my aunts, uncle and various cousins left Egypt, the family dynamics changed. Until then, I had been cherished by my father's family, as an only child but also after Nicole was born. The gap they left was never really filled. My mother was a 'good' mother, by accepted standards, but she did not give me the attention and love I longed for. I spent a lot of time at Aunt Marie's house and I was comfortable there, but again there was never the unconditional love Esther and Suzanne had given me. My aunt had lost a child at birth and I expect it must have been very difficult for her to deal with this, especially when she was surrounded by other children in the family.

There was a cholera epidemic in Egypt in September 1947, which I was too young to remember. It had started in a village and quickly spread. People were immediately vaccinated and extra precautions were taken, such as boiling the drinking water from the tap. The epidemic abated around December – about thirty-six thousand people died within a few months, but Cairo had only 32 deaths, the least of the other cities. The fellahin in the villages were used to drinking the Nile water full of germs, so perhaps that was how they got their immunity.

I still remember an incident which had a profound effect on me and happened about a couple of years later. We had an Egyptian maid who lived with us and was the equivalent of a nanny, though nothing so grand. My parents went out every evening and we were left alone with her. She took a profound dislike to me and I don't know why. She used to pinch me repeatedly and then lock me in the bathroom and turn off the light. She would also tell me that the *afrit* was coming to get me – this is the Arabic word for the devil. There were cockroaches in Egypt and lots of them in the bathroom. The secret was to turn the light on before you entered and wait a few seconds, as the cockroaches would scurry away and hide. However, I knew that was not happening as the bathroom was in total darkness and I remember being very scared.

This went on for a while until my father noticed the bruises on my arms and immediately fired the maid. She was replaced by a young girl called Amina who was wonderful and grew very fond of me, so every cloud has a silver lining. Nevertheless, I am surprised that my mother never noticed the bruises and it must have meant that the maid looked after us more or less all the time. Still, how come it had taken so long for this bullying to come to light? The bruises were probably on my arms or legs, and this was Egypt, where the weather was warm and we wore short sleeved dresses. The maid must have been fairly confident that her appalling behaviour would not be noticed.

This incident must have been traumatic, since I still wonder why she picked on me and what had I done to make her hate me so much. It marked me profoundly, though it was not apparent at the time. Nowadays such an incident would be addressed, but my parents' world was a pragmatic one. They had dismissed the horrible maid, her replacement Amina was lovely and that was the end of the matter.

We lived in a two-bedroom apartment in a street called Rue Cherifen. It was right in the centre of Cairo, near Soliman Pasha Square (today Tala'at Harb). At the centre of the square was the statue of Soliman Pasha, a large bronze horseman with a fierce look and hook-like moustaches. In my memory, this statue symbolises Cairo and my childhood. There was always a policeman dressed in white in the middle of the square. He was called *shawish* and he directed the traffic with his arms and a whistle.

Cairo was often referred to as 'the Paris of the Nile'. The main shopping streets, Fuad Street and Kasr-el-Nil Street, were only a few minutes' walk away. This was where the best shops and department stores were situated. We were also minutes away from the Groppi tearooms. Right opposite our apartment block was the Cairo broadcasting house. My aunt Marie lived in Antikhana Street, ten minutes' walk from us. There was a narrow alleyway at the corner of our building and the apartment block facing ours was so close you could see what was going on in the flat opposite.

I don't remember much about our neighbours in the building, probably because we had very little to do with them. My parents did not encourage familiarity anyway, so they would have avoided getting friendly with any of them. The exception was a Greek lady called Helène, who lived in the flat across the hallway from us and who my mother was friendly with. I remember Lena, a girl who was in the same class as me and lived on the sixth floor. My parents barely knew hers; in any case they had a completely different lifestyles – mine loved going out whenever possible, hers were the opposite and very homely.

We lived very near all our relatives and I assume that was why my father always refused to move to the leafy suburbs of Maadi or Zamalek. The latter was a residential area in Cairo, situated on an island in the Nile. It had elegant houses and apartment buildings which would have been more comfortable than our small apartment in the centre of Cairo. I remember going with my mother to visit a friend who lived in Zamalek and I was impressed with the pretty villas and gardens with bougainvillea and jasmine. However, my parents preferred to live in the heart of Cairo and, lovely as the suburbs were, they would have hated being far away from their families.

Our apartment was on the fourth floor and had a lift. As you came into the building, you were always greeted by the *bawab*, the Arabic word for concierge or caretaker. He was an institution and played an important role. Whatever his age, he had the gift of remembering faces and people. Many of them came from North Sudan, from a region known as Nubia – ours was a Coptic Christian. He sat on a bench at the entrance of the building and was always there, whatever the time of day. He looked as if he was asleep, but in reality knew everything that was going on, not just in the building, but the whole neighbourhood. He always got up when we came in and opened the door of the lift for us.

Our apartment was in a six-storey building and each

floor had two flats, which all had high ceilings and large rooms. When you opened the front door, you were straight into the lounge and beyond it was the dining room with a large balcony. On the side of the dining room was my parents' bedroom, then the bedroom I shared with my sisters and Amina the maid – she slept on a mattress on the floor. The rooms were aired out and cleaned very morning. Once this was done, the shutters were closed – partly to protect the apartment from the heat of the sun and partly because the sun would have damaged the furniture. The shutters were only opened again in late afternoon, but they could also be adjusted to give more or less light. If there is one thing that reminds me of my childhood, it is the smell of mothballs. There were a lot of moths around, so the only way to protect clothes, linens and blankets was to tuck as many mothballs as possible between the layers. Whenever you opened a wardrobe, a strong whiff of moth balls would hit you.

Beyond the bedroom, there was a long corridor leading to a fair-sized kitchen on one side and a bathroom with a toilet on the other. Each kitchen in Egypt had something called a *namliya*. This was the place where food was kept cool and away from insects. It was in effect a screened food pantry designed to allow for air circulation. People shopped daily, so the food was always fresh and only dry good were stored for any length of time. The buildings in Cairo had a slab on the roof where there were small bedrooms for the hired help. This was where the washing was done on washdays and hung to dry. There was also a Turkish-style toilet which the servants used.

All the apartments had a balcony and this was where we often sat before sunset. The heat of Cairo would have subsided by then and there was a wonderful breeze coming from the Sahara desert. The street below came alive with the cries of vendors, the sound of the muezzin calling the faithful to prayer and the music played in the cafés and many apartments – all loud and different tunes, of course, so it sounded like a cacophony but it didn't matter, I doubt we even noticed.

My father loved collecting crystal glasses, goblets and stem ones. We had what we called a *vitrine* in the dining room, where these were displayed, along with various trinkets which we called *bibelots*. There was Limoges china and Baccarat Crystal glasses, which my father used for whisky and soda, his favourite drink. His love of crystal continued when we lived in London and twice a year, he regularly went to the Harrods sale and acquired a few more items. He built up quite a collection, which my sisters and I shared after both my parents had passed away.

After Arabic, the main language in Egypt was French. Walking in downtown Cairo, you would have been forgiven for thinking that you were in Marseilles or any city in the South of France. The names of the streets, as well as above the shop fronts and on the billboards, were all in French, with the Arabic names underneath. The official day of rest was Sunday and not Friday, even though Egypt was a Muslim country. Everything was closed for the main Christian and Jewish holidays – all businesses and shops, even those belonging to Muslims, were shut for Christmas, Easter, Rosh Hashanah and Yom Kippur.

We were not rich, but we were comfortably off and my father had a strong work ethic. He was the Managing Director of John Dickinson & Co, a well-known British company with large offices in England. They were paper merchants and stationers, and he had risen up the ranks to a good position. Strictly speaking, he was the Deputy Managing Director – being a British company, only a British person was allowed to be Managing Director, but that person was merely a figurehead and my father was completely in charge. He had the use of the company car and the chauffeur, who was called Hassan. Hassan often took me and my sister to school.

As with most Jewish people in Egypt, we had two servants. Most Westerners today would not be comfortable with this and I always feel I have to add an explanation and even apologise if the subject comes up. Yet, in Egypt where I grew up, employing servants was part of the fabric of society and an integral part of the economy. My parents would have been very surprised if any criticism had been levelled at them. After all, the servants were respected and treated very well. They were part of our lives, stayed with the family for years and watched us grow up.

Most of them were quite young and came from villages outside Cairo or from Upper Egypt. They had free board and lodging and were paid a small salary which they sent back to their families. Once a month they went back to visit. The young girls eventually married and left the family when they did. Some of the maids were older widows whose children had grown up and left home and a live-in position suited them well.

We had a *khadam,* also known as *sufragi* (manservant in Arabic) called Salah and a maid called Amina. She was very young when she came to us and her job was to look after the children, make the beds, help with the laundry and general light duties. I loved her right from the start and we always got on well. I spent much more time with her than I did with my mother and she was often the one who put us to bed if my parents went out.

Salah was Nubian and his family had originally come to Egypt from Northern Sudan. He took care of the shopping, the heavy house cleaning and served at the dinner table. His first task when he descended from his attic room was to shop at the souk. His list of supplies was delivered to him orally every morning by my mother. It included herbs, different vegetables and fruit. Meat and poultry were purchased separately. Salah loved his tea, which he regularly consumed whenever he had a break. He drank it the way Egyptians still do – black, and in a glass. He would take small sips of it, whilst making a slurping sound.

When it was my mother's turn to host a card game, he served the refreshments. For the occasion, he wore the traditional waiter's garb, which was white with a large red belt around the waist. Because he and Amina were always in when any of us returned home, we never carried any keys. We simply rang the bell and one of them opened the door.

Salah also cooked under my mother's supervision – she had taught him a lot and he became a very good cook. It was mainly vegetable dishes, as well as meat or chicken and rice. Kilos of fresh vegetables were bought on a daily basis, such as artichokes, *bamia* (okra), aubergines, courgettes and peppers. The kitchen was off limits to the children. Everything started early because of the heat later on in the day, so the cleaning, shopping and cooking were done by midday.

We did our homework on the dining room table which was long and rectangular. I was often distracted by the fridge which stood in the corner of the dining room. There was no food as such in it, as everything was bought and cooked fresh on the day. Instead there were many jars of the most wonderful looking jams – dates, figs, quince, grape, strawberry – and a thick cream we called *eshta*. In those days milk was unpasteurised and had to be boiled. The top of the milk was then removed and cooled and gave the most wonderful cream.

Sharing a bedroom with my sisters was fun. I was the eldest, my sister Nicole was less than three years younger than me and Claudine seven years younger. Our beds were arranged along the walls of the bedroom and there was a dresser and a wardrobe against one of the walls. We used to have singing competitions as we lay in bed, which helped us fall asleep. It sounds silly now, but it was fun. Each one would each sing a song which was popular at the time and we would then give each other marks. We had differences of opinions about actors such as Robert Taylor and Stewart Granger. I had liked Robert Taylor in Ivanhoe and Nicole preferred Stewart Granger in The Prisoner of Zenda and Scaramouche – or was it the other way round? Years later we could not agree again; this time it was about the Beatles and the Rolling Stones.

We were only given presents once a year on our

birthday. Christmas passed unnoticed and it was not my family's custom to give anything for Chanukah. Girls were always given a doll as a present. One particular doll which was very popular in the 1950s was made of rubber and urinated if filled with water. She had blue eyes with eyelashes that would close if you lay her on her back. She came with a layette and a baby bottle. I was fascinated, even though I was never particularly interested in dolls.

We also received board games and books. Many of the games we played were outdoors – marbles, hopscotch and especially jump rope. It was not possible to play in the street, as we lived in the city centre; however, since we spent most Sundays at the sporting club, there was plenty of time to have fun there. We also played cards whenever we could; a favourite was a game called *basra,* which was popular in coffee houses throughout the Middle East. It was simple in its mechanics and easy going, but provided opportunities for strategy and skill.

I was a painfully shy and awkward little girl. On my very first day at kindergarten aged six, I cried my eyes out and refused to leave my mother's side. In fact, I hung on to her skirt and she finally had to push me into the classroom. I liked our apartment, which was my cocoon, the one place where I didn't have to talk to people or overcome my shyness. If I close my eyes, I can still visualise it.

I blushed very easily, had no confidence and going anywhere with lots of people made me nervous – I was only comfortable around people I knew. This made life difficult, since the society I grew up in was very gregarious. My family loved socialising and life would have been much easier had

I been the confident child my parents expected me to be. Instead, going to the sporting club on a Sunday was always difficult and a visit in the middle of the week required a bribery such as an ice cream. I felt different, but at the same time wanted to fit into the norm.

I didn't like what other children enjoyed. I hated clowns, the circus and children's entertainers, and could not understand why Laurel and Hardy, Abbott and Costello and Charlie Chaplin were supposedly funny – I can't remember what I actually liked! Even the game musical chairs at birthday parties was a challenge because I was always worried that I would be the first one out. I much preferred reading or playing board games.

A favourite at birthday parties was the *gala gala* man. He was an Arab conjurer who had the children enthralled as he magically made rabbits and doves appear out of hats. He also pulled out endless streams of knotted handkerchiefs from his sleeves. It was a fascinating sight, as those were bright colours of yellow, orange, green and red, striped and polka-dotted. This was the only part of a birthday party which I liked.

We had pretty dresses for parties and other special occasions. They were made by a seamstress and I had to stand on a table and twirl while my mother and the seamstress were satisfied that the hem was perfectly straight. We wore white cotton vests and knickers – the make was Petit Bateau which still exists in France today.

My parents, like all Jewish Egyptians, were very protective. They believed that it was necessary to shelter children from anything bad and assumed that, if they did not discuss any frightening situations in their presence, it would protect them from fear. They didn't understand that interrupted conversations, whispers and concerned looks are far more frightening to a child than knowing the truth of whatever was going on. Children need an acceptable explanation and communication, otherwise they get anxious and start imagining or misinterpreting things.

I did not know about men and women having sex until I was 12. It never occurred to me that my parents would do something in bed rather than sleep. I never wondered how we were born and didn't ask, I just took it for granted that a woman fell pregnant. I was not a precocious child, neither were my close friends, so we never talked or wondered about sex. My parents certainly never discussed the subject in front of us and there were no sex scenes in the movies, as there are today – films were romantic, with amorous scenes, embracing and kissing, but no actual sex acts like today. My education, when it came eventually, was through my peers, who relied on bits and pieces of hearsay.

My scariest experience was having my tonsils out. Nothing was explained to me beforehand as my parents probably did not want to make a big deal, so it was quite a shock to suddenly find myself in a hospital room surrounded by nurses and a doctor in a white coat. I remember one of the nurses putting a chloroform mask over my face, the smell was horrible but I was out cold almost instantly, The good thing was that I was allowed to have lots of ice cream afterwards.

We grew up in a bubble. That meant that I was totally unprepared when negative things happened later on life.

Politics were never discussed in front of us. All my parents' serious conversations or disagreements took place behind closed doors. Euphemisms were used whenever possible; for instance, my mother never simply said that someone had died. Instead, she referred to it as 'having lost someone'. For years, as a child I believed that the person she was referring to had somehow got lost in the woods.

It was the Jewish Aleppo way never to expose children even to the hint of death. I was never told that my paternal grandfather had died – one day, he was no longer there. I grew up believing that my parents knew everything, were always right and in a sense were infallible. It was implicit that the adults knew better. Of course, as a child you will do what your parents tell you, but I found it very difficult to shake off all these assumptions later on in life, even as an adult.

I attended the French Lycée, a non-denominational school situated in the nearby district of Bab-el Luk, within walking distance of our apartment. At the beginning of every school year, we were required to cover all our books with cobalt-blue paper and meticulously write our name at the top right hand corner. We visited a bookshop which sold everything we were required to study. I loved the feel of all these new books. We also had to buy notebooks, blotting paper and a dual-purpose eraser, one half for ink and the other half for pencil. It was exciting to return home clutching all our new purchases.

I was a conscientious student and did reasonably well in my studies. The teachers were strict, but fair. As the school was a French one, everything we learnt was based on the curriculum in France. The only national anthem I knew until the age of 14 was the Marseillaise. We did not study modern Egyptian history or literature and we lived in a French atmosphere. The only thing British about my mother's family was her passport, although my uncle Victor served in the British army during WWII. I have a photo of him in his navy uniform.

We studied all the important French playwrights, Moliére, Corneille and Racine, as well as writers such as Voltaire, Balzac, Zola and Victor Hugo. We knew the fables of La Fontaine from a very early age and part of our homework was often to learn a particular one *par coeur,* meaning by heart. We had to recite it the next day in the class and woe to the student who missed a line. Later on, it was Charlemagne the Great, king of the Gauls who, in a campaign of conquests, founded the French nation, Joan of Arc, Louis XIV, Louis XVI and of course the French Revolution. I had never heard of Wordsworth, Keats, Byron or even Dickens and Jane Austen until I started studying for my O Levels in England and Shakespeare was never mentioned. Even now, I can only add up, subtract, multiply or divide in French.

English history was never on the curriculum, so I knew absolutely nothing about the English kings and queens, when they reigned or the different Royal houses. We had to study Ancient Egyptian history in depth and became familiar with Isis, Osiris, the Pharaonic dynasties and the burial customs of Ancient Egypt. The ancient Egyptians had an elaborate set of funerary practices that they believed were necessary to ensure their immortality after death. Those rituals and protocols included mummifying the body, casting magic spells and burying the person with goods thought to be needed in the afterlife. I found it all very fascinating.

We were taught some English at school and our English teacher is the only one I still remember vividly. She was called Miss Volkonsky and claimed to be a Russian princess who had fled the country after the Russian revolution. I believe she was telling the truth and we were scared of her. She was very thin, always wore white and had a wide turban of the same colour on her head, which all gave her the appearance of a ghost. She was not a very good teacher as, after six years of being in her class, all I could say when we arrived in England was good morning.

We had an excellent French education and, whilst our French did not sound precisely like the one spoken in Paris, it was nevertheless correct. The two other languages we were taught, English and Arabic, were fairly rudimentary. Before the revolution of 1952, we only had Arabic lessons two hours a week and that was the classical Arabic, which had nothing to do with the colloquial language spoken in the street by the servants and the local population. Although we spoke French at home, both my parents spoke fluent Arabic and it was the only language my maternal grandmother knew.

After the revolution, writing and reading Arabic became compulsory and I therefore had to have some private tuition in order to satisfy the new government requirements. My parents found a *sheikh* (a Muslim cleric) who came to the house once a week. He was as uninterested in teaching me as I was in learning. He did not start the lesson until he was served with a cup of Turkish coffee – probably to keep him awake, as I think he would have nodded off otherwise. He was a patient man and didn't get annoyed if I made a mistake; he just wasn't inspiring and I didn't get very far with his teaching.

The Lycée was a vast building with a private courtyard. It was sealed from the outside world by a big gate that was kept shut, except when we arrived in the morning and when we left at lunchtime. Above the main hammered door with a Greek lintel were the names of famous French writers 'Corneille, Racine, Molière, Voltaire and Descartes'. The playground was dusty and surrounded by a fence. It was bare and we used to just walk round and round. For some girls, the main attraction was the fact that the boys' school was on the other side of the fence, so they took the opportunity to exchange a few words, until the teacher in charge of looking after us noticed and told them off.

School started at 8.00 and finished at 1.00 pm. At break at 11.00 am, we would spill into the playground. I had two friends, called Liliane and Sheila. We didn't meet in each other's houses out of school, but played at break and went to the cinema together. That should have been enough for me, but it wasn't. I desperately wanted to be part of what I considered to be the 'in crowd'. This was a group of girls and boys who were very popular and looked very grown up; they were always going to parties and seemed to have lots of fun. I was never invited and felt like I was constantly missing out.

The system in the Lycée was such that students

remained in the same room for the whole school year and the teachers went from class to class. As a result, one stayed the entire school year with the same schoolmates and then moved with them from year to year. Strong friendship bonds were thus established, though not in my case. When we moved to London, I was surprised and delighted to find out that my friend Liliane was living fairly near to me. I met with her once, but she did not seem keen to continue with our friendship and we lost touch. I never saw my friend Sheila again or heard from her after we left Egypt.

We had a prize giving ceremony at the end of every school year. We called it *la distribution des prix* and attached a lot of importance to it. This was when prizes for academic performance were given out to top students. It was held in a large hall with a stage and was attended by the parents of students and some family members. The best pupils were called up and, as I always came second in my class, I was very proud to receive my prize, which was a book. We took ballet lessons – I was not particularly good at it and it didn't last long.

Most of the children in the school were Jewish, although there were a few Muslim girls. They came from prominent Egyptian families who were considered upper class, well educated and wealthy. They were the daughters of generals, high ranking officers, lawyers and bankers. We waited impatiently for the end of the school year, as it meant three wonderful long months by the seaside. On the last day of term, we all shouted out at the top of our voice the traditional song which meant that school was out. I still remember the words and the tune – '*vive les vacances, à bas les pénitences, les cahiers au feu et les livres au milieu'.*

I was easily frightened and sensitive from a very early age. I was only two years old in 1945, yet I remember being frightened by the sound of sirens and trying to hide in an empty bottom drawer. I did not want my mother to go out then, but she always did, promising to bring me back some sweets. I used to wake up early every morning from the age of seven or eight, to go into my parents' bedroom and check that they were still alive! I never shared those fears with anyone, certainly not with my parents.

Amina our maid was very superstitious and regularly believed that the end of the world was about to happen. One day, when I was about 12 years old, she told me that this was going to take place the next day at 1.00 pm. Of course, my mother dismissed this as nonsense and made me go to school. I remember walking or rather running back after classes, trying to make sure I got back home safely before it happened. I didn't like the swimming pool at the sporting club initially, as I was afraid of the water. I repeatedly refused to even try and go in, so one day my father finally lost patience and literally threw me in. Not the best of ideas, but it worked. I must have been six or seven and that's the way I learnt how to swim.

In Egypt, middle class Jewish girls generally did not work unless they had to, with the exception of some more independent girls who aspired to something more than a life of leisure. Those who had a job were young – the pretty salesgirls at the Cicurel store and the occasional secretary or teacher. Married women in Egypt could not work; for a married woman to do so was unthinkable, as it meant that her husband could no longer take care of his family.

This changed a little after the revolution of 1952, when the military regime capriciously confiscated Jewish businesses and property, often leaving their owners in financial ruin. In addition, companies were asked to limit the numbers of their Jewish employees, leaving those dismissed without an income. However, even if the wives wanted to work, there was very little that they could do. They had only known a life of leisure and were not trained for anything, except how to be a good housewife.

Generally, young Jewish girls were expected to learn how to cook and bake, while waiting for a suitable husband to come along. Many marriages were arranged, or the future couple were introduced to each other by mutual friends. The ladies continued their life of leisure after they got married. My mother did not take us to school – initially it was Amina or Hassan, the company chauffeur, and then when I got older I went on my own.

For my mother and many other women in the Jewish community, it was a life of leisure and perhaps a shallow one, at least that is how it would be perceived nowadays. Nevertheless, these ladies did not have the stress of having to manage working full time and bringing up a family. They knew their place and where they were going from an early age – they had never known anything else and, more often than not, would not have questioned it. Divorce was practically unheard of and, rather than face the scandal of one and the ensuing gossip, the couple just got on with it – or had very discreet affairs which were referred to as a five to seven – meaning that the couple usually met in a secret rendezvous between the hours of 5.00 and 7.00 pm.

This way of life could not have lasted forever, even if the political events culminating in the expulsion of the Jewish community had not happened. That was my parents' generation, but the younger one was beginning to want something more meaningful. Girls often started working after they left school, at least until they got married. Many youngsters were sent to Europe to finish their studies – having experienced a different lifestyle and mentality, they were often reluctant to come back to Egypt after their final exams.

My mother prepared the lunch with Salah's help and went out at around 11am. I think she followed the Aleppo tradition of having meat on Tuesdays, Wednesdays and Fridays, whereas Mondays and Thursdays were reserved for dairy only. She visited her sister Marie and her mother every day. There was never a particular reason for her daily visits, she just enjoyed being with them. That was part of the Jewish Egyptian culture, when families were close and saw each other almost every day. I miss that closeness and British people don't understand this. In England, you have to arrange a visit beforehand, whereas in Egypt people just knocked on your door.

Aside from shopping at leisure in all the fashionable stores in downtown Cairo, regular visits to your seamstress were a must, although my mother excelled at sewing. She enjoyed looking for new patterns in magazines such as Modes et Travaux and Elle. She played cards with friends once or twice a week and invited them – each lady took it in turn to receive guests and they called it 'son tour de *recevoir.'* They played cards, mostly two games called *poula* and canasta. The women also exchanged gossip, talked about their children and complained about their servants. It was not a simple affair, as lunch was offered, as well as coffee and pastries. These were always homemade and only ordered from a caterer on special occasions. Salah dressed in his best *galabeya* to serve the food. Whenever my mother hosted a card game, I did not go home after school, but straight to Aunt Marie's house.

My father returned home for lunch, had a two-hour nap after his meal and woke up refreshed and energised. He went back to the office at 4.00 until 7.00. That was the norm and, because of the hot weather, evening entertainment did not start until late – my parents went out about 9.00 pm. Cairo came alive at night and the picture shows in the outdoor cinemas started at 9.00 or 10.00 pm, whereas for attractions in night clubs it was usually after the stroke of midnight.

There were times when we all went to visit Aunt Marie and my grandmother after school and stayed for lunch, with my father joining us. That was often impromptu, and my mother and aunt rustled up a last-minute dish together. My aunt never came to our house – perhaps it was difficult to leave my grandmother on her own. Children's perceptions vary – I remember my grandmother as quiet, reserved and rather vulnerable, but my cousin Doris tells me she was a little scared of her.

It is likely that I would have remained close to my father's family if most of them had not emigrated to Israel. Instead, there were only my aunts Sophie and Matty left.

We saw Sophie on a regular basis, but Matty was still busy doing her own thing. My mother's family became central to my life, so I was more exposed to their Aleppo culture. It was a judgmental, conventional one and you were expected to stick to 'the norm' and fit into the mould. If you didn't, you were pushed aside or labelled. Zaki, Marie's husband, was not a pushy person, quite the opposite. He more or less faded into the background and that was how the rest of the family behaved towards him. They were fond of him, but I am not sure they respected him or referred to him for any opinions. Nina, Victor's wife, came from a wealthy, well to do family. She had had a privileged upbringing, totally different from my mother's family and I think there was a certain resentment towards her. This was never acknowledged, of course – instead, she was made fun of behind her back and underestimated.

My father did not particularly like Marie because she had a huge influence on my mother and not always a positive one. She was a strong woman and the centre point of the family. Although he was wary of her, my father respected her opinion and often referred to her for advice. All the festivals were celebrated in her house, with all the family round the table. Oddly, we never celebrated with my father's family, although he was close to them.

They seemed to be a separate part of his life and I wish they hadn't been. Years later, when we were living in London, my father was more open about how he felt about my mother's family. He didn't seem happy when my mother invited her brother Victor and his wife on a Sunday and always made his appearance late –and he was then perfectly charming! The same thing happened when Marie came to stay with us. Clement was the exception and the only one whose company my father seemed to enjoy, probably because my uncle was gregarious, very confident and successful.

Many Jewish families considered boys to be more important than girls. This was not the case with both sides of my family, perhaps because we were all girls. Education was important and we were encouraged to do well at school. Because of the heat, we did not go back to school in the afternoon and always had lunch together as a family. We waited for my father to come back from the office and after lunch, my parents would retire to their bedroom for an afternoon nap. My mother supervised our homework, saw to it that we had an afternoon snack and then left us to carry on with her social life, going to Groppi or playing cards with her friends. She often went shopping and sometimes took me with her. She returned home around 7.00 pm, because that was the time my father finished work. Dinner was something light, yoghurt, cheese, eggs, bread with jam and fruit. My parents would see to us children and then go out with their friends until the early hours of the morning. Sundays were reserved for the children.

As well as Groppi, there were many tearooms in Cairo where friends met for a coffee, a pastry and of course some gossip. Familiar names were A L'Américaine, La Parisienne, Café Riche and the patisserie Loques. Groppi was always my favourite as, apart from the meringue with chantilly cream, I was very fond of their marquise aux marrons (with chestnut cream) and their peach melba. A L'Américaine served huge sandwiches stuffed with cold cuts. Nowadays we would never think of indulging in all those pastries and other fattening things. Things were different back then, no one worried about obesity and being healthy meant being well fed. Generally, people were not fat because on the whole the diet was healthy. We ate a lot of vegetables cooked with olive oil and lunch was the main meal.

There was a Literary Club called Les Amitiés Françaises and a library where we could borrow French books and magazines. The well-known French bookshop Hachette had a branch in the centre of Cairo in Soliman Pacha Square; a relative by marriage, Uncle Marco, worked there. The shop was like an Aladdin's cave, stacked with books for all ages and with a special section for children's books. There were some chairs and tables so people could relax while browsing.

My favourite books as a young child were Babar the Elephant and then Tintin and Bécassine. Tintin is well known outside France and the books have been translated into English. Bécassine was a French comic strip, published in a magazine called La Semaine de Suzettte. The main character, Bécassine, was depicted as a typical Breton peasant, with a lace coiffe and clogs. She was portrayed as a typical provincial girl, rather naive and her name was often used in a conversation as a way of describing someone silly. Her books were very successful. I also liked 'One thousand and one nights' and in particular the tale of 'Ali Baba and the forty thieves'. There were quite a few French newspapers and magazines printed in Egypt, the main ones being Le Journal du Caire, Le Progrés Egyptien and La Bourse Egyptienne.

Women were fussed over during their pregnancy. After the birth of a child, the new mother had to stay in bed for eight days. Everyone was at her beck and call and, in order to help her recuperate and build up her strength, she was supposed to eat a lot of sweet things. One such delicacy was called *mefataa*. It was made with a mixture of walnuts, pistachio nuts, almonds, pine nuts and fresh coconut, all soaked in hot olive oil. The mixture was then thrown into a large saucepan containing nothing but pure honey, to which a variety of spices were added. This thick mixture had to be turned constantly until it had reached the right consistency. It took a lot of time and effort, so it was always made in large quantities. The new mother was supposed to eat this many times in the day, in order to help keep her strength up while breastfeeding. It was very fattening, so she inevitably put on a lot of weight in just one week.

Giving birth was a much simpler event for Egyptian women. They usually did this at home, helped by a midwife, unless there were complications. In the villages, where giving birth was considered a natural thing, the new mother simply carried on with her routine straight afterwards.

My parents had a very good social life and went out practically every evening. They had a close-knit group of friends consisting of another three couples and they shared many things – holidays, of course, but also evenings out for a meal or dinner dancing. Restaurants stayed open very late; people didn't dine until midnight and then went out dancing. One of their regular haunts was the Semiramis hotel rooftop. The hotel still exists and is now part of the Hilton chain. They regularly went to Cairo's trendiest entertainment venue, called L'Auberge des Pyramides, a favourite of King Farouk. It had a popular restaurant, a casino and a modern nightclub featuring entertainment brought from Europe and Latin America.

The weather was always warm and it very rarely rained, so evenings out in the open air were the norm. I remember all the songs my parents danced to – Jealousy, by Frankie Lane, La Comparsita, Besame Mucho, Cerisiers Roses et Pommiers Blancs (Cherry Pink and Apple Blossom White). My father loved the song Besame Mucho and even now I get tearful when I hear it. This was the era of romance and romantic music, and it must have been wonderful to go dancing in the open air, with a great view of the Nile. The added bonus was that you never had to worry about the weather.

Until the fifties, Cairo was a major stop on tours by performing arts companies such as the Comédie Française and La Scala opera house. My parents always went to the theatre when the former was in town. They also loved tennis and went to watch all the main tournaments; famous players of the time included Pancho Gonzales, Lew Hoad, Ashley Cooper and Ken Rosewall. Cairo and Alexandria had practically everything a European capital offered. As well as an opera, symphony, concerts, horse racing and shows, there were many colonial style nightclubs with elaborate shows. The most recent movies from France, England and America were shown in various cinemas across the cities, always with French subtitles.

The Jewish Egyptian community considered itself more European than Arab. The latest fashions from Paris were displayed in the numerous Cairo stores. Most ladies had their personal dressmaker who could whip up the latest Paris design from a pattern. Clothes were very important in Egypt's two main cities, Cairo and Alexandria. The women were always well dressed, and most gentlemen possessed at least one white sharkskin suit – handmade by expert Egyptian tailors. This is what they wore when they went out in the evening, especially on holiday. Jewellery was always the preferred gift item and women collected jewellery – this applied to Egyptian women as well and even the 'fellah' woman wore 18 carat or 22 carat bangles on her wrists.

It was a privileged life for those who led a European lifestyle, but out of reach for most Egyptians, unless they were wealthy professionals. What was acceptable in Egypt in the 40s and 50s would be perceived as a social injustice nowadays. Underneath this glamorous veneer and existing side by side with it, was a lot of poverty. We were not exposed to it, but I remember the beggars in the street, many of them blind or with limbs missing.

My father was very fond of horse racing and whenever my uncle Clement was in town, they went to the racecourse together. Another one of my father's pastimes was a game called *tric-trac*. The Egyptians call it *tawla* and it's a form of backgammon. He played it with Zaki, Marie's husband, when they had nothing else to do and wanted to entertain themselves. They sat round a low table on which they opened a box of dark wood.

The game seemed shrouded in mystery and I was always curious to find out more about it, so I was interested to read a detailed description by Alain Bigio, in his book The Journey from Ismaeleya to Higienapolis. Inside the box, there were six triangles at the top and bottom of the open box. Then there were 30 round and flat chips, half of them white and the rest black. My father and my uncle placed them on the board in a manner that seemed random, although it probably wasn't. There were two small white cubes which were the dice and I liked the distinctive noise they made when they were thrown. The players then shouted words which had no apparent meaning but were supposed to encourage the dice. It was quite funny watching them play. The rules of the game were complicated and I never understood them. This game was also played by Egyptian men in cafes.

Like many families in Egypt, we did not own a dog or a cat – it would have been impossible anyway, as we lived in an apartment, but my parents would not have entertained the idea of a pet. Egyptians did not like dogs, which therefore tended to be mistreated. The only experience I had of looking after a living creature was at school. We once had to take care of silkworms. We fed them mulberry leaves and watched them build a cocoon around themselves; we were fascinated when one day the cocoon was pierced and a moth came out.

Most children were members of the scouts or girl guides. There was a Jewish sports club called the Maccabi, to which many young boys belonged. It was initially a Zionist movement established in Czechoslovakia in the 1920s to promote physical education among Jewish youth. They regularly went on excursions and played sports, but the goal of the Maccabi was probably to recruit young Jewish boys to the Zionist project in Palestine/Israel.

I was a girl guide in a Jewish group. There were weekly meetings when we learned a few things, one of which was to tie the six most important knots. We had day trips and camping holidays and slept in tents, which seemed a big adventure. I remember the wonderful smell of strawberry jam cooking, which greeted me on my return home from one of those trips. The leader of the group was a charismatic young woman who was adored by all of us. She was tragically killed in a car accident one night on the road between Cairo and Alexandria. The girl guides were never the same after that. As the school I attended was an all-girls one, some of the girls joined the Maccabi as a way of meeting boys. My parents would not have allowed it, but I was not tempted anyway.

Sporting clubs were an important part of social life. The most exclusive was the Gezirah Sporting Club in Zamalek, but there were also the Heliopolis Sporting Club and the Maadi Sporting Club. My parents were members of the Tawfikiya Tennis Club, which we referred to as the TTC. It was smaller than the others and more accessible to the middle classes. This was where my parents and their friends met most Sundays.

The Tawfikieh Tennis Club was British owned and managed by an English gentleman called Mr. Hooper. His daughter Joyce was part of the glamorous older crowd. We had very little to do with them, but in 1956, after we were expelled from Egypt, we bumped into them in Kensington Gardens. The hierarchical perception had levelled off then and they were just simple refugees like us.

The club had huge expanses of well-tended grass, where we could run and play. Families with their children, young and old, sat at tables in the gardens, joined by friends. The tables were large and all had parasols. The swimming pool was huge, or so it seemed and there were red-earth tennis courts and a restaurant serving delicious mezze, cakes and refreshments, always welcome after a swim. If I remember the chocolate meringue from Groppi, Nicole remembers a cake called L'Argentin which was the speciality of the club – it was made with layers of chocolate and cream. The gardens were well maintained by an army of local gardeners. My parents always sat with their group of friends, and children played together. The older girls looked very glamorous in their bikinis and had great figures.

The children played all sorts of games, such as hide and seek, marbles and hopscotch when we were little, and more sophisticated games when we got older. There were other activities, such as ping pong tables. One passion was collecting – cinema programmes were a favourite and also signed photos of glamorous Hollywood stars. We used to buy Coca-Cola drinks in small bottles and asked the barman to give us the bottle tops; each bottle top had a letter and, if you managed to make up the name of Coca-Cola with the ones you had collected, you won a big prize. We never did, as despite all our efforts and enthusiasm, we just kept getting the same letters again and again.

Special activities were organised at the club, such as dinner dances and New Year's Eve celebrations. For big events, there was an orchestra and sometimes just records with loudspeakers, playing American, Italian and French dance rhythms. Tennis was played on clay courts and small Egyptian children picked up the ball when the players shouted *kora* (ball). They were small, poor children and they ran barefoot behind the balls to earn some small change, instead of going to school. It sounds totally unacceptable now, but we were not aware of the social injustice at the time. We were busy having fun playing, whilst our parents gossiped or played cards.

We were friendly with a couple called Felix and Edith Ezri. They had a daughter called Mireille and I often played with her. Unlike my parents, Felix and Edith were very sporty and loved playing tennis at the club. Sometimes my parents left me with them and returned home. The Ezris lived in downtown Cairo near the Metro cinema and, as they did not have a car, we went back on the tram – that was quite an adventure and something I would not have done with my parents, as neither of them had ever used a tramcar.

Cairo was a modern cosmopolitan city, with apartment blocks, buses and trams. There were 22 tram lines in Cairo alone, carrying approximately 250,000 passengers daily. A Cairo tramcar was nothing like those you see in European cities. For a start, there was no such thing as queuing: the tram arrived and everyone scrambled to get on it. You had to buy a ticket for every trip and this could not be bought in advance. The seats were uncomfortable wooden ones and, if the tram was full, people still got on and hung on as best as they could, which could be dangerous at times. They talked amongst themselves; complete strangers started discussing politics, the government or any current topic. Women had their bottom pinched regularly and only used the tram when they had to get to work and had no other option. You also had to be very careful of the pickpockets who had a field day when everyone was packed so tightly. Mostly though, everything was good humoured, because Egyptians are friendly people who take things philosophically.

More often than not, we went to the Tawfikieh Tennis Club on a Sunday and I can't help wishing that my parents had been a little more adventurous and taken us to see some of the wonderful sights of Cairo. Perhaps visiting a mosque may have been a step too far, but there were many other places. I was taken to the Khan Khalili market just once – Cairo's famous bazaar and souk – yet it is one of Cairo's main attractions for tourists and Egyptians alike.

When we lived in Cairo, the Ezbekeya Gardens were a favourite with many Cairenes. This was where they went for walks and had family picnics on their days off and holidays. The gardens were lovely, covered a large area and were well-tended. Many relationships were forged there and that is where Amina, our maid, used to arrange to meet her husband-to-be. They were also famous because of a large theatre which was the stage for most of the monthly concerts held by the beloved Arab singer, Om Kalsoum. Unfortunately, they are only partially present now, as two multi-storey car parks have been built on large areas of the gardens.

Sometimes we left the club early and went to Groppi for a drink. The children were happy with an ice cream or a cake, but the adults preferred a drink and enjoyed the numerous mezze served with it – the black and green olives, grilled pistachios, cashew nuts, white salty cheese cubes, tahini salad and cucumber pickles. A light snack was Egyptian bread, called *shami* bread, served with tahini, humous and aubergine dips.

There were many brasseries in Cairo and if you were a regular customer in an establishment, the owner made sure that you were served a few extras with your drink, such as fried chicken livers or cod roe which was called *bastourma*. The more drinks the customer ordered, the more mezze appeared on the table. Then of course there was the constant stream of street sellers, trying to tempt the customer with more delicacies.

I liked Sundays because I spent it with my parents and we always went out for the day. If not to the sporting club, then to the Mena House Hotel. It was located five miles from the centre of Cairo and stood at the foot of the Pyramids plateau – guests had a priceless view of the Pyramids from the hotel bedrooms and restaurant terrace. In keeping with its romantic desert setting, the Mena House catered for wealthy socialites and offered luxurious hospitality. It had elegant furniture, superb restaurants, a bar that served imported drinks, libraries, rooms for card games, and a huge swimming pool.

The Mena House Hotel was not just a luxury hotel, it was a legend. Until today, it remains by far the most iconic place to stay near the Pyramids in Giza. It is famous for its harem windows, known as *mashrabia* – a carved woodwork which was introduced to Egypt during the Islamic period, from 750 AC onwards. Brass embossed doors, blue tiles, mother-of-pearl and mosaics of coloured marbles all helped to give the hotel the impression of a fairy tale palace. The great dining hall was an exact replica of a Cairo mosque.

Many celebrities had stayed there – Agatha Christie, who wrote the first pages of Death on the Nile during one of her visits, Churchill, Montgomery, Roosevelt, Cecil B. De Mille and Edward, Prince of Wales. The Aga Khan and the Begum, Jane Fonda and Om Kalsoum were amongst the numerous actors, musicians, politicians and celebrities who had enjoyed the hotel's luxurious hospitality. They were all drawn by what it offered its wealthy clients – the magic of the desert and the charm of history. The First World War brought Winston Churchill there for the first time; he fell in love with the luxury retreat and became a lifelong regular visitor, as was King Farouk, who from time to time raced his red sports car through the Pyramid Road to the Mena House for a drink.

There is an amusing anecdote relating to the Mena House. During the First World War, an Australian officer was caught naked chasing a woman through the hotel corridors. In his defence, he quoted an Australian army regulation which stated that 'an officer may wear any costume appropriate to the sport in which he is engaged'.

The hotel was a magical place for me. What I remember best are the large gardens where the scent of the jasmine flower was heady and I loved its intoxicating smell. Vendors outside sold heavily scented jasmine garlands. In addition, there was always the exciting prospect of bumping into someone famous while there. Even after all these years, I still think of the Mena House with great fondness and nostalgia. It's a reminder of a golden bygone era, a part of my childhood which I can never recapture. This was where my romantic hero Omar Sharif regularly stayed and where Charlton Heston rode a horse every day in the hotel gardens during the filming of The Ten Commandments. Robert Taylor and Eleanor Parker shot large parts of Valley of the Kings around the hotel.

My father drove there, as he had a car he was very proud of, a Ford model, which unfortunately caught fire one day on an afternoon outing in Alexandria. He didn't use the car during the week as he didn't need to – he could walk everywhere and also used the services of Hassan, the company chauffeur. I think Hassan was more my father's chauffeur than the company's and they were very fond of each other.

To get to the Mena House hotel, we left downtown Cairo by the Kasr-El-Nil bridge, the iconic one with the lion head on each side. Sometimes we had to wait while the bridge closed to let boats through. We drove along what was then the desert road to the Pyramids; it was a wonderful drive and virtually traffic-free. Along the road, we saw all kinds of crops, ready harvests and the occasional old man riding sideways on a donkey, wearing a long dress, his bare feet crossed, rocking to the motion of the donkey's walk. Eventually, the three Pyramids came into sight on the horizon – the Great Pyramid of Cheops, Khephren and Mykerinos. Today, this desert road has become an urban jungle and is sadly unrecognisable, as it's totally built up and very busy. You can hardly see the Pyramids amongst the tall apartment blocks and satellite dishes. Thankfully, the hotel is still there, but it's no longer an icon. It's been totally renovated and is now part of the Marriott chain.

Although the hotel was within striking distance of the Pyramids and the Sphinx, we never actually went to visit them and it was enough to see them from the terrace. They were part of our everyday life, something else we took for granted and we didn't look at them like tourists did. Neither did we pay any particular attention to the graceful silhouette of the camels in the distance. The Pyramids have always been Cairo's top attraction, so the site was always full of tourists, photographers, souvenir vendors, dealers in fake antiquities and guides deafening you with their entreaties. I visited them in 1994 and it wasn't a positive experience.

We once went for a ride around the Pyramids in a *yarabeya hantoor*. This is the equivalent of a ride in a horse and carriage in Central Park in New York, only it's Egyptian style and certainly not as comfortable. We never went on a camel ride and it's not something I regret. Another treat was a tour in a *dahabeya*, a boat on the Nile.

My father was the disciplinarian in the family and very strict. He never laid a finger on us – all he had to do was raise his voice, roll his eyes and pretend to take out his belt. That always stopped us in our tracks. He controlled our lives and we couldn't go anywhere without his approval. There were many films we were not allowed to see, for one reason or another, and he also checked everything I read. I was very fond of a couple of French magazines, which in fact were quite harmless romances, but not in his eyes. I tried to hide them under my bed, but he always found them and destroyed them. Instead, we used to go regularly to a lending library where everything we borrowed was carefully checked. The only magazine I was allowed to read was called *Bonnes Soirées*, a weekly women's magazine.

My mother never raised her voice and always appeared outwardly calm, even when my father occasionally lost his temper. She always seemed to accept his outbursts philosophically, perhaps because she knew that he loved his family dearly. If she was upset or annoyed, we were rarely aware of it. She was completely the opposite in temperament – she didn't show her emotions and, if anything, was rather cold and not very affectionate. Her sister Marie was very much like her, so perhaps it was a culture or a defence mechanism due to a difficult upbringing. I noticed my father's outbursts much more in London, but not particularly when we had lived in Egypt – perhaps he had been outwardly calmer back then. I realise now that my father suffered from anxiety and obsessive compulsive behaviour. He had repetitive gestures, like washing his hands several times. His anxiety often culminated in bouts of exasperation when he screamed and ranted for a few minutes, then very quickly calmed down.

We went to the cinema on a regular basis. I remember names like Cinema Rivoli, Diana, Odeon, the open-air Miami and my favourite, the Metro – which is still there but showing mostly Arabic films. On holiday, we went to open air cinemas. These were not drive-in ones, like you see in America, but had regular rattan chairs lined up in a row. Most of these cinemas have disappeared now and have been replaced by modern multi-screen venues.

The Movietone News was shown first, which I always found very interesting. That was when we got the news from abroad and a glimpse of what was going on outside Egypt. The Queen's Coronation in 1953 was the world event I remember best, as it all looked very solemn and glamorous. We saw all the American films popular at the time – From Here to Eternity, The Robe, and Rebel without a Cause with James Dean. All the films had subtitles in French. In 1955, Blackboard Jungle was released and caused quite a stir – it was the start of the rock and roll era and the film was considered subversive at the time. Much to my disappointment, I was not allowed to go and see it.

I loved Fernandel, France's top comic actor at the time and went to see all his films. The Don Camillo series were my favourite – Fernandel is well remembered for his portrayal of the irascible Italian village priest at war with the town's communist mayor. American audiences remember him from Around the World in 80 Days, where he played David Niven's coachman. Actresses like Bette Davis, Ava Gardner, Rita Hayworth and Heidi Lamar seemed the height of sophistication. Films were romantic, as crime was not so bloody or lovemaking so explicit. It was easy to imagine yourself in the place of the heroine. I was fascinated with Vivian Leigh as Scarlett O'Hara in Gone with the Wind and, like every other young girl, fell in love with Clark Gable as Rhett Butler.

The Egyptian film industry was prolific and actors like Omar Sharif and his then wife Faten Hamama were extremely popular, yet we never went to the cinema to watch an Egyptian film – at least, my family didn't. I am glad that our maid Amina went to the cinema regularly when we holidayed in Ras-El-Bar and took me with her, otherwise I would have missed out on the experience.

There were regular cinema showings on Saturday mornings, mostly cartoons with a talent competition before the main show. Some of the acts were quite good. I still remember a particular one, which was a song in a mixture of French and colloquial Arabic and very funny. My parents were never interested in Egyptian culture or music and instead knew all the popular French songs. I only learnt to appreciate Egyptian music when I was much older and had been living in England for many years.

Holidays by the sea

Summers were the best. Our school holidays lasted three months – June, July and August. Because of the unbearable Cairo heat in summer, the tradition was to escape the city and go to the seaside. For many years, we spent those summer months in Alexandria. My parents rented an apartment in the fashionable residential area of Sidi Bichr, as did their close group of friends. We were also joined by Uncle Mayer and his family and sometimes by Aunt Marie. We travelled from Cairo to Alexandria by car and stopped along the way in a small town called Tanta. The journey took over three hours. Getting ready for the holidays involved much packing, as we took everything but the kitchen sink with us. Although the apartment had many amenities such as a refrigerator and kitchen equipment, we had to take our own bedding, towels and everything else we thought we might need for three months.

The most magical moment was when we finally arrived in Alexandria and, going down a small street, my father shouted *Et voilà la mer* – 'here is the sea' – we could see the Mediterranean, shimmering in the distance, blue and sparkling in the sun. Alexandria had a special scent; it was the sea salt, which you could smell a mile away, in contrast to Cairo, which had a dry desert smell. The residential areas were along the Corniche and all the fashionable hotels, casinos and nightclubs looked towards the sea – Hotel Beau Rivage, the Casino of Shatby and Montazah Palace, set in extensive gardens overlooking the coast. The apartment my parents rented was always near the waterfront, a few minutes' walk from the beach.

Alexandria covered more than 25 kilometres of coastline. Along the coast road lay a succession of beaches which had been given cosmopolitan names – Chatby, Stanley, Glymonopoulo, San Stefano. They were all lined with restaurants, dance halls and casinos. Sumptuous villas nestled among the palm trees, as well as luxury apartment houses. As with Cairo, the city's fashion boutiques, pastry shops and fancy grocery stores vied with those of the greatest European capitals. The same could also be said of the city's schools, bookstores, cinemas and theatres. Victoria College, the oldest English language public school outside Great Britain, and the French college Saint-Marc were the establishments where the wealthy families chose to send their children. French was the language of elite social circles throughout Egypt, in Cairo as well as Alexandria. It was also spoken by middle class Egyptians, as a means of expressing their hatred for the English.

Alexandria was a beautiful city at that time, with a long winding Corniche which defined the city. It started at the Western Harbour and followed the shoreline to King Farouk's former palace at Montazah. His other palace was located in the Ras-el-Tin quarter of the city. It was built on a promontory, which in antiquity had been the site of the Island of Pharoah. The King abdicated from there in 1952. One of the grandest hotels was the Hotel Cecil, which staged grand balls during the holiday season. The majority of the buildings along the Corniche were white or pastel-coloured, as is the case in most Mediterranean towns, and the luxurious villas had red roofs. Alexandria was hot and humid in the summer, with an almost constant onshore breeze.

At the eastern end of the Corniche was the port of Alexandria. You could observe the traditional fishermen, but equally see many pleasure yachts and large cruise ships. We used to meet up with a colleague of my father's who managed the Alexandria branch of John Dickinson. His name was Jacques Jerusalmy, his wife was called Tita and their daughter Monique. Before we met them, for some reason we always sang a little refrain which went 'we are going to meet Tita, Monique and Jacques Jerusalmy'. Tita always brought with her a wonderful cherry pie. I still remember one incident involving Jacques Jerusalmy. My sister Nicole was as thin as I was chubby. One day, my mother, Jacques, myself and Nicole were walking along the beach. We were very near the water and a wave suddenly swept Nicole away. Jacques was very quick to jump into the water and catch her.

Alexandria had wide expanses of beaches, all immaculately clean and covered with a fine golden sand. The beach at Chatby had huge waves, Stanley and Sidi Bishr were known for their very fine white sand and Sporting had two beautiful bays. You were spoilt for choice, but my parents always chose Sidi Bichr. Montazah had the most beautiful beach. It belonged to the King at the time, so it was out of bounds. However, following the Egyptian revolution and the abdication of King Farouk, the beach was opened to the general public.

The Corniche was bordered by a low wall which was broken now and then by a wooden stairway leading to the various beaches below. There were long rows of cabins located under the promenade and each had its own terrace or entrance hall. There were plenty of showers near each set of cabins, and we always had to shower and change into clean clothes before going back to the apartment at lunchtime – it was important to wash off the sea salt and the sand that stuck to your body. The restaurants all had bamboo thatches that protected patrons and beachgoers when the tables were put out on the pavement. These thatches were called *hassiras*.

The beaches were patrolled by lifeguards who put up their umbrella some distance from the water. There were plenty of vendors peddling their wares along the beach. The sellers of pastries dripping with syrup carried them in a glass case balanced on their shoulders. There were also the vendors of an Egyptian favourite called *lebb*. These are toasted pumpkin or watermelon seeds, sold twisted into a newspaper or cornets. Eating *lebb* was a national pastime and people ate them while conversing, in cafés, after a cinema performance or just relaxing at home.

The beach at Sidi Bichr was a long expanse of fine golden sand, set against the background of the blue Mediterranean Sea. I loved dipping my toes in the wet sand or standing at the edge of the water, watching the gentle waves come in. I had already learnt how to swim in the pool of the Tawfikieh Tennis Club, but perfected this during the summer. The sea was nearly always calm and we were only allowed in if the flag was white, which meant that it was safe. We always found something to do and were never bored. One of our favourite pastimes on the beach was to try and catch crabs and there was much excitement when someone caught one. We held them on their belly so they wouldn't pinch our fingers and always put them back in the sea. The most evocative time of day was at sunset, when you could watch the spectacular sun slowly plunge into the sea and disappear.

It was always sunny in Egypt and it hardly ever rained. There were only two seasons to speak of: winter and summer. Winter was very mild and we did not need to wear a coat, although the evenings were colder. Summers were hot, more so in July and August when the dry heat became unbearable in cities like Cairo. We took the weather for granted as we had never known anything else – of course the sun was going to shine every day; there was no reason why it shouldn't and there was no weather forecast. However, we had to check the flag and the water when we arrived at the beach – a red flag indicated that the sea was rough and a white one that it was calm and safe to go in.

Holidays were endless days of sunshine. The men accompanied their families and initially stayed for a few days. They then had to go back to Cairo for their jobs. They returned every weekend, arriving pasty-looking on a Friday and leaving again on a Sunday. They came by train, as it was probably easier than the car journey and there was a fast train from Cairo to Alexandria called the Diesel.

We all did the usual holiday things – every morning was spent by the sea and, because the water was always warm, it was possible to go in and out of the sea constantly. The sand was very fine and felt like silk and when you came out of the water, the heat of the sun dried you in a couple of minutes. I remember the gentle sound of the waves against the shore, the shimmering blue of the Mediterranean and the warm rays of the sun on your face.

The women passed the time chatting and doing embroidery, which we called *petit point*. The designs were wonderfully intricate and lovely enough to be framed – flowers with fawns and peacocks, a prince whispering to his princess. The children also had their own needlepoint frame and would spend a little time concentrating on this, mostly to cool down from the heat of the sun. This never lasted very long, as playing on the beach and going in the sea was much more fun.

We went back to our apartments at lunch time and had a siesta after lunch. I hated this as I always woke up feeling tired and in a bad mood. Late afternoons and evenings were spent playing games outside or going to an open-air cinema. We also played board games such as ludo, snakes and ladders, and dominos. We were very lucky to be able to spend three months by the seaside every year, although everyone took this for granted, not having known anything different and having nothing else to compare it with.

On weekends, when the men were there, we went to downtown Alexandria for an ice cream or a cake in one of the wonderful patisseries. The one I remember most vividly was called Athinéos, but there were many others – Délices, Pastroudis, Trianon and many more. The best ice cream was called *dondurma*. It was made with mastik, a Greek or Turkish speciality – the mastik was chewy and gave the ice cream a unique taste.

On weekend evenings, the adults went to one of the many restaurants, Le Monseigneur, Le Romance or San Stefano, where they could have a meal, followed by entertainment and dancing. There were also numerous casinos, which were cafe-bars on the seafront. An orchestra played the latest hits and was often accompanied by a singer. In 1951, the most popular song which was heard everywhere was Jezebel by Frankie Lane. The one we knew and was played constantly was the French version by Charles Aznavour. If I ever hear it, the memories come flooding back.

There was a very well-known restaurant called Benyamine. Benyamine was a Yemenite Jew who was famous for his *ful medames* and *ta'amiya'* (falafel), both the national dishes of Egypt. *Ful medames*, a dish made with fava beans, traces its origin to Ancient Egypt. We sometimes used to go to eat fish at Abukir. This was the location of the naval battle between Napoleon's fleet and the British navy under Admiral Nelson, which ended with the destruction of the

French navy and a British victory. You could go into the kitchen to have a look at the available fish that day and choose the one you wanted, which would then be charcoal grilled. Our favourites were *doradas* (sea breams) and red mullets.

We sometimes went to a zoo with beautiful gardens in a place called Nouzha, which was located inland, near the airport. My favourite animals were the monkeys and I could have spent hours watching them at play. There was a lake inhabited by pelicans and the gardens were full of beautiful flowers.

I often went on long bike rides with my father, either along the coastline or all the way to downtown Alexandria. I had a very bad fall once, but my father encouraged me to get straight back on the bike. It was only many years later when I was on holiday in Italy that I suddenly developed a fear of riding a bike. I loved summers in Alexandria, but then something changed, which slightly spoilt my enjoyment. In the afternoon, after the siesta, all the children from my parents' group of friends played together, away from the adults who were probably chatting or playing cards. There were about 12 of us and I was the oldest. That was irrelevant because, thanks to the efforts of a couple of children, I started to get pushed out. I was upset, but kept quiet initially. When I eventually mentioned it to my mother, she didn't believe me. Her reply was that I was either lying or imagining it. I didn't dare bring up the subject again, so it was left at that.

There were reasons why it would not have occurred to me to argue further with my mother or insist that she listen. I was used to doing what was expected of me and her dismissive response did not really come as a surprise. In any case, she would not have given me the benefit of the doubt and would have preferred to believe anyone else over me. I was the difficult child who presumably exaggerated everything, and perhaps I did.

After many years spending the summer holidays in Alexandria, my parents and their friends decided they needed a change and chose a resort called Ras-El-Bar, which translates as 'head of the land'. It is located on the Mediterranean at the mouth of the Damietta Nile branch, hence the name. It is now a fashionable all year round resort, but back then it was solely a summer one and a unique Egyptian experience. During the summer the Nile was at its lowest point and at Ras El-Bar, the Damietta branch of the Nile met the Mediterranean. People took advantage of the river's low levels and constructed a whole village of reed and wood – only for it to be taken down at the end of the summer, when the Nile would again rise and flood the entire area. This temporary summer resort made of straw huts on stilts suddenly became fashionable. People liked living on top of each other, but I much preferred the comfort of a summer apartment in Alexandria.

The accommodation consisted of cabanas erected just for the summer season – we called them *huttes*, or *eshash* in Arabic. My parents, together with their friends, rented what amounted to a two-bedroom cabana in a pavilion of six or eight. Each family had their own, but they were next door to each other, so there could not have been any privacy. It was all very basic and my parents and their friends liked this rustic charm. Because this was where the Nile met the Mediterranean, the sea was not blue but was dark in colour and so was the sand. There was only one Jewish hotel in the resort, called the Aslan. It was open to non-residents and there were evening dances on the terrace every night. A small orchestra played tangos, waltzes and other dances, and everyone converged on the dance floor. The men always wore white suits and the women low cut dresses.

Meals were taken outside on the verandah and this was where the street vendors came into their own. They started early in the morning selling *ful medames* (a stew of cooked fava beans served with oil and lemon juice and a hardboiled egg) and *ta'amiya*, the Egyptian word for falafel (deep fried balls made from chickpeas). The *ful* seller stopped with his cart outside our pavilion, we handed him a large pot and he filled it up. A special treat was something called *foulade*, which we sometimes had for brunch. It was *ful medames*, served with olives, tomatoes, feta cheese and bread. Later on in the morning, there were the vegetable sellers and the men selling freshly caught fish. Once the daily 'shopping' was done, the maid started preparing the lunch.

My favourite sweet was called *lokomadis*, deep fried doughnut balls soaked in a sugar syrup and served warm. I finally found something that resembled them in a Turkish supermarket in North London, but they did not taste as wonderful as the ones I remember from our holidays in Ras-El-Bar. Sometimes, Amina took me to see an Arabic film with her, which I loved. Omar Sharif and his then wife Faten

Hamama were very popular and Amina also liked the films of Samia Gamal who, until today, remains the best known and loved Egyptian actress and the greatest belly dancer.

Apart from the daily siesta, we spent all our time outside. The beach was a few minutes' walk away and we rushed there as soon as we had finished our breakfast. We had cabins where we could change after a shower. In the afternoon we played games and went to the open-air cinema. Meals were simple as the cooking facilities were basic. From 4.00 pm, after the siesta, the street vendors started again, chanting the praises of what they were selling and generally making a lot of noise. You could get anything from them – fizzy drinks, fruit juices, pastries, ice creams and all sorts of sweets. These sellers did not work for themselves, but for someone who paid them a percentage of their earnings. The most famous of them was called Mohamed Eid. The seller chanted whatever he was selling and added the name of his boss; I especially remember the chant of *kaimak kaimak Mohamed Eid'* – that was ice cream.

We went to bed late, but the adults partied well into the night. They played cards or went to the open-air dancing. There was a small train which went round the resort and ran until the early hours of the morning. All the shops, cafes and restaurants stayed open until at least 3.00 am and the night life continued beyond that. Music could be heard from the open-air dancing.

Helwan (from the word *helw*, which means nice or sweet in Arabic) was a small town south of Cairo. It was known for its pure air and its mineral water springs. People went there for a few days of relaxation, to smell the 'good air' and take the cure, which consisted of drinking glass after glass of the mineral waters and soaking daily in the mineral springs. It was believed that this could fortify and cure any ailment under the sun. There was an astronomical observatory in Helwan, the Khedivial Astronomical Observatory, built in the 1900s. It was from there that scientists had observed Halley's Comet.

We never went to Upper Egypt, probably because it was too hot and it was far more preferable to spend summer by the seaside. Although we studied Ancient Egyptian history at school, I never got the chance to visit any of the famous temples in Luxor and Karnak, but finally got the opportunity during a Nile cruise in 1994. It was very interesting, but also very tiring – we had to get up at the crack of dawn every morning, as the heat would make any visit later on in the day very uncomfortable.

Egyptian and Jewish festivals and customs

I have great memories of the many festivals in Egypt – there always seemed to be one in progress, as some saint had to be honoured or a rite performed. The first ten days of the sacred Moharram, the opening month of the year, were celebrated. In the second month, the pilgrims returning from Mecca were welcomed with a picnic celebration. Many of the festivals did not derive from Islam, but from Ancient Egypt pagan rites and customs. Egyptians liked to enjoy themselves and any occasion was a pretext for fun and merry-making. There was dancing and singing in the streets, and glass and fire eaters. Women and young girls wore brightly coloured dresses in purple, lilac, orange and scarlet. Even the sweet pastries sold in the street were brightly coloured in yellow, pink and green. Housewives prepared mountains of assorted pastries, which they sent to relatives and neighbours.

An important Egyptian festival I remember clearly was Sham El Nessim. Literally translated it means 'smelling the breeze' and it commemorates the arrival of spring, ushering in the agricultural season. Because it coincided with the Orthodox Easter Monday, both Muslims and Coptic Christians came together to celebrate the festival. It was a national holiday which dated back to Ancient Egypt, where families gathered for picnics. Children loved it because they got to throw lots of petards which did not need to be lit, but were made in such a way that they exploded the moment they hit the ground. The noise was constant and always made me jump. Apart from hating the sound of those petards, I remember Sham El Nessim as a joyous occasions when people headed to parks and gardens to celebrate it. Families gathered together for picnics and brought traditional food. As it was a holiday, and schools and businesses were closed, we often used to go away for a couple of days, always with the usual group of friends. Sometimes we had a picnic or went on a boat ride on the Nile.

After fasting for 30 days, the holy month of Ramadan ends with a period of celebration lasting three days. It's known as Eid-el-Fitr and it was, and still is, one of the biggest celebrations in Egypt. Egyptians greeted it with hearts full of joy, and families gathered and came together to cook and eat various delicacies. The first day of the holiday was spent visiting and receiving guests, but the last two were all about outings. Large crowds gathered in public places like parks and gardens, and many people spent the day cruising on the River Nile. The *dahabias*, the floating houses on the Nile, were all colourfully decorated. Kids proudly donned new dresses and attires and loved this holiday because they also received gifts, usually new clothing and a gift of cash known as *Eidyah*. After dark, large crowds filled the streets, which were lit up with lanterns and other festive decorations. There were mobile carnivals, performers and story tellers who knew how to keep the crowd enraptured with their tales. It was a truly magical time and I have not seen any celebration like it since.

Mouled El Nabi, which celebrates the birth of the Prophet Muhammad, was an important religious festival in Egypt. It falls on the 12th day of the third month of the Islamic calendar, around October/November and dates back to the Fatimid era (10th - 12th century), when the ruling families organised large feasts for the poor and needy and handed out large amounts of *Halawet AL Mouled* sweets. There were many traditions associated with this festival and weeks before the event, stores and street vendors began selling sweets made of different types of nuts and honey. I liked the small square ones made of roasted nuts held together by a sugar syrup and also the ones called *malban*, which were similar to Turkish delight – they were made of starch, sugar and water, stuffed with walnuts and dusted with powdered sugar.

A vivid memory of this festival – and a tradition unique to Egypt – is called *Arouset-al-Mouled* (Al Mouled bride). It was a peculiar shaped doll in different shapes and sizes, which was sold to children. The colour of the doll's dress was never white, as that would have been too bland. Instead, they were all very brightly coloured, made of paper or cheap material. Some people thought that the dolls were sold to encourage young people to get married on that day, so the streets were filled with brides and happiness.

A celebration I have vague recollections of is called Wafaa El-Nil. Since time immemorial, the Nile and its flooding have been the lifeline of its inhabitants, and the focus of their social and economic activities and ceremonies. The Ancient Egyptians believed that the Nile flooded every year because of Isis's tears of sorrow for her dead husband, Osiris, and one of the myths was the custom to offer a virgin as a sacrifice to the river Nile every year, in order to instigate a flood. However, Egyptians have never thrown a human sacrifice into the river to celebrate this ceremony, often referred to as 'the bride of the Nile'. The ancient legend has survived into an ongoing tradition where a wooden doll dressed as a bride is thrown instead. Girls were given sugar dolls painted in different colours and dressed in frilled multi-coloured tissue and silver papers.

We didn't take part in any of the Egyptian celebrations, but we were very much aware of them, because of the local population around us and the joyous excitement in the streets. These festivals were taking place against the background of our daily lives and we were often able to witness the merriment in the streets. I think Amina took me out a couple of times, and I remember watching children throwing wooden dolls in the Nile and little girls proudly displaying brightly coloured dolls. On all those occasions, there were lots more stalls in the busy streets, selling an innumerable variety of sweets, pastries and drinks.

Egyptian Jews were mostly Sephardim and considered themselves superior to the Ashkenazim – there were about 75,000 Sephardim and only about 5,000 Ashkenazim. The Abbassieh Jewish quarter was where most Jews lived. There were a large number of synagogues in Cairo, including an Ashkenazi and a Karaite one. Some wealthier Jews had moved to the leafier suburbs of Maadi and Zamalek, but my parents and the rest of my family preferred the hustle and bustle of downtown Cairo, where everything was within a few minutes' walk. The Sephardi and Ashkenazi Jews had different religious and culinary traditions; for instance, the Ashkenazim usually named a child after a dead relative, whereas the Sephardim gave the name of a living relative, except the child's parent.

There was a small community of around 8,000 Karaite Jews in Egypt. They were a sect within Judaism who strictly adhered to the Scriptures. They did not follow the Talmud and the Mishnah, and only recognised the Five Books of Moses. Most of them lived in the Jewish Quarter called Haret El Yahoud. They only spoke Arabic and the men usually dressed in *galabeyas*. They did not have benches in their synagogues; instead, they knelt on carpets and prayed by touching the ground with their forehead, much like Muslims do. Their names were Moussa, Mounir, Wahba,

Wassef and Abdallah – again, Muslim-sounding names. The Karaites tended to be the poorest Jews.

In Egypt, it was normal to be known as Jewish. The average Egyptian was not anti-Semitic and was tolerant. We did not feel threatened, probably because my family never got involved in politics. I don't have any bad memories of Egypt and don't remember ever being frightened, apart from the Saturday in January 1952, when Cairo burned down.

We were secular Jews, as were the rest of our family and friends. We did not follow strict kosher dietary rules and didn't light the Shabbat candles. Nevertheless, we were faithful to our religion and led a Jewish life – although my mother's observance of the Shabbat consisted in not sewing on that day and my father's in not smoking. Apart from the servants, the locals we came across and a handful of Muslim girls in my class, all the people I knew were Jewish. I was aware of Christianity as a religion, but I did not have any Christian acquaintances. As a young child, I assumed everyone who was or looked European was Jewish. I led a very sheltered life and that perception was part of it.

Not all Egyptian Jews were secular. In the predominantly Jewish areas, on Friday nights the streets were filled with men on their way to the temple, dressed in elegant suits and carrying the small satchels which contained their prayer shawls, books and skullcaps. The Arab population had no problem with this, at least until 1948. They were tolerant and accepted other religions. Many girls in these Jewish areas celebrated their Bat Mitzvah, but it was not the custom in the community I knew. Those ceremonies looked a little like the confirmation in the Catholic religion – it was not an individual one, as it is now, but rather about a dozen girls celebrating together and all dressed in white.

There was a large Coptic community in Egypt. Copts believe themselves to be the descendants of Egypt's ancient Pharaonic people and are Christians – the caretaker in our building was a Coptic Christian. They considered themselves Egyptian, since their Church had existed long before the Arab conquest. There was nothing to distinguish them from the rest of the population; they belonged to all the different social classes, looked Arab and only spoke Arabic. When we lived in Egypt, they used to live peacefully side by side with the Muslim population, as we did. Unfortunately, this is no longer the case and recently Copts have been the victims of attacks and discrimination.

In the 1950s, there were 39 Sephardic synagogues in Cairo alone and only a couple of Ashkenazi ones. We went to the main synagogue twice a year during the High Holy Days, for Rosh Hashanah (the Jewish New Year) and for the eve of Yom Kippur, the Day of Atonement, as well as for weddings and bar mitzvahs, which were always a grand affair. For Rosh Hashanah we always had new clothes and new shoes.

The main synagogue was the splendid Ismailieh Temple in Adly Pacha Street. It was known as the Grand Temple and on High Holy Days it was packed with people who had come to hear the Chief Rabbi's sermon – Rabbi Nahum's speeches in French were famous. It was a tradition for the Prime Minister of Egypt to attend the Kol Nidre service. The synagogue was majestic, and had magnificent chandeliers and velvet drapes. It was usual for the man to start praying from the beginning of the service, no matter what time he arrived, resulting in a cacophony. The women watched from the balcony, dressed in their best outfits, as were the children.

The honour of carrying the Sefer Torahs for the Kol Nidre service was auctioned off and the size of your bid determined your rank in the procession to the Ark. The magnificent Torah scrolls, which were stored in large wooden cylinders, stood erect when opened. The parchment was kept in an upright position when read – in contrast, Ashkenazi scrolls just have an embroidered cover and the scrolls are read while lying flat on a table.

Many weddings took place at the Ismailieh Temple and it was always a grand occasion; there were at least two or three bridesmaids and the temple was packed. Bar mitzvahs were also regularly celebrated there and it was common for the family of the Bar Mitzvah boy to donate an embroidered Torah cover to the synagogue.

The Maimonides synagogue in old Cairo had a special significance. Rabbi Moshe ben Maimon, also known as Maimonides, was born in Cordoba, Spain, in1135. He lived for around 40 years in Egypt, where he practised medicine and served as a rabbi. People believed he performed miracles, saving the lives of poor people and well known personalities alike. After his death in 1204, his tomb in Cairo became a shrine where the desperate sought cures.

Egyptian Jews believed that the synagogue had miraculous healing powers. Legend had it that Maimonides had performed many of his feats of healing inside the temple walls. It was known as the Temple of Miracles and became a kind of Jewish Lourdes in Cairo. Small alcoves were transformed into sleeping areas, where people spent the night, bringing with them sheets, pillows, blankets and even mattresses. Mothers brought their sick children and women who had trouble conceiving came to pray for a child. You had to lie down, make your wish and sleep. If the rabbi appeared in your dreams, it meant that he had heard your request and your wish would come true.

My father could read Hebrew and knew all the prayers. The men went to synagogue to pray, the women to meet up with their friends and catch up with the gossip. The majority would not have been able to follow the service. They sat in the women's gallery upstairs, stood up when they were required and chatted away the rest of the time. When a wedding was celebrated, the groom was honoured with an Aliyah to the Torah (being called up) on the Saturday Shabbat service after his wedding – Ashkenazi grooms are called up to the Torah the Shabbat before the wedding.

The Brit Mila (the circumcision of a boy on the eighth day after birth) was an important ceremony in the Jewish community. It was customary to give the honour of godparents for the first newborn male to the grandparents on the father's side and for the next male to the mother's side. At the ceremony, a special ornately embroidered cloth was draped over a chair, Elijah's chair. It was believed that Elijah, as an eternal witness, cast positive blessings over the ritual. In some communities, the chair was left empty, in others the godfather sat on the chair. The godmother carried the baby, who was placed on a pillow and dressed in an embroidered white gown. She handed the baby over to the godfather, who held the infant during the ritual. The words 'Bo Hatan' (Come, Groom) were recited three times. The mohel – surgeon – performed the circumcision, during which the mother was not present. The baby was then named, and a festive breakfast followed.

The Pidion Ha Ben – Redemption of the firstborn male child – was performed on the thirty-first day after the child's birth. According to the Law of Moses, the firstborn male child, if not born to a Cohen or a Levy, belongs in spirit to the Priesthood until the Pidion Ha Ben is performed. In the ceremony, it was customary for the boy's father to redeem his son by paying five silver coins to a Cohen, who gave the baby boy a priestly blessing.

Jewish holidays were always important occasions, when we visited family and friends. Pastries and sweetmeats were offered in every house you visited, and it was a competition as to who made the best. Although the basic recipe was the same, every hostess had her own way of making something or a secret ingredient.

Traditions were very important to my father. We observed all the festivals and the customs that went with them. On High Holy Days, my parents did what was known as the Kapparot of Yom Kippur. This is the old Jewish custom of offering a chicken (for girls) or a rooster (for boys) to atone for one's sins. It is considered a blessing and a good action. In the Judeo-Egyptian culture, the sacrifice of a chicken, which was then given to the poor people, was thought to bring good fortune to the person in honour of whom it was made. That is probably why we had two live chickens every year as special guests in our bathroom before the High Holy Days! The chickens were then slaughtered by the shochet, the ritual butcher.

Kapparot also had its roots in a ceremony which I don't remember, so maybe my parents did not practise it. It was based on a kabbalistic custom, in which the sins of the person were transferred to a fowl. The fowl was held above a person's head and swung in a circle three times, while some Hebrew selections were recited. It was hoped that, in this way, the fowl would take on any misfortune which might otherwise occur to the person who had taken part in the ritual. It was then slaughtered.

If something broke accidentally, my father always said *kapparah*. I had heard the word many times and was used to it, so I never thought of asking what it meant. I have since learnt that, in Jewish lore, kapparah was the necessary catastrophe that precedes an unforeseen windfall. It was the experience of bad luck, but with the understanding, or rather the hope, that for each blow you received, you had averted a significantly worse one; it was hoped that the minor loss would offset the occurrence of something worse.

Rosh Hashanah was a festival celebrated with all the family around Aunt Marie's dining table. All the traditional foods were present, each one symbolising something. Black-eyed peas were cooked with a neck of lamb and were meant to ensure that we multiply. Pomegranate seeds were served in sugar syrup and rose water, in the hope that our virtues would accumulate like the seeds of the fruit. Leek omelettes, my father's favourite, were associated with the hope of crushing our enemies. A popular dish was called *pritades*, eggs cooked with vegetables, or with spinach or zucchini. *Almodruta*, made with aubergines and eggs, was another Sephardic favourite, but it was not customary to eat it on Rosh Hashanah, since the eggplant is black and this symbolises bad luck for the coming year.

In keeping with the theme of sweetness, it was customary not to have salt or lemon on the table. *Ka'ak* (called *roskas* in Ladino) were also made for the festival. They are savoury biscuits in the shape of small bracelets, covered with sesame or aniseed seeds. Their circular shape symbolised a well-rounded New Year and the seeds represented hope for a fruitful year.

There were jars containing apple jam for sweetness and golden filaments of zucchini (marrow) jam. I loved it and have tried to make it but have so far been unsuccessful, as I think it was a special type of marrow only grown in Egypt. The jam was served in the hope that our virtues might swell like the marrow and that we would discard the lesser elements of our character, as we had thrown away the seeds in making the jam. The Judeo Spanish custom was to serve sugary delicacies in order to bless the New Year – orange marmalade, marzipan and *travados,* sweet pastries made with walnuts, sugar and honey.

In the synagogue, the deeply moving chant of the ancient hymn Kol Nidre, was sung at the commencement of the fast of Yom Kippur. The Spanish liturgy included poems by Spanish medieval poets, Shlomo Ibin Gabriel and Yehuda Ha-Levy, where verses were sung in Ladino. Towards the end of the service, the men covered their heads with their prayer shawls, while 30 blasts of the ram's horn, the shofar, were blown.

Before the fast on Yom Kippur, it was customary to have a very lightly seasoned meal – okra and rice with tomato sauce, or chicken with potatoes. Spices were avoided, so as not to increase thirst. Fresh fruit such as melon, coffee and a final cup of water were served last. The fast was broken by eating bread with olive oil, followed by the cheese savouries such as *borekas, roskas* and *pan di Spania*, a dry cake. Pastries with walnuts, honey and sugar were also made.

We celebrated Chanukah – my father always lit the first candle on the chanukiah, the next day my mother lit the second one, on the third day it was my turn as the eldest child, and so on. A Syrian tradition involved lighting an extra candle. A Syrian rabbi once explained the reason for this; during the Spanish Inquisition in 1492, the Jews dispersed all over Europe and the Middle East. When some fled to Syria and were once again able to live in peace, their rabbis claimed that they should all light an extra candle, because the fact that that they had once again found a place to live was like a second miracle. Some of their descendants still follow this tradition.

Tu B'Shvat, the Jewish New Year for Trees, was also called Las Frutas. It was particularly important to the Sephardim and involved a ritual meal, where four categories of fruit were served in successive courses. On this festival, an abundance of sweet treats, including halva and marzipan, were offered.

Purim, which celebrated the triumph in the fifth century BCE of the ancient Persian Jews over their enemy Haman, was a festive occasion. We did not make hamantaschen, the traditional Ashkenazi pastry for Purim.

The shape of it is said to represent either Haman's ears or his stuffed pockets, which were filled with the bribes or lots he had hoped to use in deciding the fate of the Jews. Instead. we had a three-cornered filo pastry stuffed with a sweet ricotta filling and topped with a rose water syrup.

Baklava was also served, because the sweetness of the syrup signified the good luck of the Jews in the past and their hope for survival in the future. Purim was a time when homemade cakes, biscuits and sweet confectionery, called Purim plates, were given to relatives and friends. One of the favourite Ladino Purim songs was *Kuando Haman se emboracho,* meaning when Haman became drunk. My father also bought us some special sweets and he continued to get the same assortment when we lived in London.

For Tish'a B'Av, the Fast of Ab, which commemorates the destruction of both temples in Jerusalem, we had *megadarrah.* The dish is a combination of cooked rice and brown lentils, topped with crispy fried onions and eaten with yoghurt. Rice pudding with honey was served for Shavuot – there is a line in the Bible's Song of Songs which reads 'Honey and milk are under your tongue'. This is understood to mean that the knowledge of the Torah will enrich one's life with sweetness, like honey, and nourishment, like milk.

The apartment was thoroughly cleaned before Passover, in order to rid the home of all traces of leavened food. All the metal utensils and saucepans were sterilised, making them ready for Passover use. They were stirred three times in boiling water, plunged into a basin of cold water and dried. Cupboards were cleaned and all traces of crumbs removed. The rice was not like the one we get nowadays in supermarkets. It was dirty and full of black particles and dead insects, so it had to be sifted carefully before use – for Passover, following the Sephardic tradition, it had to be cleaned three successive times.

Each religious festival brought its obligations, as well as its specific foods. In contrast with Ashkenazi custom, Sephardic Jews are allowed to eat rice, beans and corn during the festival of Pesach. At the Passover Seder, the entire Haggadah was always meticulously read, the reading shared between the men. Inevitably, the children would get impatient and start chatting, while the men tried to keep order and proceed with the prayers. All the rituals were observed and there was always much discussion as to what was the right way to do something or what followed next. This never ceased to amaze me, considering it was the same prayer in the same order every year. However, it was part of the fun, and we were starving by the time all the prayers were finished.

Ritual required the presence of a shoulder of lamb, complete with knucklebone, on the Seder table. The bone was used to represent the lamb that was sacrificed during the Jews' exodus from Egypt. We also had celery instead of parsley as one of the symbolic foods on the seder plate. Chicken soup with matzah balls is the first thing served by Ashkenazi Jews at the start of the meal, but we had *borekas* and *pasteles* (pastries filled with minced beef). In keeping with the Syrian Jewish tradition, lamb shanks were served as a main course. The apple and nut mixture used in Ashkenazi communities for charoseth was replaced by a thick date-nut mixture, also called *silan*.

The preparation of the charoseth, the traditional Passover jam used for the Seder, was a laborious task. Dates had to be pitted and raisins thoroughly washed several times. These were then put into a large pot and left to simmer on a very low heat for 24 hours. Sugar and vinegar were added, and the result was a thick, reddish brown, delicious charoseth – I used to look forward to the jam all year. The Passover cakes were made using lots of ground almonds, hazelnuts and orange blossom water. My favourites were the biscuits because of their crunchiness and my mother's were just right.

As well as the charoseth, my mother made a sweet, creamy coconut jam which was served to guests in crystal bowls with a long handled silver spoon and a glass of iced water. A favourite of mine was the *nareng* and Aunt Marie's were always the best. They were half inch long rolls of orange rinds, soaked and cooked to a sticky rich syrup. The oranges used were a special variety called Seville, which were only available between January and February, so large quantities were therefore made and stored away. Their taste is quite special and I have managed to make some recently, fairly acceptable but not as good as my aunt's. For Shavuot, we had a dessert called *sahlab* – it was white and made using milk and cornstarch, topped with ground pistachios.

Some of our traditions were different from those I have encountered in Seders in England. For instance, when the time came to recite the plagues, instead of each guest removing 10 drops of wine from his glass, as is the Ashkenazi custom, the Sephardi one was for the head of the Seder to pour wine into a separate bowl. My uncle

Mayer would have probably done this in Cairo, as he was the oldest member of the family. After the naming of each plague, some wine was poured into the bowl, with the person holding this having to look away – as the oldest child, I was the one entrusted with this task. The wine in the bowl, believed to be cursed, symbolically distributed the plagues to other nations who are enemies of the Jewish people. There was always some argument about what to do with it; someone would suggest emptying it into the kitchen sink but, because it was believed to be cursed, in the end it was always dumped into the toilet.

In 14th century Spain, the Seder leader walked around the table three times with the seder plate in hand, tapping it on the head of each guest. The tradition was thought to be connected to the Talmudic custom of 'uprooting' the seder plate so that guests might ask questions about the Jews in Egypt. That is probably why, living in Egypt, my family did not feel the need to keep this custom, although many Moroccan, Turkish and Tunisian Jews did. The Jews from North Africa also used to break the matzah into the shape of the Hebrew letter 'hey', which corresponds to the number five.

Orthodox Sephardic Jews started the Seder with a symbolic knock on the front door. Dressed in biblical garb and carrying a sack over his shoulder, the leader of the Seder entered the home. The children followed him to the table in an opening procession symbolising the Jews going out of Egypt. This, and other sights, tastes and smells were designed to transport the participants back to the time when the Jews were slaves in Egypt.

It must have seemed strange to read about the Exodus from Egypt, sitting at a dining table in Cairo, surrounded by all the family – we were thanking God for saving us from bondage, while we were in living in Egypt! As a child, the Haggadah was just a nice story, at the end of which we had a wonderful meal. Passover was a special week when bread was replaced by matzoh and we had different food and cakes. Nowadays, the reading of the Haggadah has a special meaning and is particularly poignant, because my family actually experienced the exodus from Egypt.

Although we observed all the traditions, they were never explained to us, so we followed them without knowing exactly why. For instance, my father always recited a special prayer whenever we tasted the first fruit of the season and the only word I caught was *shehecheyanu*. He never explained the meaning or the reason why he did this and I never thought to ask, which sounds strange now. I found out later that the Shehecheyanou blessing is a Jewish prayer said to celebrate special occasions, expressing gratitude to God for new and unusual experiences or possessions.

There were special foods for every festival and every family had a different tradition, depending on where their ancestors had originated. Although a secular Jew, my father was a deeply religious man, as his father had been. His beliefs were also steeped in superstitions; for instance, we were not allowed to go anywhere fun or buy anything new on Tish'a B'Av, the 9th of Av, which is considered the saddest day in the Jewish calendar as it commemorates the destruction of both temples in Jerusalem. I think my father thought it was bad luck not to respect it. My mother, on the other hand, was not religious or spiritual. She followed the traditions because that was how she had been brought up and she enjoyed the family gatherings.

A historical context

1948 to 1952 – the creation of the State of Israel and the beginning of the end for the Jewish community

On November 17, 1869, Queen Victoria opened the Suez Canal with great pomp and ceremony. Overnight, Egypt became the new Eldorado as the Canal and modern means of transportation shortened the route to the Orient by many months. These new means of communication sealed the end of the old caravan routes which had been very profitable to the Jews of Aleppo and Damascus. This also coincided with the decline of the Ottoman Empire.

Jews from Aleppo, Damascus and the Ottoman Empire, realising the decline of their communities, left in search of new economic opportunities which they found in Egypt. They settled mainly in Cairo and Alexandria. They established religious, educational and charitable institutions. Although in 1929 the Egyptian government published a new law granting Egyptian citizenship to all those born in Egypt, only 5000 Jews out of approximately 60,000 living in the country by that time succeeded in obtaining an Egyptian passport. Even then, this was confiscated in 1948 after the establishment of the State of Israel. My father was stateless, as were all his family members. Fortunately, my mother had a British passport, which is how we were allowed to come to the UK in 1956.

Because of great corruption in the government, Egypt became bankrupt only seven years after the inauguration of the Suez Canal. The European powers imposed a severe economic recovery plan and gradually took control of the country's economy. The Egyptians revolted in 1882, under the leadership of Ahmed Orabi, but they were quickly subjugated by England. The British took advantage of that fact to occupy Egypt and turn it into a 'protectorate'. The country was essentially under British control thereafter and this continued even after the formal recognition of Egyptian independence in 1922, with British troops remaining around the Suez Canal zone, in spite of continued efforts to force them out of Egypt. Full Egyptian self-rule was not realised until the revolution of 1952.

In 1929, Egypt enacted a nationality law which stripped the majority of Egyptian Jews of their nationality and their citizenship rights and protection. Some families had lived in Egypt for centuries and this law forced them to seek the protection of foreign governments by proving some tenuous lineage to these countries, or otherwise remain stateless. To possess a British or French passport did not require the holder to have lived in Britain or France, or even to speak the language.

In 1947, the Egyptian government enacted the

Company Law, which required Egyptian citizenship for 90% of employees and 70% of management in any private or public company. This law, in one fell swoop, deprived many Jews – as well as Greeks, Armenians and other ethnic minorities – of their livelihood. Greeks and Armenians were targeted for their nationality, Jews for their religion. This went further in 1954, when the Nationalisation Law stripped Jews and even some well-to-do Egyptians of their businesses, and nationalised their assets.

In spite of this, until 1948, Jews, Muslims and Christians had on the whole lived peacefully side by side. There was a Jewish quarter in Cairo called Haret El Yahoud (The Jewish Street) and a Jewish community had inhabited the area since the 12th century. One famous resident was Maimonides, the renowned philosopher and scholar. Haret el Yahud was a centre of residential and commercial life, and middle and lower class families lived in the labyrinth of streets that made up the Jewish quarter. Unlike the Jews who lived in downtown Cairo and the leafy suburbs, they spoke Arabic amongst themselves and at home. They lived in the vicinity of the business district called Mouski and the Khan Khaliki market, home to many Egyptian artisans and workshops involved in the production of traditional crafts and souvenirs.

The formation of the State of Israel in 1948 changed the dynamic between Arabs and Jews in the Middle East. Overnight, things deteriorated for Egyptian Jews, and generations of peaceable interaction and tolerance disappeared. Violence began to occur against them, stimulating hatred, and the government did little or nothing to prevent it. The hostilities began in the Jewish quarter, where shops were burnt and ransacked, and some Jews murdered.

During the summer and autumn of 1948, Jews and their property were attacked repeatedly. On 20 June 1948, a bomb exploded in the Karaite district of Cairo, killing 22 and wounding 41. Several buildings were severely damaged. Witnesses on the scene reported that the response of the police and firemen was sluggish and negligent. On July 15, Israeli planes bombed a residential neighbourhood in Cairo, killing civilians and destroying many homes. The attack took place during the Ramadan Iftar (meal to break the fast), which undoubtedly amplified the anger of the victims, who began an angry march on the Jewish quarter. On September 22, an explosion in the Rabbinate quarter in Cairo killed 19 and wounded 62 victims.

The government's response to these attacks was inept, not because they actually encouraged these assaults, but because they were frightened by the apparent strength of the Muslim Brotherhood. Since its foundation in 1928 in Ismailia, Egypt, the Brotherhood had spread rapidly through Egypt, Sudan, Syria, Palestine, Lebanon and North Africa. The movement advocated a return to the Quran and the Hadith as guidelines for a healthy modern Islamic society. At its height in the 1940s, it was estimated that it may have had some 500,000 members in the Arab countries.

There were many detentions and sequestrations of Jewish properties in 1948. However, these were erratic and some notable Zionist leaders were not arrested, while others were interned for months. The inconsistency of the

Egyptian government gave rise to many interpretations – the relatively modest scale of the detentions and the fact that a few Zionists escaped them altogether encouraged some Jews, notably the bourgeoisie, to believe that their future was not threatened, and they could therefore continue the comfortable and privileged lifestyle many of them had led for generations. The troubles had left them relatively untouched, and they carried on frequenting clubs and cafés and spending their summers by the sea.

In contrast, some began to realise that their future in Egypt was imperilled. Whilst Jews worldwide rejoiced that we would at last have a homeland in Israel, those of Arab countries were aware that their safety and way of life was being threatened. At five years of age, I was of course too young to understand all this, but I nevertheless suffered emotionally when the two people closest to me, my aunts Suzanne and Esther, suddenly disappeared from my life because they had emigrated to Israel.

In 1948 an emergency law was declared, which forbade Egyptians and Jews from leaving the country without a special permit, called an exit visa. I am sure my family and other Jews were deeply worried as it was a turbulent time and I don't know how my aunts managed to leave Egypt; I think you had to pretend to the Egyptian authorities that you were going somewhere in Europe and then make your way to Israel from there. Most people left from the port of Alexandria on a ship bound for Italy or Greece.

The first exodus of Egyptian Jews took place that year. About 20,000 of the 80,000 Jews – or as many as 90,000 – living in Egypt emigrated. In the following years, some realised what was happening and began to make preparations to leave, others were forced to depart in 1956 and the last remaining Jews left in 1967. Eventually the Jewish community in Egypt was reduced to 100 people who couldn't leave – some were too old, a few were married to Egyptians, others simply could not bear to leave the country of their birth.

With the rise of Arab nationalism and the onset of the UN partition debate over Palestine, the political environment in Egypt grew progressively more hostile towards the Jewish community. Between 1948 and 1952, there were riots and targeted bombings of the Jewish community and businesses. Over 200 were looted and there were some injuries. Some Jews were placed in detention camps, just for being suspected of having Zionist sympathies or being undercover spies for Israel. A few were lucky and were allowed a private bathroom and conjugal visits; however, most inmates endured having to sleep in a crowded cell, often head-to-toe with other prisoners. In hard labour jails, exercising was mandatory and the prisoners had to run in circles chanting anti-Israeli slogans.

1948 can be considered the beginning of the end of the golden era of Egyptian Jewry, culminating in the mass exodus of 1956 and 1967. The process to expel the Jews and other minorities from Egypt started with one slogan 'Egypt for the Egyptians'. This spanned many years and entailed many steps to achieve this goal – loss of citizenship rights and protection, loss of jobs in the public and private sectors, no prospects of future employment, dispossession of assets and, ultimately, expulsion.

From then on, it became increasingly evident that a Jewish presence in Egypt was an alien one. The Jews gradually became regarded as the enemy and no longer an important part of Egyptian society. In the end, Egypt, along with all other Middle Eastern countries, has succeeded in ridding itself almost entirely of its Jewish population. This mass exodus has not been well documented and sadly, a whole culture and way of life will vanish forever and hardly make the history books.

Farouk's father, King Fuad, had been educated in Geneva and the Turin Military Academy. Farouk himself had spent his happiest years in Italy and, on returning to Egypt, had retained a number of Italian servants. They had always been kind to Farouk, who kept them in his immediate entourage. Antonio Pulli, the palace electrician, became Farouk's shadow and accompanied him everywhere when he was off-duty. The palace Italians cushioned Farouk's sense of inadequacy with a back-slapping bonhomie, spiced with schoolboy pranks and smutty jokes; theirs was the only companionship in which the young Farouk felt at ease. His emotional stability was not helped by the behaviour of his mother: once her husband King Fuad was dead, Queen Nazli took on a new lease of life and on holiday in Europe, she was seen at the theatre, in restaurants and at parties.

It was one of Farouk's great misfortunes that he had barely turned 16 when he found himself the richest and most powerful person in Egypt. It was an immense burden for a young boy who had not yet begun his adult life and was emotionally weak. As Head of the Royal family, he could only be advised, not told what to do. The isolation of his position and a deep sense of inadequacy made him awkward and given to absurd boasting in the company of his own social class.

Farouk succeeded his father in 1936. Initially, he was extremely popular with the Egyptian people. His accession was encouraging, both for the populace and the nobility, due to his youth and good looks. He dismissed all the British servants employed by his father, while keeping the Italian ones. He made a handsome couple with his bride, Queen Farida. In the early days of his reign, Farouk was very good looking. Tall and well built, he also had the light hair and blue eyes admired in the Orient; this made him an ideal of masculine beauty to his subjects, who were deeply proud of him. In July 1937, more than two million people from all over the country poured into Cairo to celebrate his crowning. Queen Farida became very popular and appeared in many magazines.

For a long time, one of the most spectacular scenes on the streets of Cairo was the long line of red and black Rolls-Royces that streamed down Malaka Nazli Avenue every time King Farouk travelled from one place to another. Advance cars, sounding their sirens, announced the motorcade. People lined the pavements, applauded and blessed their young and handsome king.

There were two principal figures in Farouk's public life: his staunch political supporter, Ali Maher Pasha and the British Ambassador, Sir Miles Lampson, who stood an impressive six foot six. Sir Miles had very little respect for Farouk, whom he referred to as 'the boy', not only in his diaries but in public as well. To Farouk, who called Lampson 'the Schoolmaster', the British Ambassador represented everything he hated most – an authoritarian father figure and the foreign occupation of his country, something he yearned to get rid of.

The Wafd, founded by Saad Zaghloul, was a nationalist liberal political party. It was Egypt's most popular party, from the end of World War I through the 1930s. However, the King's rising popularity was undermining that of the democratic Wafd. In December 1937, the Prime Minister, Nahas Pacha, attempted to block Farouk's power once and for all. The result was a massive anti-Wafd demonstration, mounted by the Islamic University of el Azhar and the students of the secular University of Cairo. Thousands of people gathered outside the Abdeen palace, shouting for the King. Nahas and the Wafd party were pushed out of power; the Palace had won and in August 1938, Ali Maher became the Prime Minister.

Unscrupulous courtiers played on the King's naivety and seedier appetites. He ballooned into an obese, tyrannical monarch with debauched tastes. During the hardships of World War II, criticism was levelled at Farouk for his lavish lifestyle. He insisted on keeping all the lights burning in his palace in Alexandria, during a time when the city was blacked out due to Italian bombings. The King never seemed satisfied with his wealth and often travelled to Europe for grand shopping sprees. It was reported that he began pilfering objects and artefacts while on state visits abroad. Even the common people were the victims of his kleptomania and his penchant for thievery earned him the name of 'The Thief of Cairo'. These excesses would later prove to be the leading sparks which triggered the 1952 military coup.

After a hopeful start, Farouk proved to be a dissolute monarch with rampant corruption in his government. He was totally unscrupulous – he once arranged for an army officer to be killed in order to take that man's wife as his own. He liked playing poker, but he also liked to win. It is reported that in one game, when he had three kings, he declared that he had four, counting himself as one. No one dared argue with him and he would readily shed ministers of his government. Farouk divorced Farida because she had only given him three girls. He married his second wife Narriman, who was a commoner, in the hope of regaining the popularity he had lost after divorcing Queen Farida. His attempt failed, because the people still loved Farida and remained loyal to that love. Narriman gave him one son, Fuad II, who was six months old when Farouk was forced to abdicate and leave Egypt.

Israel's victory in the Arab-Israeli war had a devastating effect on King Farouk and his government, which still depended on British support to stay in power. The relationship between the British ambassador, Sir Miles Lampson, and Farouk further deteriorated. This eventually culminated in a standoff in 1942 between Farouk and Lampson known as the Abdeen Palace incident, where Farouk was humiliated. The incident caused the Egyptian people to rally round their king, who was seen at the time as the victim of British bullying.

After the humiliation of the Abdeen Palace incident, Farouk lost interest in politics and abandoned himself to a lifestyle of hedonism. He became a frequent visitor of night spots and casinos and was obsessed with 'collecting' women. His eye for beautiful women was common knowledge and no woman was safe. He only had to make his desire known and denial was dangerous, as Farouk did not countenance any refusal. His reign, which had begun with such promise, was now widely resented. The Egyptian population despised him because of his dissolute lifestyle, which went against Islamic teachings.

Throughout the city, popular restaurants and dance halls used to set aside at least one table for the king and his love of the nightlife was well known. He had his valet bring fair-skinned women from the dance halls and brothels of Cairo and Alexandria to his palace for sex. Any woman was fair game for Farouk and that included Egyptian society ladies and European ones. A husband who had a beautiful wife was afraid when the king's eyes rested on her. Farouk put on a lot of weight and looked gross. What further alienated the people were the vast amounts of money Farouk spent, either on trips abroad or at home. He even ate gargantuan amounts of food in the day during the holy month of Ramadan.

In December 1951, Farouk backed General Sidi Amer for the presidency of the Cairo Officers' Club. In a surprise upset, Amer was defeated by General Mohammad Naguib, a member of the Free Officers Group. On 25 January 1952, a confrontation between British forces and policemen at the Ismailia barracks caused 40 Egyptian policemen to die. The outrage felt by the Egyptian people culminated in what is now known as Black Saturday and the Burning of Cairo.

1952 – seminal events and the rise of Gamal Abdel Nasser

On Saturday 26 January 1952, a crowd of Egyptians, led by the Muslim Brotherhood, attacked the monarchy and foreign companies; this was in retaliation for the British massacre of Egyptian policemen in Ismailiah the day before. The riot was made to look like a spontaneous uprising. In reality, it had been organised by a group called The Young Egypt Party and another called The Green Shirts. These groups were anti-Western, anti-British and anti-Jewish. The fires were a seminal event in Egyptian political history.

Large Egyptian mobs, carrying butcher knives, axes, sticks and torches, walked from the poorest and most populous quarters to the wealthy part of the city. The crowd marched through downtown Cairo and torched all the symbols of luxury and foreign excess. Most of what Ismail the Magnificent had built in the style of Paris was burnt down. The crowd set fire to hotels owned by foreigners, British companies, as well as businesses owned by Jews. Targets included the department stores Cicurel, Chemla and Orosdi, as well as the Groppi tearooms, Barclays Bank and the Shepheard's hotel, where British officers loved to meet. Every major establishment associated with the British, the French and the Jews such as banks, cinema houses, airline offices and outdoor cafés, were attacked and burnt down. The Shepheard's hotel, which had become a quintessential symbol of British colonial rule, was destroyed beyond recognition. Gone was the large terrace which had been the place to go if you wanted to be seen; also the two bars which were the favourite haunts of British officers, the lavish lobby and the tea salon.

The fires started early in the morning. I remember we were sitting on our balcony whilst the events unfolded. We watched Cairo going up in flames, acrid smoke burning our eyes; it was a terrifying spectacle, especially when the crowd passed through our street. There was no telling what they would attack next. We lived opposite the main Cairo Radio station, so they did not touch our building. The next day, the extensive damage caused during the riots became apparent – shops, cinemas, department stores, all burnt down and in ruins. Although the angry crowd had taken care to escort people out of buildings before setting those aflame, 76 people had died in the riots. Sadly, one of the victims was a young Jewish girl visiting from Alexandria, who had died in the fire at the Shepheard's hotel.

For a few days afterwards, we stayed home, too frightened to go out. Whilst the anger of the crowd had been aimed at foreigners – and the British in particular – we still felt very vulnerable. We had never seen such a large crowd so incensed, and we feared that they would also regard the Jews as aliens. When we finally ventured out of our house, the scene downtown was one of unparalleled devastation. The Cicurel department store had been reduced to ashes, as had the major cinema houses like the Miami and my favourite, the Metro. Inevitably, looters began to ransack stores and banks, bagging merchandise and cash.

Eventually, the government regained control of the city. Initially, it had been assumed that the devastation had been caused by an unruly mob. As time passed, it became clear that it was more the result of a strategic and coordinated attack by some of the King's enemies, of which Farouk had many. In spite of numerous investigations, the mystery remained unsolved, though the chief suspects remained the Muslim Brotherhood.

The Free Officers took charge, with Mohammad Naguib as their leader. However, it soon became apparent that Naguib was just a figurehead and that the real power behind the throne was a young and ambitious officer called Gamal Abdel Nasser. The Free Officers' intention was not to instal themselves in government, but to re-establish a parliamentary democracy. Nasser did not believe that a low-ranking officer like himself would be accepted by the Egyptian people and so selected Naguib to lead the coup.

During the six months after the burning of Cairo, Farouk frequently shuffled prime ministers in an attempt to quell the demands for reform. However, by then it was too late to turn the tide of change and Farouk was widely condemned for his corrupt and ineffectual governance. This, coupled with the continued British occupation and the failure to prevent the creation of the State of Israel, meant that public discontent against the king rose to new levels.

In July 1952, Farouk was forced to relinquish the throne, the victim of a military coup. The organisation called The Free Officers, anti-monarchist and anti-British, occupied Ras-el-Tin, his palace in Alexandria, and overthrew him. The revolution was launched and declared a success the next day. The Free Officers seized control of all government buildings and radio stations, as well as the army headquarters in Cairo. Farouk asked various foreign powers for help, but the most they were willing to do was to ensure that he left the country alive. The American government guaranteed his safe exit from Egypt and he left on his yacht, the Mahroussa, with 20 million Egyptian pounds. Suddenly, he was an exile. He settled in Rome with his wife and son, and subsequently divorced Narriman, who returned to Egypt.

On 18 June 1953, the monarchy was abolished and the Republic of Egypt declared, with General Naguib as its first President. Within days of Farouk's abdication, an edict was passed eliminating royal titles. There were no more pashas and beys – even the distinctive red tarboosh, which had been worn by *effendi* (gentlemen), was abolished and disappeared virtually overnight. Ironically, the origin of this iconic headgear had been Turkish, but it had come to symbolise Egypt, as much as the Pyramids and the Sphinx. The new military government wanted nothing that was seen as vaguely reminiscent of the royal family and proceeded systematically to eradicate all traces of the monarchy. Within a couple of years, even the street names which paid tribute to various royals were changed.

Testaments to old heroes also had to be abolished. Thus, Soliman Pasha Square – which paid tribute to a Frenchman who had built the modern Egyptian army, whilst also converting to Islam – was renamed 'Talat Harb', after an industrialist who had founded the first bank of Egypt. We carried on referring to the square as Soliman Pacha, but Cairo became a confusing mess of streets with official names and unofficial ones.

On Yom Kippur 1952, General Naguib visited the Jewish community at the Great Temple of Ismailia, where he was received by the Chief Rabbi of Egypt, Rabbi Nahum. The visit was widely publicised and the two were photographed beaming outside the Temple. Naguib also visited the Jewish hospital and toured the wards. He was trying hard to show that the new regime would be as loyal to the Jewish population as the monarchy had been. Naguib was a highly respected officer who wanted to create a democratic Egypt and live in peace with Israel. He tried to reach out to non-Muslims, visiting schools, hospitals and synagogues in Cairo and Alexandria.

Egypt seemed to be entering a new era of tolerance. The Jewish community was reassured and, for a while, it seemed that their life in Egypt would not suffer as a result of the fall of the monarchy. Eventually, it became clear that the young officers of the Egyptian army, in particular a group of colonels led by Gamal Abdel Nasser, were the true instigators of the coup that had overthrown the king. Both Gamal Abdel Nasser and Anwar El Sadat had participated in the war against Israel in 1948 and had felt humiliated by the Arab defeat.

Our life changed after the 1952 revolution, although as a child I would not have been aware of this. Fear and an uneasy feeling persisted. The government first started to nationalise all the assets of people who had more than 100,000 Egyptian pounds in net worth. They also nationalised shops like Groppi and movie houses, as well as the financial institutions and pharmaceutical companies. Foreigners could not hold jobs in banks, which could only hire a limited number of non-Egyptians as employees.

The Jews of Egypt saw the writing on the wall. Some

were left with little choice – having no job, no money and no prospects meant that they could not stay, even if they had wanted to. About 5,000 left Egypt between 1952 and 1956. Their reasons were varied – the loss of public sector jobs after independence, Nasser's nationalisation of properties, industries and services, and the economic hardships some of them suddenly found themselves in when their assets were seized. Some Jews still remained optimistic, thinking they were citizens in the country of their birth.

The failed Lavon affair in 1954 exacerbated an already tense situation and increased resentment against the Jews. Code named Operation Susannah, it was part of a covert Israeli military intelligence operation, where a group of Egyptian Jews were recruited to plant bombs inside Egyptian, American and British owned civilian targets. The bombs were timed to detonate several hours after closing time. The attacks were to be blamed on the Muslim Brotherhood and the aim was to create a climate of sufficient violence and instability to induce the British Government to retain its occupying troops in the Suez Canal Zone.

The operation failed and two members of the cell committed suicide after being captured. It became known as the Lavon affair after the Israeli Defence Minister, Pinhas Lavon, was forced to resign as a consequence of the incident. It endangered Jews in Egypt and several innocent men and women were arrested, interrogated, tortured and imprisoned.

After World War II and with the resurgence of nationalist activity in Egypt, the Communist Party had sought to widen its base, making affirmative efforts to attract members from the popular classes. Despite some successes, the Communists were not able to create a mass movement and never became a dominant political force. However, their importance and influence were larger than their numbers imply. They had a significant ideological impact on Egyptian society, especially amongst the intelligentsia. They were present at key moments of nationalist, student and trade union militancy. They also contributed to the destabilisation of the constitutional monarchy, helping to pave the way for the emergence of Gamal Abdel Nasser and the military movement of 1952.

Henri Curiel was an Egyptian Jew and a left-wing political activist. His family had been expelled from Spain by the Inquisition. Born in 1914, he had helped found the Egyptian Communist Party. He led the Communist Democratic Movement for National Liberation until he was expelled by King Farouk in 1950. He was exiled to France and was gunned down in his Paris home in May 1978.

Both Nasser and Naguib looked for secular rather than religious solutions to Egypt's problems. This angered the Muslim Brotherhood, a Sunni Islamist religious, political and social movement which had been the largest and best organised political force in Egypt. Their goal, as stated by its founder, Al-Banna, was to drive out British colonial and other Western influences and institute Islamic Sharia law, including strict codes of behaviour. In October 1954, a gunman belonging to their organisation attempted to assassinate Nasser while he was delivering a speech in Alexandria. In the wake of this failed attempt, which strengthened Nasser's position, the Muslim Brotherhood was officially dissolved and outlawed, its headquarters burnt and thousands of its members arrested. Naguib was accused of having been a tool of the Muslim Brotherhood. This led to his dismissal in November 1954, when he was placed under house arrest. He remained so for the next 16 years, until Nasser's death in 1970.

Nasser formally took power in July 1955. From the very start of his presidency, he introduced reforms that were meant to develop an Egyptian middle class, as well as reduce economic inequalities. This was done through expanded employment opportunities, land redistribution and, most importantly, the sequestration of the assets of wealthy foreigners. Nasser truly believed that his reforms would level the playing field for the Egyptian masses.

Jews depended on the goodwill of the authorities. The laws requiring that 90% of employees and 70% of management in any public or private company must be Egyptian had deprived many of them of their livelihood. They could own small businesses or work in a small business owned by other Jews, but they had no career prospects or possibilities in large companies. Many Jews left. My father could see that the situation was gradually deteriorating and he was becoming increasingly worried. Not worried enough to leave though, and I believe he would not have left Egypt in 1956, had he not been forced to do so.

By the late 1940s, only 5,000 Jews were Egyptian citizens. Some 30,000 were foreign citizens and the majority, about 50,000 Jews, were stateless. This situation worsened when, as a result of the Suez crisis, Nasser brought in a new set of regulations imposing rigorous requirements

for residency and citizenship as well as forced expulsions –
these affected British and French nationals and Jews with
a foreign nationality, as well as many Egyptian Jews. Over
25,000 Jews left in 1956, mainly to Israel, Europe, the
United States and South America.

For the remaining Jews, Nasser's fervent nationalism
and his imposition of a no-return policy meant that they
were trapped between a rock and a hard place. They were
forced to abandon their nationality if they ever wanted to
leave the country, but few of them wanted to. However, as
the country turned increasingly intolerant, they were left
with little choice. Many tried to stay as long as possible, but
police detentions and religious fundamentalism meant that
life in general was becoming unbearable.

As children, we were not aware of the political events
unfolding around us, but the adults certainly were. They
must have felt the wind of change after 1948, when
acceptance by the Muslim population was not always there
– though I must add that I never experienced this first hand.
Some Jewish men were accused of Zionism and spying for
Israel and were from time to time thrown in prison and
even tortured, but fortunately this did not happen to any
members of my family or our acquaintances.

If my father had any views on political issues, I never
heard him express them. Politics was not discussed at home
and certainly not in front of the children. Similarly, any
discussions or concerns they wanted to share with family
members were done when we were not around. My father
must have had strong views about Israel, especially as most
of his family members were living there. However, he never

expressed them and always seemed to be on his guard. He knew deep down that we would eventually have to leave, and I remember that he was becoming increasingly edgy. During our last holiday in Alexandria in 1956, I often caught him looking nervously at the horizon and across the sea.

Nasser was an ardent nationalist who believed that Egypt belonged to the Egyptians. In 1954 a law was passed which authorised the arrest and detention of anyone who threatened 'public order and security'. This led to the arrest of some leaders of the Jewish community. Nasser implemented a nationalisation programme in the country and was vehement in his criticism of the West. He allied with Russia, who had agreed to provide him with arms and an unconditional loan towards the Aswan Dam project.

1956 – the Suez crisis and its consequences

On 25 July 1956, Nasser addressed a crowd of 250,000 people in Alexandria, when he announced the nationalisation of the Suez Canal company as a means of funding the Aswan Dam project. One of his cherished projects was to build a high dam in Aswan, to rein in the waters of the Nile. He had asked the United States for financial help. Secretary of State John Foster Dulles had initially promised American support, but later reneged in the light of various actions which Nasser had taken.

Until 1956, the Universal Company of the Suez Maritime Canal had been jointly owned by the British and

French governments. France and the UK felt that they had to protect their long-standing interests in the Canal and saw its nationalisation as yet another hostile measure aimed at them by the Egyptian government. In addition, Nasser had made it clear that he would not allow Israeli ships to transit the canal. The announcement of the nationalisation was followed by an affirmation by Nasser that Egypt had decided to cleanse the land of Palestine of its Jews and that he would send terrorists or fedayeen to engage in hostile action against Israel. On October 25, 1956, Egypt signed a tripartite agreement with Syria and Jordan, placing Nasser in command of all three armies.

Sir Anthony Eden, the English prime minister at the time, absolutely hated Nasser. He compared him to Mussolini – even Hitler – and was determined to overthrow him. In a secret meeting with the French prime minster, Guy Mollet, and Israel's David Ben Gurion, they agreed to send their armies into Egypt, take back the Suez Canal and topple Nasser. On 29 October 1956 at 20.30, the tripartite attack by the British, the French and Israeli army was launched, called Operation Musketeer. The aims were to regain Western control of the Suez Canal and remove President Nasser.

Israeli forces crossed the Sinai Peninsula, overwhelmed Egyptian posts and quickly advanced to their objectives. They swept across the desert, capturing virtually the entire Sinai as far as Sharm-el-Sheikh and the eastern bank of the Suez Canal. Two days later, British and French planes followed, landing their own troops near Port-Said. They bombarded Egyptian airfields in the canal zone. About

2,000 Egyptian soldiers were killed during the engagement with the Israeli forces and some 5,000 were captured by the Israeli army.

Despite the relative ease with which Sinai was captured, Nasser's prestige at home and among Arabs was undamaged. He sought the help of his Russian allies, who threatened the use of atomic weapons. Throughout the conflict and broadcast through amplified speakers, Nasser's speeches filled the streets of Cairo. He denied Egypt's defeat and promised deadly fights, inciting the population to defend their land against Western colonialists and Zionists. His compelling voice and emotional appeals rallied the Egyptian people behind him.

After the fighting had started and it looked like the attackers were about to achieve their aim, political pressure from the United States, the Soviet Union and the United Nations led to a condemnation of the tripartite invasion and a demand for the withdrawal of their troops. The United States and Russia, who were unwilling to let the conflict ignite another world war, imposed an immediate cease-fire. The threat of Russian involvement had added another dimension to the crisis and had forced Eisenhower and Dulles to intervene forcefully to put an end to the conflict. If the British and the French had expected to march triumphantly into Cairo, they were disappointed. Instead, their ill-fated intervention left British and French citizens, not to mention the Jews, at the mercy of the Egyptian government.

In return for the withdrawal of Israeli, British and French forces, Egypt and the UN guaranteed Israel free access to the Red Sea through the gulf of Aqaba and the freedom to use the Suez Canal. In practice, however, this remained closed to Israeli shipping. Encouraged by Nasser's success in nationalising the Suez Canal, a wave of nationalistic euphoria and patriotism swept Egypt. Songs praising him, the revolution and the army blasted from loudspeakers all over the city. Popular singers and musicians composed slogans vilifying the Western infidels, especially Israel. Being European and Jewish suddenly became very uncomfortable. We were reluctant to go out, as we could quite possibly be attacked.

By the end of December 1956, British and French forces had totally withdrawn from Egyptian territory, while Israel completed its withdrawal in March 1957 and released all Egyptian prisoners. In a way, Nasser was the major winner of this war, as he had managed to nationalise the Suez Canal, expel 'imperialists and colonisers' and turn a military defeat into a political victory. The episode humiliated the United Kingdom and Eden's capitulation in Suez had a profound historical significance; symbolically, it signalled the end of the British Empire. Eden resigned two months after the end of the conflict on the grounds of ill health.

Some 900 Jews were arrested in November 1956 and sent to prison and detention camps. Of the 500 interned in the Jewish school at Abbasiya in Cairo, half were stateless. Of the 300 kept at Les Barrages prison, also in Cairo, half were stateless, the other half were UK or French subjects. Since they were accused of spying for Israel, no one could visit them. Most of the time there was no substance to any of the accusations, but for those Jews, it must have been a reminder of the horrors of Nazi Germany. Many of them returned from internment to find that Egyptian Muslims had taken their jobs. Jews running private companies were stymied by the denial of trade permits, export and import licences and other administrative facilities essential to the conduct of their business.

On 23 November 1956, a proclamation signed by the Minister of Religious affairs and read aloud in mosques throughout the land, declared that 'all Jews are Zionists and enemies of the state' and promised that they would soon be expelled.

The events precipitated by Nasser's nationalisation of the Suez Canal shattered the lives of Egyptian Jews and destroyed the work of generations. There had always been a significant Jewish presence in Egypt and it was where the great Maimonides had eventually settled and taught after leaving Spain. A hitherto privileged community of 80,000 Jews was gradually forced to leave the country of their birth and was scattered around the globe. Close friends ended up in different parts of the world and, in many cases, never saw each other again. Our friends the Ezris left for Sao Paulo, as Brazil was one of the few countries who accepted stateless Jews. We lost touch with them.

A mere footnote in history, the Suez crisis of 1956 is little known in the larger world. Yet it created the shockwaves which uprooted my family and friends, scattering us in different corners of the world, from Europe and Israel to South and North America and as far afield as Australia. We left with few possessions, no idea of what the future held and a history and culture that no one understands or appreciates. A political blunder by the French, the British and the Israelis decimated a deeply rooted, ancient community that had had its roots in Egypt for centuries.

On 29th October, when war broke out, my father ordered us to pack a few clothes each, as we were all going to stay at Aunt Marie's house. We lived right opposite the main broadcasting station and my father feared that it could be a target, as it was a strategic building. My aunt only had a three-bedroom apartment, but fortunately Uncle Clement, who normally lived there, was away in Europe at the time. We must have managed to all squeeze in somehow and the fact that we were all together was reassuring.

The ongoing war was a frightening situation which deteriorated quickly. Even the children could feel the tension. We had to cover all the windows with blue paper because of the nightly curfew. Every evening, someone went round the streets shouting *taffi el nur* which meant turn off the lights. It sounded menacing, even though we knew we had made sure that all the lights in the flat were switched off. We heard the sounds of sirens and thought that bombs were being dropped. We could hear muted gunfire and rifle shots and also guessed that there were tanks and armoured vehicles being convoyed nearby. It was always a relief to hear the all-clear when we could turn the lights on again.

My father insisted that the curfew was only so that the Egyptian army could move its dead and wounded soldiers. His view was that the Egyptian government was doing things under the cover of darkness because they didn't want us to know the truth. I don't know whether he believed what he was saying or was just trying to reassure us. I remember that planes flew very low, and we could hear the sound of anti-aircraft fire as we all sat in total darkness in the lounge. The blackout curtains added a further dimension to our anxiety.

Coupled with the fear of the battle outside, there was a far more pervasive one – that of the retaliation of the Arab population, egged on by the exhortations of the Muslim Brotherhood and the passionate cries of the muezzin from the minarets of every mosque in Cairo at the hour of prayer. Large groups of eager believers gathered in the streets and coffee shops to listen to fiery anti-Semitic denunciations of the Jewish population. The campaign called on all citizens to watch for spies who might have infiltrated the country. Jews were at the mercy of neighbours and business rivals. An anonymous letter or a complaint was enough to result in imprisonment, peremptorily and without due process. The words Shalom and Salam, meaning peace, are used by Jews and Muslims alike in their daily greetings and everyday prayers, but that would not have stopped us being killed.

We knew that we were at the mercy of the local population around us. The Arabs had resented, if not hated, Israel since 1948 and they might well have used the current precarious situation to unleash that resentment. It is a testimony to their inherent peaceful nature that they didn't. Not everyone was as fortunate though – we heard later that some Egyptian Jews had been arrested in the dead of night, suspected of being Zionists. They were imprisoned in detention camps and sometimes tortured.

During the short conflict, life as we knew it stopped

and took a different rhythm. The grown-ups huddled around the radio every evening to listen to the BBC World Service – not officially allowed, of course, but it was the only way to get genuine news, otherwise you had to rely on the propaganda broadcast by Egyptian radios. Radio Cairo was jubilant, announcing the victory of Egyptian troops. Very different news was emanating from the BBC, whereby the combined British, French and Israeli forces were making headway and beating the Egyptian army. My aunt Marie did not have any live-in servants, so it was much easier to listen to foreign radio stations without the fear of being denounced. We had never believed any information emanating from the Egyptian government anyway, as they were known to lie with impunity. According to their propaganda, the foreign 'invaders' had been forced to withdraw because of the victorious Egyptian army and the actions of its glorious soldiers.

I got used to those evenings when we were all together and missed them long after. For a short while, everything had been suspended in time. The film 'The Man who knew too much' with James Stewart was the last one we saw in Cairo and the theme song Que Sera Sera became very popular. Whenever I hear it, I am reminded of that period. That was the last time we were together as a family in Egypt.

When the Suez war ended, we returned to our apartment. Hundreds of Jews, as well British and French citizens, were given as little as 48 or 72 hours to leave the country. Families who had lived in Egypt for generations and knew no other way of life, suddenly found their lives shattered. We had lived close to aunts, cousins and other friends and relatives, and were used to seeing them every day. Now we had to face the possibility that we may never see them again. It was heart-breaking.

Land and businesses owned by Jews were seized, confiscated and appropriated by the Egyptian government. If they were paid anything at all, it was a pittance and many previously wealthy Jews left Egypt with nothing – although I suspect that those who could see the writing on the wall had astutely transferred some money abroad through the years. There are still outstanding claims by ex-Egyptian Jews against the government and very few of them have been settled. It's a thankless task – not only do you have to have proof of what you claim you owned, but inevitably, the claimant will hit his head against the brick wall that is Egyptian bureaucracy and red tape. Add to this the endless queues, the prevailing corruption and the lack of a sense of urgency. It is no wonder that many have given up.

Between November 1956 and March 1957, more than 500 Jewish businesses were seized and had their accounts frozen, and 800 more businesses were put on a blacklist. In addition to depriving owners of their property and livelihood, the sequestration measures also affected a broader circle of Jews, as firms such as Cicurel, Gattegno and Chemla were required to discharge all employees who were Jewish.

It has come to light that these sequestrations were premeditated – the Jewish division of the Egyptian Ministry of the Interior kept files on every Jew and Jewish-owned business, even before the Suez crisis and there was already a team in place to manage the confiscations, proof that these would have happened eventually and the Suez crisis was merely the catalyst which precipitated events. Egyptian Jews had no choice but to leave the country and seek refuge elsewhere. Due to the French influence of their educational and cultural background, France was a natural choice for immigration for many members of the Jewish community.

Between 23,000 and 25,000 Jews are estimated to have left Egypt between November 1956 and the end of 1958. By 1957, more than 6,000 had left by ship with the assistance of the Red Cross. Other relief groups, The Hebrew Immigrant Aid Society (HIAS), the Central British Fund, the Joint Distribution Committee (JDC) and the Jewish Agency helped refugees resettle in Israel, Western Europe, the US, Central and South America and Australia. UN Secretary General Dag Hammarskjold was said to have interceded to soften the harsh treatment meted out to departing Jews. There were so many leaving Egypt and some were in such distress that, for the first time, the UN High Commissioner for Refugees, Dr August Lindt, recognised Jews leaving Egypt as bona fide refugees under his aegis.

Several Jewish organisations in the West reported that Egypt had taken anti-Semitic measures reminiscent of Nazi Germany – internment, denaturalisation, dispossession and expulsion. Perhaps the comparison with Nazi Germany is a little extreme, but Nasser certainly used the Jews and their property as scapegoats in his programme of nationalisation. His treatment of the Jewish community was also partly revenge for Israel's part in the Suez crisis. Egyptian Jews were not Israeli citizens and most of them were not Zionists, yet they were made to pay for Israel's actions.

By 1961, only 7,000 Jews remained in Egypt, of which 2,000 were Karaite, mostly unskilled labourers and small artisans. There has not been a proper Jewish community in Egypt for many years. The last exodus was in 1967, after the Six Day War. Yet there is still much evidence of Jewish life – in synagogues and cemeteries, though they are mostly in ruins. Department stores, such as Cicurel and Orosdi, still bear the name of their original owners.

My family had no option but to leave Egypt. As result of Israel's involvement in the crisis, Jews had suddenly become a potential target. The rise of Nasser's pan-Arab nationalism, the propaganda, the confiscation of property, all ramped up by exhortations from the Muslim Brotherhood, finally forced the Jews out of the country which had been their home for generations. This sudden and abrupt departure was traumatic and the worst thing that had happened to me until then.

After our exodus, whenever the name of Nasser was mentioned in a conversation, it was always with a lot of anger and animosity. We were jubilant when Israel triumphed in the Six Day War in 1967, but it was as much about Nasser losing the war as it was about Israel winning it. Regardless of this treatment of the Jewish community, Nasser was a true man of the people and his mission was to 'give Egypt back to the Egyptians'. He began a series of major socialist measures and modernisation reforms and thought that, with such a powerful ally as Russia, he could not go wrong. He called for Pan-Arab unity under his leadership, which culminated in the formation of the United Arab Republic with Syria – unfortunately, this only lasted three years, from

1958 to 1961.

Nasser remains an iconic figure in the Arab world, particularly for his strides towards social justice, modernisation policies and Arab unity. He was responsible for the launch of large industrial projects, including the Aswan Dam and Helena City. Nowadays, I understand better what Nasser was trying to achieve. My resentment has shifted towards the British Government's handling of the nationalisation of the Suez Canal, leading to the Suez crisis. The then Prime Minister, Anthony Eden, did not have the full support of his government when he made the decision to attack Egypt. Nevertheless, he went ahead, arrogantly assuming that he would have the backing of the United States. He made a series of blunders, especially not realising the depth of American opposition to military action.

The European community in Egypt, and the Jewish community in particular, were collateral damage in a politics game, which was really all about power and financial gains. A short war, which was a major setback for British foreign policy and over which we had no control and no say, changed our lives irrevocably. At the same time, departures of Jewish communities were happening all over the Middle East – in Libya, Algeria, Morocco, Tunisia, Yemen, Iraq and Iran. The Jews suddenly found their position untenable in countries where they had lived harmoniously with their neighbours for generations. Sadly, they left behind magnificent synagogues, schools, hospitals and a way of life that would disappear forever. The historical injustice experienced by the Jewish communities in the Arab world is real, but not always recognised or acknowledged.

In Egypt, it was the Jewish community that was the most affected by the consequences of the military intervention led by France, Britain and Israel. All along, the aim of Nasser's government had been to purge Egypt of foreign influence and of its Jewish community and to replace foreigners and non-Muslims in key positions with Egyptian Muslims. Some were requisitioned by the Egyptian government to train Egyptians for positions they had previously occupied, delaying their expulsion by a few months and even years.

I once came across a statement which resonates with me – ' a calamity is only a calamity when your response to it is to accept victimhood'. I am proud that Egyptian Jews didn't. They survived the trauma and prospered in all the countries where they settled. They were forced to start a fresh life as refugees in a new country, with very little money in their pocket, yet they did not see themselves as victims because they were survivors.

My mother and Aunt Marie with friends, 1937

Mum and friend, 1937

My parents' wedding, 1942

My mother and me, 1943

Aunts Matty and Sophie with me, 1943

Viviane, age 1

*Uncle Victor in his Navy
uniform, World War II*

My father and me, Alexandria, 1947

Mum and Dad, Alexandria, 1948

*My mother, Sophie, Leon and
Nicole, Alexandria, 1948*

My sister Nicole and me, 1949

Matty and Albert's wedding, 1949

Viviane and Nicole as bridesmaids, 1950

Victor and Nina's wedding

Aunt Suzanne and Benjo

My parents at the Tawfikieh tennis club, 1951

Group photo, Ras-El-Bar-, 1951

Dad and Uncle Zaki, 1951

With friends by the seaside, 1951

My father's family, Cairo, 1953

Viviane, Nicole and Claudine,
Ras-El-Bar, 1953

Claudine, age 4

My parents and friends, New Year's Eve, 1955

Viviane, Nicole and Claudine, Alexandria, 1955

Cousins Doris and Monique with my sisters and me, 1955

My mother's passport photo, 1956

My father's passport photo, 1956

My father's LAISSEZ-PASSER, *December 1956*

Aunt Nina, 1956

Family photo, Alexandria, 1956

EXTRA

 Mirror News

YOUR INDEPENDENT NEWSPAPER

WEST'S LARGEST HOME DELIVERED AFTERNOON CIRCULATION

TURF RED STREAK

COMPLETE STOCKS

Vol. IX—No. 18   In Three Parts   PART 1   3¢   WEDNESDAY, OCTOBER 31, 1956   6★   MA 5-2311—145 S. Spring, Los Angeles 53—TEN CENTS

BRITISH BOMB 5 EGYPT CITIES

THE SUEZ CANAL—FOCAL POINT OF NEW WORLD TENSION
Port Said, Cairo and installations along canal zone area threatened.

Incendiaries Dropped in Combined Sea-Air Action

LONDON, Oct. 31 (AP)—British and French air and sea forces today assaulted Egypt. Cairo radio said British jet bombers dropped incendiaries and high-explosive bombs on five key Egyptian centers including Cairo where seven persons were reported killed.

Britain's Foreign Secretary Selwyn Lloyd told the House of Commons tonight that "It is quite untrue that Cairo has been bombed." He said the attacks were restricted to airfields.

British officials in London insisted that Cairo, a city of 3,000,000, was not considered a military target. They said the bombers were operating against military targets only.

However, Cairo radio said:

"At 8:50 p.m. local time British bombers carried out attacks on Cairo, Alexandria, Port Said, Ismailia and Suez.

"Seven persons were killed in the second attack.

The broadcast said Cairo was bombed twice with casualties resulting in the second attack.

There was no mention of ground-force operations. Israel radio reported a one-hour air-and sea-and-air raid at Port Said, at the Mediterranean mouth of the Suez Canal.

Earlier the British Defense Ministry announced:

"An air offensive by bomber aircraft under the command is at this moment being launched against military targets in Egypt."

The two generals named Gen. Sir Charles Keightley, formerly commander in chief of Britain's Middle East land force, as commander in chief of the expeditionary force. Vice Adm. P. Barjot of France is his deputy.

The Defense Ministry said their job is to "intervene to restore peace" and end the fighting between the Arab-Israel cease hostilities and the fighting forces of both sides keep clear of a zone 10 miles on either side of the canal, had replied 12 hours earlier.

Egypt had rejected the ultimatum. Israel had accepted it on the condition that Egypt would agree.

The French and British contended that fighting between the Sinai Peninsula endangered the canal because of the vital negotiations safely in the canal and Britain for the canal and Britain's stopped shipments.

Britain Prime Minister Eden told the House of Commons, during angry question

LATE BULLETINS

TEL AVIV, Israel, Oct. 31 (P)—The Israeli army said tonight an armored task force has driven across Egyptian territory in a move to cut off the Egyptian-held Gaza Strip on the Mediterranean. It said the Israelis pushed from El Arish, south of Gaza, 49 miles southwest of El Arish on the seashore. The operation would seize the Gaza Strip from Egypt. Israeli radio said the Gaza Strip is being encircled.

WASHINGTON, Oct. 31 (P)—White House aides Secretary Hagerty said today aides at the air attack on the British and French governments urge the United States an advance note that they were momentarily disenchanted against Egypt. Hagerty said President Eisenhower received his first word of the action from U.S. intelligence services.

SAN FRANCISCO, Oct. 31 (P)—Air Force bases watch since Monday because of the Middle East situation. Maj. Gen. Roy B. Lynn, commander of the Western Air Defense Force at Hamilton Air Force Base, emphasized that the watch is not an "alert" and he stressed that "no airplanes have been moved up and no leaves have been canceled."

WASHINGTON, Oct. 31 (P)—Units of the U.S. 6th Fleet moved to Mediterranean ports of Egypt and Israel today to help evacuate Americans. More than 1000 already have left.

BONN, Germany, Oct. 31 (P)—West Germany has started evacuating its citizens from Jordan and Syria, the Foreign Office said today. German citizens will be evacuated out of Egypt, but this has not yet started.

ALEXANDRIA, Oct. 31 (P)—Three hundred and fifty Americans, mostly women and children, left for Europe today aboard a U.S. transport. Motor convoys brought them to port from Cairo.

OTTAWA, Oct. 31 (P)—Canada today decided to suspend "for the time being" all shipments of arms, including 24 Sabre jets, to Israel, Prime Minister St. Laurent would not say whether the suspension implies criticism of Israel's invasion of Egypt.

Ike to Meet With Leading Military Men

WASHINGTON, Oct. 31 (P)—The nation's top military leaders will attend tomorrow's regular meeting of the National Security Council with President Eisenhower for a full-scale review of the Middle East crisis.

President Eisenhower's talk on the Middle East crisis will be televised over KRCA (4) at 6:15 p.m. and broadcast again over KMPC at 9:15 p.m.

The announcement said combined aerial and naval bombardment began at 6:00 p.m., Egyptian time (7:00 a.m. PST) against points in the Suez Canal area.

A British-French action which began today, demanding that Egypt and Israel cease hostilities.

Secretary of the Army Brucker, Secretary of the Air Force Quarles, Adm. Arthur W. Radford, chairman of the Joint Chiefs of Staff; Adm. Arleigh Burke, chief of Naval Operations.

Turn to Page 3, Column 3

Stocks Take Sharp Drop in Reaction to Hostilities

NEW YORK, Oct. 31 (P)—again today on news of British bombings in Egypt, with the latest advances centered in grains, cotton and crude vegetable oils.

World prices for chiefly near metals tobacco higher with renewed vigor.

The biggest clean scene in the hours before noon went after Prime Minister Eden announced that his country would protest its interests in the Near East. This brought a flood of sell orders to the market, which had been continually sluggish up to that time.

There was a further and less active decline on later reports of British and French bombing in Egypt. Toward the end of the session prices recovered slightly.

In the commodity markets prices against edged up.

(Details Page 28, Part 1)

Jet Crashes; Pilot Bails Out

ORINDA, Oct. 31 (P)—a Navy Cougar jet fighter upon its march, exploded and burned in an open field yesterday. The pilot bailed out safely.

He is Lt. J. E. Greeley, 31, of Onywalk, CO., assigned to the 844rd Fighter Squadron, Naval Air Station, New York. Greeley was checking out the F9W jet before flying it to New York.

Russ in Full Retreat Out of Budapest

BUDAPEST, Hungary, Oct. 31 (P)—The Russian retreat from Budapest appeared in full swing today.

Soviet tanks—leaving their dead and wounded—headed away under a shower of anti-tank fire from Hungarian patriots plan thundering to all corners of the town.

Russian armored forces guarding the Danube River bridges withdrew at dawn today, retreated throughout the morning.

The Hungarian army, now completely on the side of the revolution, tracked in fresh platoons to relieve street patrols of the ragged insurgents.

The army took over the Citadel, a fortress commanding the entire city, and ringed it with antitank guns.

Rebel anger which had been directed against those who directed the detested State Police force, had been channeled to work for the most part against the remnants of the detested.

Turn to Page 8, Column 4

A MISSING LINK

Where Does It All Leave U.S.?

BY JAMES MARLOW, Associated Press News Analyst

WASHINGTON, Oct. 31 (P) — The missing link in the fighting in Egypt is this: Did the British, French and Israelis plan it together? It looks that way. All three stand to gain by what they did.

What the Israelis wanted was to help wreck Egyptian President Nasser, who for beyond their move to wipe out Israel. They wanted to wipe out him, the way the Italians pledged to work with and uphold the United Nations, although hold the world organization.

French wanted war to wreck Nasser and get back the Suez Canal.

But the effects of what the United Nations would soon see, telling Secretary of State Dulles nothing of their plans to go into the Suez area and then ignoring President Eisenhower's personal plea not to.

They made their move at a time when the West might have profited by the Russian killing of Hungarians in the Budapest.

Turn to Page 2, Column 1

Poulson Gets Hospital Exam

Mayor Poulson today entered St. Vincent's Hospital for a checkup.

Mayor is not ill, and will be examined as a routine.

TODAY'S POLITICS

Eisenhower makes major campaign address in Philadelphia tomorrow night on Middle East crisis. Page 5.

Stevenson says Eisenhower administration bears "heavy responsibility" for crisis in Middle East. Page 3.

Nixon charges Stevenson is politician first and statesman second in comment on Middle East crisis. Page 7.

Knowland charges Eisenhower with "oil and power" in Middle East. Page 4.

Political Analyst Lockwell wonders how many voters are swayed by campaign oratory. Page 12.

MIRROR-NEWS INDEX

	Pt.		Pt.
Bridge	26	Horoscope	31
		Hamburger	21
Classified	7-11	Knight	4
Comics		Labor	14
Crossword		Markets	28
Deaths		Mitchell, Alma	8
Crosby	27	Sport	16-20
Editorials	3	Theaters	29
Financial	28	TV-Radio	31
Gudson	26-25	Vincent	12

Suez Crisis, 1956

*Victor and Nina, outside
Bridgend hostel, January, 1957*

*A family photo, outside Bridgend
hostel, January, 1957*

*Uncle Zaki with cousins
Rony and Daniele*

Uncle Clement, Milan, 1958

Fortunee Gubbay, my grandmother

My grandmother and Aunt Marie by the seaside

Everyday life

Mores, customs and superstitions

I have lived in the UK most of my life. Culturally, I am still French and feel perfectly at home with the language and culture. I am very familiar with the literature and history and the names of Paris streets remind me of this. I also love Italy and lived in Milan for three happy years. I have been in England for longer than I care to remember and do not wish to live anywhere else; yet I don't feel English and can only describe myself as British.

The truth is, I can't identify with one single country, as most people do. I am not French and have never lived in France. I am not Egyptian as I am Jewish and was forced to leave and I don't feel English as I was not born here. I speak four languages fluently, but none of them like a native – English with a slight accent, French with an English accent now (or so I am told), Italian with a French accent and Arabic with a reasonable vocabulary, but I would never pass as Egyptian. Egyptian Jews call themselves citizens of the world, so perhaps that is what I am.

The older I get, the more I realise that my heart is still

in Egypt. It is the country of my birth and I will never forget it. Even though, towards the end, the government rejected and hated the Jews, we still belong to the land and we still love its people, most of whom were honest and decent. I am proud to say that I was born in Egypt and I am not unique in feeling this way. Most people my age remember their native country with the same fondness and have many good memories of their childhood there. Perhaps we were too young to understand the political events that were unfolding, in the way that our parents did. Nevertheless, we are lucky to have had a privileged childhood. Egypt lives on within us and it will continue to dwell in our memories.

This is the general consensus amongst Egyptian Jews who have written or spoken about what they remember. Coupled with a feeling of outrage, as they had no choice but to succeed elsewhere, they all feel the same sense of nostalgia, loss and regret. I have tried to be as truthful as I can in my recollections, but I am aware that I was seeing things through a child's eye. I wish I had had the wisdom and the foresight to ask questions when the older generation was around because I am sure that, in spite of my efforts, a great deal of information has been lost.

Whenever I meet people with the same background, there is an instant connection. Somehow Egypt has stayed with us – in our habits, our comfort foods, our customs and in the way we interact with others. The expressions we still use make us laugh and we have many shared memories – the places where we lived, studied or spent the summer holidays are the same. Whether it was Cairo or Alexandria, we had roughly the same experiences.

Today, we are the older generation and our children cannot share those memories. For them, Egypt is just another country and they can't comprehend how we can possibly still love it, since we were forced to leave. They don't understand our special affection for the country we were born in. Sadly, we are the last generation to remember a thriving Jewish life in Egypt and the same goes for all the Jews who were born and brought up in Algeria, Morocco, Tunisia, Iraq, etc. Jewish life has ceased to exist in Arab countries.

We were uprooted when we were forced to leave Egypt suddenly. Perhaps our parents had a harder time because they had the responsibility of making a new life in a strange country, with next to nothing in their pocket and a whole new culture and way of life to adapt to. Nevertheless, the children experienced a trauma, especially if they were old enough to understand. For years I did not allow myself to think about Egypt and was too busy having to cope with the problems life throws at us.

I have looked at some photos which were taken in Alexandria in 1956, during our last summer holiday by the seaside. We are all smiling and on the surface appear relaxed. Even if the grown-ups were anxious about the unfolding political situation, no one imagined that this would turn out to be our last holiday. Fast forward a year, and we were all scattered in different parts of Europe, the US or South America. Added to the nostalgia, there is a certain anger. We were born in Egypt, so were our parents and in many cases generations before them. Jews had lived there since biblical times. However, the Jewish people are destined to wander and there have been countless times throughout history when they have been expelled from the country they called their own, sometimes tortured, always singled out, solely because of their religion.

Egypt was once a beacon of hope for hundreds of Jewish immigrants who found a new and often prosperous life there. One hundred years later, their children and grandchildren found themselves rejected and expelled from the country that had welcomed them with open arms. Mixed with regrets for the old life and nostalgia, Egyptian Jews are nevertheless proud of the fact that, wherever they ended up, they have managed to build a new life and have become upstanding members of their community.

What is hard to accept and makes me sad is the Jewish cultural holocaust which has taken place in Egypt. Hundreds of synagogues have shut because of lack of attendance, cemeteries have been looted of their headstones, and of the numerous Jewish-owned shops, not a single one remains. The names of some buildings and department stores are still the same, but the Egyptians who shop there have no idea that these establishments were founded and owned by Jews. Why would they, since the history of the Jews in Egypt is not included in their school curriculum? Most of them do not realise that there was a large Jewish and European community living in Egypt not so long ago, but perhaps the older generation remembers us with some regret – my hope is that one day the average Egyptian will realise what their country lost when we left and acknowledge that, not so long ago, there was a thriving Jewish community in Egypt, which was vital to the economy.

Egypt in the 1940s, 50s and 60s was not the place it is today. It was a Muslim country, but not an Islamic one and a place of tolerance where women had many rights. They could dress as they pleased and show off their figures. There were swimsuit competitions, which Egyptian women, as well as European ones, entered. In 1954, Miss Egypt went on to win the Miss World title. Egyptian cinema was the third largest in the world and its music flourished. Foreigners dreamt of spending their holiday exploring, especially the temples of Luxor and Karnak.

Although I am not an Egyptian Muslim, I can still identify with Egypt, the country of my formative years. I think of it as a special place, with warm and hospitable people. I miss the streets of Cairo, noisy but vibrant and full of life. I remember many things – the sound of the muezzin calling the faithful to prayer, the wonderful scent of the jasmine flower, the blue of the Mediterranean, the warmth of the sand under your feet, the palm trees fluttering in the wind and the small doughnuts called *lokoumadis,* dripping with sugar syrup. I miss all the smells that always hit you when you walked along any street, sizzling butter, Egyptian bread and kebabs, Turkish coffee and the aroma of garlic and turmeric coming from the kitchens.

There is a saying in French '*Celui qui a bu de l'eau du Nil en reboira*', which translates as 'he who has drank from the Nile will drink again'. Figuratively speaking of course – taking these words literally would be impossible, as the water of the Nile is dirty and polluted. Nevertheless, the Nile has been an integral part of my childhood, always in the background and often taken for granted. It's the lifeblood of Egypt, without which the country would be a desert. The Nile changed colour according to the seasons and the tide. Feluccas, the traditional wooden sailing boats, were a familiar sight and so were barges carrying all sorts of goods. The Nile was always a busy waterway, which linked Cairo with the fertile delta, as well as Luxor and Aswan in the south of Egypt with the North. Although Ancient Egyptians believed that the flooding of the Nile was the result of the goddess Isis's tears flowing as she wept for her dead husband, it was in fact the results of monsoons in the highlands dumping rain into the Nile. This started in spring and continued through most of the summer.

The rain was such a rare event that it's only associated with one incident in my mind. We had an office building in front of our apartment and, as it had been raining, the *bawab* (caretaker) of the building had gone up on the roof, probably to check something. Tragically, he slipped, lost his balance and fell to his death. Egyptian women wail very loudly and repeatedly whenever something bad happens. Many of them stood outside the building, probably professional mourners as well as family, friends and neighbours, and their wailing went on for ages. They kept shouting *ya sater ya Rab, ya sater ya Rab*, which translates as God forbid, all the time slapping their face.

In contrast, Egyptians in general loved celebrating. The birth of a child was an event to rejoice about, especially the first son. After the birth, the mother and father were often called by the title *Abu'* and *Om* (meaning father and mother) followed by their son's names. Some families also arranged for the slaughter of an animal – two for boys and one for girls – one week after the birth to mark the event. Weddings were a particularly joyous occasion, especially in the popular areas. There was music, dancing and singing and everyone joined in. You didn't have to be invited and everyone was welcome. The women loved to ululate at any happy occasion. They made the traditional joyous Middle Eastern sound called *zaghlat* in Arabic – by putting their hand in front of their mouth and emitting a long, wavering, high pitched vocal sound.

Life in Egypt may have been wonderful, but it was not always easy. The humidity rose in summer and you had to be careful of heat rash. We kept medicated talcum powder at hand to relieve the itching. There were no vaccines for childhood illnesses, such as measles and whooping cough. Typhoid was still endemic and there were things you could not eat. We had all the childhood illnesses, whooping cough, measles, German measles and chicken pox. Water had to be boiled and also milk because it was not pasteurised.

There were many home remedies used for various ailments. Some of them have turned out to have some scientific basis for their curative properties, whilst others seem to belong more in the realm of superstition. Either way, they often seemed to work and I still remember a few.

For discomfort from a toothache, brandy or clove was applied onto the tooth to numb the pain. It tasted horrible, but it worked for a short while, you just had to keep applying it. For colds and flu, it was hot tea and of course the Sephardic chicken soup with rice. For stomach ache, anise-scented ouzo was massaged onto the area of the stomach and then wrapped with an ouzo-doused cloth for a few hours. An extreme way of curing fever and headaches was called *shakayika* – slices of raw potatoes were tied to the forehead with a handkerchief to draw out the fever or pain.

Respiratory infections which had gone to the chest had to be treated in an old fashioned way, since there were no antibiotics at that time. The most common method was a form of cupping called *ventouse* or *meter ventozas* in Ladino. A tray was brought in, bearing a number of small, heated downturned glasses, covered by a clean cloth. The hot glasses were then placed mouth down on the sick person's back and left for a few minutes. As it cooled, the air contracted, creating a vacuum and suction effect on the surface of the skin. This increased the blood flow to the surface, drawing out the toxins. When removed, they left a series of red circles all over the back. The idea was to draw out the mucus from the bronchial tubes, but it was not a pleasant experience. The less extreme treatment was to massage the chest with warm camphorated oil but, although this was gentler, the smell was overpowering and unpleasant.

Earaches were also cured in a rather unorthodox way. My mother used to put some paraffin oil in a teaspoon and light a match to heat the bottom of the spoon. When the oil was warm, she soaked a small piece of cotton in the oil and inserted it in the ear that was hurting. Sometimes this was too hot. Eau de Cologne was thought to have magical powers – wherever I hurt, she put some on a handkerchief and applied it to where the pain was. It was quite soothing, but really didn't make much difference to the pain. We often had lice and the remedy for that was to put paraffin on our hair. It seems incredible now and dangerous, but there were none of the lotions available nowadays and some remedies were quite primitive. To top it all, we had to go to school the next day with paraffin still in our hair. This was quite embarrassing, as it was then obvious to everyone that you had lice!

There was an interesting Egyptian old wives' tale – it was believed that in order to ensure a young child's eyes stayed strong and healthy, compresses of warm water and onion juice had be applied to the rims of the eyelids. Some people said that it worked, but the onion juice should definitely be avoided! In ancient Egypt, women used kohl from an early age, in order to protect their eyes and enhance their beauty, and women continue to use it to this day throughout the Middle East.

Summer brought a plague of mosquitoes, so we had a film of white netting over our beds every night to prevent the bites. The rooms were sprayed with a Flit gun containing an insecticide called DDT, which released a pungent mist everywhere. The irony is that DDT would be considered poison now. The mosquitoes did not always wait till the night and we often got bitten in the early evening. There were flies everywhere and sometimes flying ants. One year there was an invasion of grasshoppers. The sky became dark all of a sudden and the grasshoppers were everywhere – on the ground, the cars, the pavements and the road. It felt and looked like a biblical plague, ironically one of the ten plagues brought down on Egypt during the first Exodus of the Jews. However, all these were incidentals in what was otherwise a good life.

Once a year, we had to put up with the khamsin season.

Khamsin means fifty in Arabic and the khamsin wind was supposed to last fifty days, although it probably did not last that long. The wind brought with it the desert sands and a fine dust which went into just about everything. All the surfaces and furniture got covered, even with the windows closed and the shutters down. Being out and about could get quite unpleasant if the wind started blowing in your direction.

I often ask myself – what if the Arab countries had not been so hostile to the creation of the State of Israel and what if the Jews had been able to continue to live peacefully side by side with their Muslim neighbours, as they had done for generations? Would I have enjoyed this lifestyle? It was certainly far more leisurely and less stressful, but not very challenging. It suited my mother and all her friends, but the new generation was asking for something more and by the 1950s many young women were employed, though this stopped after they got married. What I miss most is not having all the family living so close by. If I close my eyes I can trace the route from our flat to Aunt Marie's, which was only about 10 minutes' walk away. Another 10 minutes from there and you were in Tahrir Square, where Uncle Mayer lived with his family. My father's family lived a few minutes' walk from us, turning right instead of left from our apartment building.

There were many communities in Egypt – Jewish (mainly Sephardic), Italian, Maltese, Spanish, French, British, etc. There was also a large Coptic community, a Greek Orthodox and an Armenian one. Many of the Sudanese people living in Egypt were employed in lower paid jobs. We maintained cordial relations with the other communities, but we did not mix socially. Each community had its own customs, traditions and way of cooking. Egypt at that time was multinational and multicultural. French was the main language spoken by Europeans and was what was heard in the streets, apart from Arabic of course. We got on well with the local population and I don't remember any conflict.

All religions were tolerated. We co-existed peacefully side by side with the local population, but there was a clear distinction between the so-called Europeans and Egyptians. Commerce and industry were exclusively in the hands of Europeans. Apart from the Banque Misr, all the banks were British or French. Many Jews had a foreign nationality, which their ancestors had somehow acquired in the past – mainly French, British and Italian. Cinemas, restaurants, cafes, night clubs, department stores, banks, and so on were run by Europeans, only the waiters were Egyptian and there were many establishments where the locals were not allowed. I realise that in the light of today's society, this reeks of colonialism and it's not surprising that the Egyptian population was initially so inspired by Nasser's nationalism.

By the time Nasser came to power, things had been changing gradually. It was compulsory for companies to employ Egyptian nationals and an educated middle class was establishing itself. The upper class in Egypt was extremely wealthy. I had a classmate called Malka who invited all the girls in her class to her birthday party. A chauffeur driven car came to pick up each of us and took us to her sumptuous villa. We were all very impressed and perhaps a little surprised.

There were three words which Egyptian people liked to use as often as they could – *bokra, inshallah* and *maaleche,* and their philosophy can be summarised in those words. *Bokra* means tomorrow. They had no sense of urgency, most things could wait and, if it could be done tomorrow, why rush around and do it today? If an Egyptian told you that something would be ready the next day, you would have been foolish to take this literally. It may have happened the next day or perhaps the day after or the day after that. All you needed to remember is that you had to learn to be patient and it would happen eventually.

Inshallah means God willing and everything is in His hands. They accepted their fate and had faith that God would provide and sort everything for the best. Most sentences ended with the word *Inshallah,* which could also be a vague answer to a question. So, if you asked if your order would be ready to be collected the next day, the answer may very well have been *Inshallah* – it was vague, it didn't mean yes, but it didn't mean no, it just meant let's hope for the best. This sense of fatalism was part of the Middle Easter culture, including that of Egyptian Jews. We often used to say *'l'homme propose et Dieu dispose',* which roughly translates as 'man makes plans, but God decides'.

Maalech means it doesn't matter and it's not important. It's much more than that though and it's a whole philosophy. Egyptians shrugged their shoulders and probably suggested that getting worked up about something was not good for your health. They were quite sincere if they said that it was not the end of the world and you should calm down – it didn't matter if something had not been delivered in time or if you had missed your train or an important appointment because of the traffic.

Another word which had a particular meaning in Arabic and cannot be translated is *mazaag*. It meant something that pleased one, but covered just about everything – something you ate or drank, something you did or something that satisfied a mood. You only had to say *da mazaag* and that summed it up.

Proverbs and sayings were often used in conversation, to convey a message or a thought. It was a means of providing a common ground and including everyone in the conversation. They were like mantras and are also used to explain, to cheer up or to console. Egyptians were fatalistic and accepted everything philosophically. For them, nothing lasts and everything passes. They looked up to the sky and said that it's God's will. Again, just one word said it all – *maktoub*, which means 'it is written', therefore it was meant to be. This belief meant that they were able to accept everything that happened to them, even tragedies. God would provide and hopefully make things better.

Like the Jews, Egyptians were renowned for their hospitality, but they took it much further. If they liked you, they gave you the shirt off their back. They welcomed you into their house, however humble it was, as though you were the most important guest in the world. They insisted you shared with them whatever they were eating and went without themselves if need be. That was done discreetly and the guest was not aware of it. They were tolerant on the whole and had a good sense of humour. Although they liked their food, for the average Egyptian eating and drinking was done without ceremony. They could have their sandwich sitting on the pavement, with their plate placed on top of a sheet of newspaper.

Egyptian weddings in the popular areas were totally different from our Jewish weddings, very picturesque and much more fun. To seal the engagement, it was customary for the fiancé to give his intended what was known as a *shabka* – usually a full set of gold jewellery, such as a pricey necklace, earrings, rings and bracelet. He was also expected to provide somewhere to live. A few days before the wedding ceremony, all the furniture was moved to the couple's apartment which, until then, had been empty. All the moving, the heavy furniture, beds, sofas, kitchen utensils, was done by friends and neighbours. When this was finished, the bride brought her own trousseau, along with the bedding, pillows, bedcovers and finally all the presents. All this took place with a lot of noise and music.

Wedding ceremonies required a great deal of preparation. On the day itself, a ceremonial tent was set up. The men started early, setting up lamps, laying down large carpets and carting dozens of folding chairs inside the tent. The whole street was lit with brightly coloured baubles and was decorated for the occasion. A platform was erected, where two chairs were placed. This was where the bride and groom sat after the marriage contract had been signed, high above and set apart from everyone. A band was specially hired for the occasion and contributed greatly to the celebrations by playing non-stop.

There was much merriment, with people clapping

and dancing and the interminable ululating by the women called *'zaghlouta'*. All sorts of refreshments and pastries were offered to the guests – aside from those invited, anyone who wished to attend was welcome. The children loved these occasions because they got lots of sweets thrown at them. The weddings of the wealthier class took place in swanky hotels or clubs, specially hired for the occasion and it was still a joyous and noisy celebration, with much music and dancing.

In contrast, a memorial service after a funeral was a very sombre occasion, where all the women dressed in black and the men wore dark costumes. There was no music and all that could be heard was the wailing of the professional mourners. The memorial service in the tent outside was attended by men only. The women mourned indoors. The bereaved person sat in the middle of the room, surrounded by relatives. Female acquaintances, neighbours and friends arrived in turn to pay their respects.

In Egypt at the time – and to a certain extent this continues to be so – the way in which society considered and treated individuals depended more on their family background and the circumstances in which they were born than on their individual qualities. In time, of course, these qualities were recognised, but the person often continued to be called *'ibn'* meaning 'son of' – so they were still always identified as so and so's son.

Tipping was an institution. It was called *bakchich* and you were expected to tip everywhere and for any reason. It had its origins in the disparity between rich and poor and was considered, perhaps subconsciously, as a small way of making up for that disparity. Aside from the beggars in the street, you often encountered poor children who looked for any reason to ask for a *bakchich* and they persistently ran after the person until they got it. Adults also expected to be tipped – it was not considered begging, because in their eyes they were not asking for charity. They were performing a small service for which they expected to be rewarded, like helping someone who was having difficulty parking his car, fetching a coffee from the nearest bar etc.

In restaurants, bars, cafes and other public places, this was known as a tip and you were expected to do so generously, though it was never clear what that meant. In Europe, there is a certain code for tipping which the customer generally knows beforehand, 5%,10% or 15%, depending on the establishment. Not so in Egypt, where the amount of the tip was left to the customer's discretion.

On a Friday, Egyptians greeted each other with the expression *'gom'etak khadra'* – may you have a green week. The colour green was supposed to bring good luck and happiness. Marsim, also known as rue or herb of grace, produced strong aromatic green leaves. People rubbed them on their hands and then smelled them as a good omen for a lucky and joyous week, a 'green' week. The Sephardic Jews favoured aruda – which was a strong-smelling evergreen shrub bearing small yellow flowers. It was believed to bring protection to one's home and to ward off negative energy. It was also often placed on a bridal tray with marzipan sprinkled with gold leaf.

Egyptians were very superstitious – as were the Jews of Egypt. They feared the evil eye and they saw it everywhere.

This encompassed everything – envy, jealousy, resentment, hatred, in short any negative feeling. Starting from this, anything bad which happened, trivial or major, could be traced back to someone 'giving you the evil eye'. If you were paid a compliment, that was considered bad luck, as it may have attracted the evil eye. Everything and anything could draw the attention of this towards you and everyone had their own superstitions. Your good fortune, your health, your relationships, could all be threatened by the so-called evil eye. This could come from just about anyone, a jealous friend, an envious colleague, someone who just did not like you and so on.

These practices extended to all parts of Egyptian society and, rich or poor, you also heard phrases such as *inshallah* and *alhamdullilah* (if God wills it and Praise be to God respectively). The former was added when discussing an event that was to happen in the future and the latter to express joy or contentment over something which had already happened. This reminded Egyptians of God's presence and influence over all matters and also that God had the power to alter anything at any time, so nothing should be taken for granted.

Egyptians and Jews alike were careful never to praise the beauty of a child or its achievements, without adding the phrase *mash'allah,* which means 'thanks be to God'.

Direct compliments were greeted with anxiety and suspicion, as they were associated with attracting the evil eye. Some took the fear of being accused of this to the extreme. Upon seeing a newborn baby, rather than do the normal thing and compliment the mother, they commiserated with her as to how ugly or thin the baby was. The more they said this, the happier the new mother was, relieved that the evil eye had been averted. An admiring compliment was always met with a negative statement from the receiver. English people will happily say 'you are so lucky' to someone and mean it as a compliment. The well meant sentence would make an Egyptian Jew – and especially a Sephardic Jew of Spanish descent – feel uncomfortable. I grew up with all these superstitions and they still influence the way I think or react.

The Sephardic belief in the evil eye, called *ojo malo*'in Ladino or *nazar* in Turkish, had developed significantly during the years of the Ottoman Empire. It had certainly had a strong influence on my father and his family. It was believed that one could unintentionally or intentionally cause harm to a person simply though thinking or expressing praise. To shield one from envy, the protective custom when making a compliment was to precede it with '*sin ojo*' (without evil eye) or *nazar no*. It was important to downplay success to avoid triggering envy.

Some people – this was certainly the case with my paternal family – took this fear of the evil eye very seriously. An expression often used was '*mil mueren de ayinara y uno de su muerti*' which translates as 'for every thousand that die from the evil eye, only one will die from natural causes'. On hearing the news of a tragedy, death or fatal illness, the immediate exclamation that it should not happen to one's loved ones was often '*Barminan!*' (GOD forbid!), "*Leshos y apartados*' ('Far and apart') or "*Pishkados I lemon!*" ('Fish and lemon!'). I have no idea of the reasoning behind the last expression, but I often heard my family say *Barminan*.

One way of dealing with the evil eye was to wave five fingers in the air, as the number five was also reputed to work as an antidote. Some people just muttered *khamsa khamsa* under their breath (the Arabic word for five.) Both Egyptians and Middle Eastern Jews believed that the number 5 was a good luck number which had the power to ward off anything bad. In fact, the number 5 represents the five fundamental dogmas or Pillars of Islam – faith, prayer, fasting, charity and pilgrimage. *Khamsa* acted as a shield between the person fearing the evil eye and the person potentially capable of giving this. Syrian Jews wore elaborate pendants representing a hand (as a symbol of five because of the five fingers). To protect their family and their home, they also had a large *khamsa* hanging on the wall somewhere in the house.

It was believed that a negative power or harmful energy could be cast through envy and that amulets afforded protection. There was an array of protective talismans to choose from, often worn on a gold chain. As was the custom in Sephardic families, my sisters and I were given a turquoise stone at birth, along with a shaddai, with the three letters of the mystical name of God written across in Hebrew and I still wear mine. My father always wore a ring with a large blue pearl; blue is the colour of the sky and joy, of light and air, the opposite of which being envy and the dark forces at play.

In addition to the evil eye and the power of the blue pearl, Egyptians were afraid of something they called *afrit*. Demons – djinn – are mentioned in the Qur'an.

They are evil spirits which are omnipresent and, in order to protect themselves, Egyptians used all sorts of amulets and talismans. If I ever did anything naughty, Amina the maid would tell me that the *afrit* or the '*baboula*' would be coming to get me – this was supposed to be the bogeyman and Egyptian children were afraid of it.

Egyptians sometimes went round a dwelling with something called *aattar*, which was a mixture of aromatic herbs and incense. The mixture was put into a small brazier like utensil, was lit and then paraded in every room of the house, where it was hoped the smoke would chase away the evil eye. Very superstitious people even called on a professional exorcist to perform this ritual.

Added to the above were the superstitions associated with certain gestures. I have lost count of all the ones my father had – never put a box with new shoes on the table, or leave a pair of scissors open, or cross someone on the stairs or drop your keys on the floor. I could go on and on. I tried not crossing anyone when going down the stairs to catch the tube in London and soon had to give up. One of my aunt's habits was to put a coin in a handbag if it was a present, because that meant that the recipient would always be prosperous. If she accidentally dropped a piece of bread on the floor, she picked it and kissed it, as a gesture of gratitude for having had it. The funniest superstition was the one when, if we sneezed, we had to pull one of ours ears many times – my parents would always remind us to do so if we forgot by saying '*tire ton oreille*', pull your ear.

An old Judeo Spanish superstition was the one which said that you must not point at a star. It is possible that this warning is related to the Spanish Inquisition. In order to find out whether the Sabbath had ended, Jews who had outwardly converted to Christianity, but secretly continued to observe Judaism, counted the first three stars in the sky by pointing to them. The agents of the Inquisition knew this custom and were able to identify secret Jews this way – every superstition has a story. It was thought that salt absorbs evil spirits, so this would sometimes be scattered under someone's bed to ward off the evil eye. In the morning, the salt was carefully scooped onto a dustpan and poured down the toilet, whilst murmuring something in Ladino.

Along with my family's many superstitions (only on my father's side, I hasten to add), I have acquired some time honoured Egyptian ones – such as stepping in with your right leg when entering new place or a new house. Egyptians believed that doing so could bless the house and bring in health, happiness and prosperity. Most Egyptians did not like black crows, because they believed that if a crow stood on the roof, something bad would happen to the house or its people. The turned slipper was another one. Whenever they saw a turned slipper, they immediately put it back to its right position, as they believed that the turned slipper would bring Satan inside the house.

For Egyptian Jews, Middle Eastern folklore, religious ritual and superstitions became so closely entwined that it was difficult to define the roots of a particular custom or tradition. There were those we were supposed to observe and others we were prohibited to do, but it was not always clear why or where that had started. It had simply become the norm.

There was no rhyme, reason or logical explanation for any of these superstitions and you either believed in them or you didn't. Some of them were just habit – If I see a turned slipper, I will still automatically put it back in its right position, which to most people may appear strange, quirky or OCD. I have successfully tried to challenge some of these superstitions, but then I hear of a new one and I am back to square one.

This list is endless and it's a shame that so many of them are lodged in my brain as it can make life difficult. My husband Mike and my children, who are not superstitious in the least, do not understand why I often go to great lengths to do or avoid doing things. They see it as somewhat weird, if not frustrating. For instance, I refuse to open an umbrella indoors, as this is considered bad luck. So, the umbrella will just be left outside, where of course it will never dry. To most people, all these superstitions sound ridiculous but it's something much deeper than that – perhaps they all stem from my childhood fear of the unknown. In simple terms, if a superstition is a way of avoiding a perceived danger, then it's easier to comply.

The Jewish community often called on an old rabbi if a child had been ill for a few days and the doctor's visits had made no difference. The rabbi was called Hakham and it was thought that the older he was, the wiser he would be. He sat by the bedside of the patient, took his hand and then mumbled endless prayers. The monotony of this liturgy meant that the old rabbi eventually fell asleep, which made the women happy as they attributed this to the fact that the old man had exhausted himself trying to chase away the evil eye.

Some of the everyday expressions we used were also steeped in superstition. If someone was talking about something they were hoping or planning to do, they always ended the sentence with *Si Dieu veut* meaning God willing. Asked how they were, the person would inevitably answer that they were okay *Grace à Dieu* – God be thanked. With some people like my mother, who was not superstitious, it was just an automatic answer. We believed that when bad things happened, they came in threes. The expression we used was *jamais deux sans trois.* If something unpleasant had already happened twice, the only way to avoid a third occurrence was to break a match.

Aside from all the superstitions, I remember the numerous blessings and well-wishes my family used. Paramount were prayers and blessings for a healthy life – a common saying to this end was *Saludozos siempre.* Blessings of gratitude were also said at every sacred occasion, for example the saying *Bendichio el Dio.* In time of adversity, my father or aunts would say *El Dio mos dara buelta y alegria,* 'May God visit us and bring us happiness'. As one was to embark on a journey, a wish was made by both the travellers and the ones being left behind, *Kon bueno ver las karas,* 'May we only meet again in happy circumstances'. When a new purchase was made, the expression used was *Kon salut ke lo gozes,* 'May you enjoy it in good health'.

The Jewish community in Egypt was a closed, goldfish bowl society, which many people would find suffocating nowadays. It was also very narrow-minded. A woman's role in life was to marry and have children and it seemed that things were always done with the objective of finding a husband. Gossip was rife, as everyone knew everyone else and it did not take much to set tongues wagging. Details of any whiff of a scandal were passed by word of mouth, with all due exaggeration and embellishments. Appearances were important in the Jewish community. You were expected to behave in a certain way and conform to the norm.

The constant preoccupation was with 'what will people say' or 'what will people think'. The fear of being the subject of gossip meant that you never strayed from the straight and narrow, at least outwardly. I am sure that there were many things going on under the surface, which we were unaware of. A person was often referred to as *comme il faut,* which meant that he/she was as 'one should be'. One was expected to know what the right thing to do was in every situation and how to do it. The rules were unwritten, sometimes they were not even known, but they became part of one's personality, almost second nature.

I was lucky to have had a privileged childhood in Egypt, but I am sure that, as I got older, I would have found the society I grew up in shallow and stifling. It was a narrow minded one and rather intolerant. Most people had never travelled outside Egypt and were therefore quite insular, in spite of being au fait with the popular French culture and going to the theatre and the opera whenever touring companies performed in Cairo.

There was a certain mindset in this society. You had your place within it and, rich or poor, you were expected to stick to the script. We had a neighbour in the block of flats opposite ours and the space between our buildings was so narrow that you could see right into someone's living room. This lady was on her own (I don't think she was widowed) and had two young daughters, one of them a couple of years older than me. Cairo in the 1950s didn't look kindly on a woman without a man. My parents were not friendly with the family, quite the opposite. It seemed they disapproved, probably because this lady did not seem to care about conventions and was perhaps regarded as 'loose'. She simply didn't fit into the expected code of behaviour.

Divorced women were few in the Jewish community and were not well thought of. They were often ostracised, mostly by the women, who thought they were out to grab their husbands. Divorce was therefore extremely rare. Families always interfered in marital disputes and usually succeeded in persuading one or both parties that divorce was against their interest and not advisable – especially in the case of a woman, as there was no such thing as a woman's rights and alimony. There certainly were no high powered divorce lawyers and the rabbis acted as marriage counsellors.

These rabbis exerted a formidable influence on the mores and lives of Egyptian Jews. They were known as Hakham, the honorific title for a rabbi. The Hakhamim were well respected in the community. The educated classes, as well as the impoverished ones who lived in the poorer areas, were all taught from an early age to revere them and defer to their judgment. When consulted in marital disputes, which was always the case, the rabbi would strongly encourage the couple to reconcile and remain together. Whilst there were a few divorces amongst the wealthier classes, it was still taboo and often cost one side of the family a fortune, usually the wife's parents. Under Jewish law, the husband had all the power with regard to a religious divorce and it was up to him to consent to give his wife a 'get', which is a formal document of separation. Without this, the woman would find herself unable to marry again under Jewish law.

Money was never discussed, certainly amongst friends. It was considered vulgar and impolite. As children, all we knew about money were the couple of Egyptian piastres we were sometimes given to buy some candy after school. We didn't need to know, as we had all we needed at home and everything was bought for us. That also meant that we did not understand the correlation between work and money, and never questioned how things got there.

Young girls had to be very careful how they behaved, otherwise they ran the risk of ruining their reputation and being called 'an easy girl'. Typical of the mindset of a Middle Eastern society, this did not apply to young men. They were allowed much more freedom, in fact this was encouraged and probably seen as a sign of sowing their wild oats. Some wealthier guys had a *garçonnière*, where they entertained loose women, prostitutes and even married women bored with their marriage and seeking a diversion. These young men usually lived with their parents, for all the conveniences of having their needs taken care of by their mothers. They went to work and didn't come home in the evenings – Middle Eastern culture favoured and encouraged this.

In contrast, girls were supposed to stay home and help their mothers. If they met a boy they liked, they had to play 'hard to get', because that was the way to get him interested. The only time young girls and boys had any physical contact was through dancing. Young people never held hands in public or went out openly as a couple and all outings were done in a group. Sometimes, the girl was accompanied by her sister or a young relative. The fear was that, if she did not observe all those conventions, men would not consider her as a possible wife-to-be. Even if a girl was tempted to say yes, she usually said no. This was a game most of them played and it's also true of all Middle Eastern societies.

In 1952, the government issued the new Egyptian morality code, in stark contrast to the loose and lewd behaviour of the deposed King Farouk. The military government enacted strict laws concerning public behaviour between the sexes; couples could no longer hold hands in the movies and could not be seen seated close together in public places. This rule also applied to married couples. There were plainclothes policemen and power-hungry uneducated soldiers, with rifles slung over their shoulders, trying to enforce the new law. Any inappropriate behaviour meant a march to the *karakol* (police station in Arabic). Egypt had a military government and people with high ranks in the army had extensive authority over other branches of the government. They did not hesitate to exercise their power over people below their rank.

Egyptian Jews were very hospitable. They opened their house to visitors and always offered them something to eat. If someone dropped in, even for a short visit, it was a selection of small pastries such as *ma'amoul* (date filled pastries), accompanied by a cup of Turkish coffee. The custom in Egypt was to serve a glass of iced water with the coffee. The lady of the house also served guests some of her homemade jams. There was always a certain rivalry between the ladies as to who made the best jams or the best pastries.

In the Middle East, there was a form of etiquette amongst the Jews not only to be a courteous host to your visitors, but to be a gracious guest as well. The host offered many things to the guest in order to make him or her feel welcome. The guest, on the other hand, had to know how to modestly accept what the host was offering. There was a balance between showing restraint so as not to appear greedy and not wishing to insult the host by declining too much. If the lady of the house offered something, such as a pastry, the guest was supposed to refuse the first time; she would insist, the guest would refuse again and would eventually be persuaded to accept. This long-winded exchange may seem silly and unnecessary now, but it was part of the accepted etiquette at the time. My mother continued to observe these rituals whenever we had guests in England, and I used to find it irritating and amusing at the same time.

Etiquette also required a guest to be welcomed with a warm smile and a look of pleasure, even if he or she had come unexpectedly. It would have been considered rude on the part of the host to ask the reason for the visit, going to great lengths instead to remark what a pleasure and an honour it was. The guest would never divulge the reason for the visit right away and instead enquire about the family, friends and the general health of his host. In England, we are accustomed to ask visitors whether they would like a drink. In Egypt, that would have been considered rude – instead, refreshments were automatically provided.

The Jews originating from Spain often used something

called a *kucharera* – or *tavola di dolci* in Ladino. It was a silver vessel used for presenting sweets to welcome guests. The custom had its origin in the need to express joy over the visit and was one of the characteristics of hospitality amongst Jews of the Ottoman Empire – one of my aunts had one. The tray was made of silver and had an ornamental container in its centre, a *kucharera* (the word *kuchara* means spoon) with a place for hanging spoons and forks. On the tray there were two or more small plates containing two kinds of marmalade and water glasses. The guest took some of the sweets with a fork or a spoon and placed it in the centre of the container when he/she had finished eating, then drank the water.

The kind of fruits presented were usually fruit marmalade like *naranjes,* an orange marmalade or *kayisi,* an apricot one. My aunt still used the *kucharera* on special occasions, but nowadays it serves more as a decoration than an everyday kitchen utensil.

White sweets made of water with sugar, almonds and walnuts were also served – they were called *sharopi* and were often given to guests at a wedding in a candy dish called a *bonbonière;* in ancient times, this was connected to the custom of using sugar and sweets to attain good luck.

The weather was always good in Egypt, warm in winter and very hot in summer in cities like Cairo. The heat was a dry heat, not like the humid one of West Africa and Asia. The sky was always blue, a clear and pure blue – at least it was before the Aswan dam was built – and the nights were always starry. The khamsin wind was sometimes a problem, as the light dust created by the wind got literally everywhere and created a haze on the horizon. We used to keep the shutters down all the time during the khamsin season.

There always seemed to be a lot of shouting going on, but this was simply people talking loudly. They shouted at one another from balcony to balcony, from balcony into the street, and from one end of the house to the other. People in the Middle East generally, and Egyptian Jews in particular, speak in loud voices and are very animated, constantly gesticulating with their arms and hands. English people, my husband included, mistakenly think we are fighting, arguing or are angry, and it is difficult for them to understand that this is our normal way of talking. Shouting and gesturing was how we like to express ourselves. In Egypt, the fact that our conversation, mostly in French, was sprinkled with Arabic, Italian or Greek words made it even more expressive.

The street where we had lived when I was growing up had been a busy one, as it was in the city centre. Outside the building there had been an Egyptian café – these were nothing like their European equivalent. They were quite basic, consisting of tables and chairs and nothing more. They were frequented solely by men and it just was not done for an Egyptian woman to be seen in a café. The men played *tawla,* the game we called *tric trac* (backgammon), smoked the *shisha* and chatted. The old men spent hours watching the world go by. They wore a *galabeya,* the traditional Egyptian garment – it's a loose, full length gown with wide sleeves, often decorated with embroidery on the hem and collar.

The weekly washing was done by a *ghasala, a* laundry woman, assisted by Amina the maid. She came once a week early in the morning and her method of washing was the oldest, though not the most comfortable. She squatted in front of two large washbasins – called *tocht,* with both feet flat on the floor. The basins were large and shallow, about one metre round and 20 cm deep. One was for boiling hot water and the other was filled with cold water. Boiling water was added to the cold one in the basin until the desired temperature was reached.

The laundry woman then proceeded to wash, scrub, rinse and wring out every item of clothing. She attacked the laundry with her bare hands, as though it was an imaginary enemy, twisting and turning the fabric. It must have been exhausting, especially in the heat up on the rooftop, which is where the washing was done. By midday, this was finished and was hanging up. It dried very quickly and always smelt fresh. The sheets were made of white Egyptian cotton and there were none of the polyester ones available in different colours which can be bought nowadays. Because they had been dried in the heat of the sun, they always remained sparkling white.

No ironing was done at home. Everything was sent to a *makwagi,* a man whose sole business was ironing clothes. He was part of our everyday lives, as everything was ironed, even the little romper suits toddlers wore which we called *barboteuses* and the little girls' dresses with intricate embroidery on the front. We had a *maqwagi* a few doors from our building and when I was older, I was allowed to go and collect the ironing. The man had a tiny shop with a very small front. The back was full of irons and clothes waiting to be tackled and you could see the steam in the air. It must have been very difficult and exhausting to work in such a heat in a small space.

Rugs were regularly cleaned. There were no vacuum cleaners, so this was done the old fashioned way. The rugs were lifted, flung over the railing of the balcony and vigorously beaten with a small wicker hand broom, a special contraption which looked like a tennis racket. The floor tiles were scoured with a stiff brush and soap; this was done by the servants on their hands and knees, barefoot, soaping and washing the floor. No cleaning products were used, just soap, water, vinegar and Eau de Javel for the bathroom. Twice a year, the apartment underwent a thorough spring cleaning. A man was hired to do the big jobs. All the furniture was moved, cupboards and wardrobes were cleaned inside out, and blankets and linen aired.

The *makwagi*, the *ghasala*, the waiters in the cafés and the errand boys, were all part of an army of locals who worked tirelessly for us and never complained. They were used to hard work and didn't know anything else. We took it all for granted and never gave it another thought – it was just the way the economy worked in Egypt at the time. The month of Ramadan must have been particularly difficult when it fell in summer, as all those people had to carry on working as usual whilst fasting. Every evening, a loud cannon shot announced the time for devout Muslims to eat after the long day's fast.

Once a month, the ladies had to suffer the ritual called the *halawa*. This was the Arabic practice of boiling sugar and water until it formed a thick, caramelised paste which was then applied to women's bodies to remove body hair. It was very uncomfortable and extremely painful, but it was very effective. It was not very nice to watch the *halawista* prepare the paste as, whilst kneading it, she would spit into it several times until it had achieved the desired consistency. The skill was in applying short, determined pulls that sounded like paper being ripped off and then tearing off the paste as if it were a huge bandage. It left the skin smooth and silky, though very red for a while.

The importance of food

Food played a huge part in our lives and we turned to it to mark and celebrate important events such as engagements, weddings, Bar Mitzvahs, circumcisions, religious festivals, new arrivals, etc. Many occasions called for a particular dish or delicacy, and there was always pressure on the host to do the right thing, as criticism was very much feared. Parties, although lavish, tended to have the same dishes and the usual range of delicacies; no buffet table would have been complete without stuffed vine leaves, ma'amoul or baklava.

Cooking was mostly passed on from mother to daughter and was based on respect for custom and tradition. Each community had its own way of cooking and its favourite recipes. In addition, there was the typical Egyptian food which was cooked in homes and sold in the street. The Judeo Egyptian cooking embraced this but, in addition, each family had the cooking inherited from their ancestors – Spanish, Turkish, Tunisian, Moroccan, Iraqi and so on. Young Jewish couples brought the food they had grown up with to the marriage.

When my parents married, two different styles of cooking merged. My father liked the Judeo Spanish dishes that he was used to, so my mother learnt how to make them – many dishes used onions and leeks and were drenched in lemon, garlic and olive oil. Garlic was supposed to protect from the evil eye and spirits. My father loved leeks (called *prasa* in Ladino), so we had many leek-based dishes. He also liked thick vegetable omelettes, called *fritadas* and the Sephardic way of preparing vegetables, which was to combine them with cheese and eggs, when the dish would be referred to as *con keso*, 'with cheese'.

Little pies are the trademark of the Sephardi table – they are called borekas, borekitas, boyos, pasteles, pastelikos, empanadas or sambusek, depending on the shape, filling and where they originated. Each community had its own special pies with different doughs and shapes. There were cigars, triangles, fingers, half moon turnovers, crescents, corners and circles. My father's family mainly made borekas with a traditional cheese filling. These pies required skill and time, but in Egypt women had all the time in the world.

Although my mother was a good cook, she did not do much cooking, preferring to leave this to our servant Salah. Her speciality was cakes and she made wonderful ones when it was her turn to host a game of cards. Her style of cooking was completely different to the Judeo Spanish one. Syrian Jews like to use fruit in many of their dishes, especially apricots. Sour cherries, tamarind paste, olives and above all fresh apricots were more often than not added to anything and everything. My father learnt to appreciate the

Syrian dishes my mother made, but he never liked having dried fruit added, as the sweet and sour combination did not suit him.

Kibbeh, known in Egypt as *kobeba*, is one of the great classics of Syrian cuisine. They are golden torpedo-shaped bulgur shells filled with spiced ground beef or other savoury fillings. The word means 'dome' in Arabic. Making kibbeh from scratch is very difficult and time consuming, as it requires a certain skill in shaping the delicate shells. In Aleppo in the olden days, it was said that a woman could not marry unless she could make kibbeh. It was only served on very special occasions in my family – my mother, her sister and my grandmother were all excellent kibbeh makers. I have not inherited their skills, probably because I don't have what they used to call 'kibbeh' fingers.

A popular way of preparing poultry or meat was called *sofrito*. The chicken, beef or lamb was braised in oil and a small amount of water, to which lemon, cardamom and turmeric were added. The dish was cooked very slowly and towards the end cubed potatoes, which had been deep fried beforehand, were added. The most popular *sofrito* with Egyptian Jews was the one cooked with a shin of veal we called *mosa* or *mosata*. It was my favourite cut of meat, but unfortunately it is not readily available in England. Cumin and coriander were added to most dishes and rice was served with every meal. It was not the same as the one we buy in packets nowadays from supermarkets. It came in jute bags and contained many impurities, and therefore had to be cleaned several times in order to ensure that all those were removed.

For lunch, we had vegetables with everything – in stews, with meatballs, mashed with cheese and eggs and also stuffed. It is interesting that the same vegetable will have many variations in the way it's cooked, depending where it originated. In England and in other European countries, a meal will usually comprise a starter, main course and dessert. This was not so in Egyptian or Jewish households. Everything apart from dessert was served at once. Dessert was always the fruits of the season, never a cake or a pudding, which we had in the afternoon as a snack.

I have a special memory of the stuffed vegetables we called *mah'shi*. My father's aunt, who was called Rebecca, had left for Israel in 1948 with her daughter Esther. However, her husband stayed behind in Cairo; I am not sure why. The plan was that he would eventually join them, but in the meantime he was living on his own and in restricted circumstances. We called him *Oncle* Charles. My parents often used to invite him for lunch, out of kindness and also because he was a lovely man. I remember he always arrived early and waited patiently for us to return home. He sat at the head of the table and his favourite dish was those stuffed vegetables. Salah proudly made his entrance in the dining room with a large tray and always made sure that he was served first. He eventually joined his wife and daughter in Israel, and I missed him.

A popular dish with my mother's family was called *hamud* – that is the word for 'sour' in Arabic and it consisted of vegetables cooked in a very lemony sauce, mainly potatoes but carrots were often added. It wasn't a dish I was particularly fond of at the time, perhaps because the lemon was too sharp for my tastebuds. I often used to go to my aunt Marie after school and stay there for the afternoon, since we had no classes after lunch. Sometimes my parents used to drop in at lunchtime and, if my aunt had not cooked anything, she would turn to my mother and say 'what shall we make for lunch'. More often than not, the answer was *hamud*. I have changed my mind since then and often make it, also adding other vegetables.

Some staples could be found in every household, for the children to snack on or to be offered to guests – *kaak*, crunchy pastry bracelets brushed with egg and scattered sesame seeds, *sambousek,,* small pastries in a semi-circular shape filled with cheese and the wonderfully melting *menenas* made of crumbly short pastry stuffed with a date paste or with nuts and sprinkled with icing sugar. Each family had its own special way of making a dish and, if asked for the recipe, the lady would politely give it, but would usually leave out the crucial ingredients which made her dish special!

For Egyptian Jews, visiting friends and entertaining were popular activities and pastries had a very important place. Every household kept stocks of those and jars of fruit preserves, to be offered to guests who turned up unexpectedly and were always graciously received. Housewives were proud of the variety they could magically produce, along with the traditional small cup of Turkish coffee. Sometimes a cold syrup like almond milk or tamarind were also offered. Sweet things were a symbol of joy and happiness and at every Jewish holiday, wedding, engagements or any celebrations, a huge variety of pastries would always be displayed on the buffet table.

We had no supermarkets and food was bought fresh on a daily basis, mostly from the market. There were some grocery stores, owned mainly by Greeks and my father used to stop at his favourite one on his way home from work in the evening. He always bought a Greek cheese called kashkaval and some olives. Although Salah usually prepared the lunch under my mother's instructions, it was my mother who did all the baking.

Every morning, on Salah's return from the market, my mother shared her plan for the day's menu with him and they then proceeded with the cooking. Salah chopped the vegetables and koshered the meat in water and generous amounts of coarse salt, leaving it for the prescribed amount of time and then rinsing it. There was no beef mince of the kind you get in supermarkets nowadays. Instead, chunks of beef were ground in a meat grinder to make stuffed vegetables. It was a fascinating spectacle – at the turn of the handle, the pieces of beef were swallowed in the machine, the chunks being forced down to the perforated plate. Worms of meat and fat dangled from the holes and fell into an enamel bowl. Peas were bought fresh and the green pods had to be opened one by one. Herbs were finely chopped with something called a *makhrata*, a curved knife with two handles similar to the Italian mezzaluna.

In Egypt, each kitchen had what we called a *sandara*. It was a low ceilinged room, a loft on top of the kitchen, which was reached by climbing a drop-down ladder. It was typically used for storage – of canned goods, bags of rice and sugar, as well as books, knick-knacks, old pots, basically everything and anything which we wanted out of the way. It was the equivalent of our modern day loft and, inevitably, lots of clutter would end up there – which we called *karakib*. This was a general term for things which were no longer used and took up space.

The cooking was generally done over a type of Primus stove called *fatayel*, which was lit by kerosene. It was a long, slow procedure which sometimes required pans to be left to simmer overnight. We had a small oven in the kitchen, but larger dishes, mostly pastries, were sent to be cooked in the ovens of the local bakery. People hurried about in the street, carrying huge trays or casseroles and sometimes balancing them on their heads. These activities always took place with a lot of humour. Salah was responsible for taking the trays to the bakery and he had probably received strict instructions from my mother beforehand as to what position she wanted her trays to be placed in the oven.

We ate a lot of stuffed vegetables – aubergines, peppers and courgettes were my favourite. Vine leaves were often served, stuffed with rice, tomatoes, onions and parsley. Artichokes were abundant in Egypt and Salah spent hours in the kitchen laboriously removing the leaves, until only the artichoke hearts were left. It was a laborious task, but worth the time and effort – I loved them stewed in olive oil.

My father often bought something called *batarekh* from the Greek grocer, as it was a favourite of his. This was the roe from the grey mullet and was considered a delicacy. The roe was in a sack which was removed intact from the fish, salted in rock salt and left in the open air to dry for a few days – Egyptian *batarekh* was appreciated throughout the Middle East. The pressed smoked roe fish was then cut into slices and served over bread, with a squeeze of lemon juice, spring onions and a drizzle of olive oil.

Fresh fruit and vegetables were plentiful and varied – aubergines, courgettes and peppers were consumed on a daily basis. There were melons, watermelons, pomegranates, guavas, all varieties of mangoes and the most wonderful fresh dates. According to the season, you could get yellow dates, red ones or the black variety. The latter was the sweetest and the red ones, called *zaghloul* were slightly drier – I have not seen them outside Egypt. We always had fresh fruit for dessert and were spoilt for choice. My favourites were fresh figs, dates and different varieties of grapes, melons and watermelons.

There was a special fruit called *citron doux,* which is sometimes available here in Turkish supermarkets. It's a sweet lemon and can be eaten, as it has a mild sweet taste of its own and my mother made jam with it. Another favourite was called *eshta,* which resembled a custard apple, but much sweeter. The outer skin was mottled brown and knobbly but, cut open, the fruit revealed a central stem, on either side of which were a multitude of black pits that contained succulent white pockets of sweet flesh. It took a lot of patience to eat it, but it was fun and was well worth it.

Ready made jams were not available, so it was always homemade in great quantities, in large copper saucepans. The fruit used was the one in season and at its best, so as to maximise the taste. We had grape and fig jam, as well as all the different varieties of dates. The latter was particularly delicious, as the dates were kept whole. A special treat was some jam topped with the cream obtained after boiling the milk. The jars were kept in the refrigerator, as they would not have lasted long outside with the heat.

The best variety of mango was the Alfonso. The season was short and having one was a treat. My father used to sit me and my sisters at the dining table, cover the front of our dress with a large towel and place a fragrant cut mango in front of each of us. You could scoop out the flesh with a spoon, but we preferred to tackle it whole, so we dribbled mango juice all over the towel. Grapes were always available; my favourites were the tiny grapes without pips called *enab banati*.

Unlike today, it was virtually impossible to find out of season fruit, but the advent of the first of each variety and the *shehecheyanu* blessing by my father were always a special occasion. We lived by the rhythm of the Jewish and Muslim festivals, as well as the appearance of the first fruits of the season. It didn't matter if a particular one was no longer available, as a different variety, or another just as tasty, soon appeared at the dinner table.

All kinds of fruit and vegetables could be grown in Cairo, thanks to the fertile Nile delta and the permanent sun. The best variety of melons was the Ismailia one, incredibly sweet and fragrant. Figs were abundant, in all colours and shapes – brown, black and green figs, round or oblong. Guavas were so fragrant that you could smell them as soon as you entered a room. I have found them in some Middle Eastern stores, but they are never as sweet as the ones we had in Egypt.

Quails were a delicacy and every autumn, they

descended on Egypt from as far away as Siberia. As soon as they caught sight of land, they dropped from the sky, exhausted. They were an Egyptian delicacy and their flesh was delicious when cooked. It seems cruel now, trying to imagine these defenceless little birds running frenetically trying to escape being caught.

Rice was served with everything, so it was always on the table at lunch. It was fluffy and the best part was the bottom layer, which was crispy and brown. That is because the rice was first fried in a tablespoon or two of oil before the broth was added and was then allowed to burn at the bottom. My mother continued to make it this way after we left Egypt and were living in London.

Every morning brought a stream of merchants pushing their wheelbarrows laden with fresh produce. Sitting in your balcony watching their comings and goings must have been fascinating, but back then, it was something we took for granted as we were so used to it and this folklore was part of our daily lives. Most of the vendors were poor Egyptian fellahin. They came from nearby villages and the sale of the contents of their carts was their only income, and a meagre one at that. They could barely eke out a living with the few piastres they made off the sale of their produce. Every morning they loaded their wheelbarrows with as much of what they could pile on – grapes, figs, courgettes, okra, tomatoes and mountains of fresh fruit.

Some of them couldn't even afford a wheelbarrow. Instead, they carried their heavy load in a large straw basket perched on their head. To the uninitiated, this looked precarious, but these were seasoned vendors and they managed to walk gracefully, in spite of the heavy burden on their head. They moved along the streets for hours, singing to announce their arrival and chanting the praises of their wares at the top of their voice. The watermelons were always as sweet as sugar and the melons tasted like honey, or so they promised.

The first seller in the morning was the fava bean vendor who appeared on his enormous tricycle, pedalling his large, steaming clay pot of beans. These beans, called *ful medames,* were always served with tahini; this was a thick sesame paste covered in oil, which paradoxically got thicker with the first addition of water. It was only after more water and lemon juice were added that it turned into a smooth paste, which was poured over the bowl of fava beans. The average Egyptian man in the street didn't hesitate to eat from the same plate or drink from the same cup and did not seem afraid of germs. The immune system of the native population must have been strong.

The most evocative was the vendor of scented rose petals. To prevent the petals from blowing away in the wind and to keep their freshness, he used to cover them with a damp white cloth; this dried quickly dry in the heat, so now and then he had to stop and refresh it with water. He wandered the streets chanting *el ward, el ward,* which means roses, roses. Rose petals were a favourite amongst housewives and my mother used to buy them to make jam (our special *confiture de roses)* and *maward,* rose water which, along with orange blossom water, was an essential ingredient for baking. These were not made in the kitchen at home, but on the roof terrace. It took ages and a lot of patience, so on that day it was all hands to the pump. The aroma released by the rose petals was wonderful. The best quality was only available one month of the year.

A novel and unique way of shopping was done without having to leave your house, the forerunner of modern online shopping. There were lots of street merchants selling just about everything. If you were sitting in your balcony and wanted to buy something, all you had to do was call out to the vendor. The first thing to do was to agree the price and a lot of bartering took place.

Once the price was agreed, the buyer lowered a basket which was attached to a rope – the rope ran to the street from the balcony. The seller weighed the goods and put them in the basket, which was pulled up. The buyer inspected the goods and if he/she was happy with them, put the money in the basket, which was again lowered. Our favourite thing to buy was the sugar cane. The seller peeled it before sending the basket up and we then sucked all the juice out until there was nothing left. I can't think of a better pastime than sitting in your balcony watching the world go by, with the added bonus of buying what you fancy without moving from your seat.

Another attraction was the rag and bone man. He shouted *robabecchia* from his cart – this comes from the Italian *roba vecchia*, meaning old clothes or clutter. The cart was usually pushed by a young child and they stopped every few yards. When someone called them from the balcony, they went up to their flat and the bartering started. The rag and bone man took any unwanted rubbish, whatever it was, as he was always going to find a way of disposing of it. In Egypt, as in all other developing countries, nothing was thrown away and everything had its value, even old magazines and empty bottles.

Amongst the numerous street vendors, there were those carrying big containers of *er el sous* (tamarind juice). This had a tap in front and the vendor called the attention of passers-by jingling brass castanets. There were numerous sellers of fizzy drinks – a lemonade called *spathis-gazoza,* my favourite called *sinalco* and of course Coca-Cola. The vendor kept the bottles in a huge cool box full of ice blocks. This was very distinctive, with its red background and the letters *Coca-Cola* in white italics.

The itinerant salespeople sold their wares by shouting out the quality of their products at the top of their voice, creating a cacophony. They sold almonds, pistachios and *dora* (corn grilled on charcoal), sweet potatoes, prickly pears, as well as blocks of ice – not everyone had a refrigerator in those days and Egyptians bought ice daily to conserve their food. Before we had a refrigerator, the iceman delivered large chunks of ice daily, which Salah immediately placed in an icebox. My parents eventually bought a Frigidaire and we no longer needed the iceman every morning.

I would be hard pushed to name all the street vendors you could find walking the streets of Cairo and Alexandria. Everything and anything was sold – fresh fruit and vegetables, Egyptian bread, *ful medames,* falafel, ice cream and all sorts of pastries and sweetmeats. I always looked forward to buying *semit* from the vendor who stood outside the cinema at the end of the performance – it was shaped like a pretzel, but was softer and the top was covered with sesame seeds. You could also buy broiled corn on the cob, roasted peanuts (*soudanis*), and boiled yellow beans (*termes*). All sorts of beverages were sold – amongst them, liquorice and sugar cane juice. There were also many stationary vendors to tempt us outside the school gates.

Buying a watermelon was always a difficult operation. How could you choose the perfect watermelon from the dozens and dozens of fruits displayed on the seller's cart? One way was to touch the fruit and then tap it several times. If it made a hollow sound, then the fruit was likely to be ripe. There was always a sense of anticipation when you made the first cut. Was the watermelon going to live up to your expectations and be as delicious as the seller had promised – even sworn on his life – or was it going to disappoint? Some people were experts at choosing the right watermelon.

There were flies everywhere, but we were used to this and we didn't take much notice. Nowadays, this would be considered very insalubrious but back then, it was what you expected in a hot country. Sometimes, not very often thankfully, we had to suffer swarms of flying ants. I remember coming back from school one lunchtime and opening the door of the dining room – the large window was literally covered with them.

Many other favourites were sold by street vendors. *Amardeen w*ere sheets of dried apricot paste – we made a cone out of the paste and sometimes put an ice cube inside. The sellers of prickly pears pushed their heavy carts along the streets and cut the skin of the prickly fruit with their bare hands before handing it to us. The first thing we did after school was to rush to the stall of the guy who sold *caca chinois*. It was a small stick of tahini and sugar and owed its name to its yellow colour.

Milk was bought daily from the milkman. He carried it in a large barrel and had to go up to every apartment. He knocked on the door and poured the milk from his big aluminium container into a pot which the customer held out. The milk was then boiled immediately and the flame turned off as soon as it rose – that was the way it was pasteurised. The cream which had formed at the top was collected, placed in a small bowl, then in the fridge when cooled. We called it *eshta* and used it to accompany jam or a dessert called *khoshaf* – a mixture of dried apricots, prunes and other dried fruit, soaked overnight with orange blossom water, then cooked until the syrup had thickened. It was delicious when served with the cream.

In Egypt, there was no council responsible for collecting the rubbish. Instead it was done by a corporation of dustmen called the *zabbalin* – *zabbal* is the Arabic word for dustman. The collection of rubbish was methodically divided amongst the members of the corporation, who did not have offices or written plans. They did not need these – every day, without fail, the *zabbal* appeared in our street. He had a cart driven by a measly looking donkey and he knocked on the door of every apartment building, starting at the top floor. Someone passed him the pail of garbage, which he emptied into his bassinet. He did the same on every floor, then emptied the contents into his cart, stomping on it to make more space, and proceeded to the next building. There was no such thing as keeping garbage overnight; it would have created a haven for the cockroaches.

The Copts – the Egyptian Christians who claimed to be descendants of the Pharaohs and were the largest Christian minority in Egypt – were mostly of the upper and middle classes, but surprisingly some were also *zabbalin* (garbage people). They lived in apartments in garbage dumps on the Mokattam Hills on the outskirts of Cairo, known as Garbage City. The recycling of all the city's garbage was done by them and some became very wealthy. This probably fuelled the antagonism against them felt by some of the Muslim population; this was not directed against Christians in general, only against the Copts, probably because they considered themselves superior as the direct descendants of the Pharaohs.

Bartering was a tradition and something that was expected in the markets, shops and with the street sellers. Whatever the asking price was, beating the vendor down by even a couple of Egyptian piastres was a matter of pride – the currency was the Egyptian pound and there were 100 piastres in a pound. If the seller asked 5 piastres for a kilo of figs, the buyer would probably offer 3 and, after much bartering, they would settle for 4. Successful bartering was a matter of pride for both parties; you had to be authoritative, as there was no fixed price on the fruits and vegetables, and one was expected to haggle for everything. The vendor always had an answer and made extravagant promises – he would swear on his mother's tomb that he would never swindle you, or would suggest you bring back a watermelon you had bought if it wasn't to your liking. You had to act confident for people to respect you, that was the motto in the Middle East – it was forbidden to be meek and weak.

The most consumed beverage is Egypt was Turkish coffee. The coffee houses were an institution in Egypt. They were traditionally visited by men only, who sat and drank coffee or tea, played *tawla* (backgammon) and smoked the water pipe called *shisha* – the pipe was filled with tobacco which was flavoured with honey, apple, mint or other sweet flavours. Men also gathered to listen to the radio. A typical Egyptian coffee house consisted of an area furnished with tables covered with red gingham tablecloths, surrounded by black wooden chairs. Along the wall, on either side of the door, were wooden chairs with wooden straw seats; a *shisha* was placed next to each one.

Egyptians and Jews alike drank numerous cups of Turkish coffee in a day. This was served one of three ways – no sugar (*sadda*), just right (*mazbout*) or very sweet (*soccar ziada*). It was always served accompanied by a glass of cold water. In the home, this was the first refreshment offered to a guest, along with some homemade jam. The jam was served in a small crystal bowl with several spoons and a glass of water, where the guest could deposit the dirty spoon. After the coffee, several pastries were offered, rather than a cake.

Making a good Turkish coffee is an art which is difficult to master. It takes a lot of practice and my mother could make one blindfolded. For a start, you have to have a *kanaka* – it's a small, but tall pot with a long handle and a pouring spout, designed specially to make Turkish coffee. It's filled with water and sugar and, as soon as the water has boiled, it's taken off the flame. One or two spoonfuls of fragrant Turkish coffee are added and the kanaka is returned to the flame, where the contents foam rapidly and suddenly to the top. The pot has to be removed rapidly from the heat and tapped sharply three times to bring the content down. This procedure is repeated again and the coffee is then poured very slowly into small cups. A proper Turkish coffee must have a light brown froth on the top, called *wesh*.

Often, someone offered to read your future after you had drank the coffee. This was especially common with Egyptian ladies. The saucer was placed on top of the empty cup by the person who had drank the coffee, turned upside down and rotated in a complete circle three times. It was then left to dry out for a little while and the cup upturned. The fortune teller looked inside the cup with earnest concentration, while all the while the recipient anxiously observed her facial expressions to try and guess what she was seeing. People took all this seriously, even though they pretended to make light of it.

There was no such thing as instant coffee and it probably would not have been popular had it been available. Aside from Turkish coffee and cold beverages, a popular drink was tea, especially with Egyptian people. It was like the one we are used to in England, mostly made with milk – Egyptians drank theirs either black and strong with sugar, or flavoured, like chamomile, cardamom or hibiscus tea, called *karkade,* the most popular one.

The Egyptian breakfast of the middle class was usually taken at home. It consisted of a variety of dishes. Apart from the ever present falafel and *ful medames,* there were hard boiled eggs, cheeses and pickles. The popular class often had a quick breakfast outside – it was a simple sandwich of *ful medames* or falafel. The national Egyptian bread was called ai*sh baladi* – *baladi* means traditional and *aish* life. Inside the flatbread, the seller put a ladle of *ful medames* and some falafel, to which he added two spoonfuls of green salad, a spoonful of tahini and finally oil, lemon juice and salt. The whole sandwich was prepared at the speed of light and handed to the customer.

There were also many restaurants serving this, but the street sellers were favoured by those who were on their way to work or school and pressed for time. During Ramadan, as soon as they heard the cannon which signalled the end of the fast for the day, our servants Amina and Salah went in the kitchen to have their meal. Sometimes it was what was left over from lunch, other times *ful medames* and falafel, which they had with a very finely cut salad seasoned with oil and vinegar – known as Egyptian salad.

Our breakfast at home was much simpler, just bread rolls, jam and milky coffee; no one had heard of cereals or porridge. We always had a sandwich in our satchel to eat at break time, usually cheese. One day I was having this in the playground and a crow came and snatched it from my hand, much to my fury. It's the sort of silly incident a child remembers.

The popular class in Egypt ate their meals from a low table called *tablia*. They sat on straw mats around it and the dishes were put in the centre; instead of cutlery, they expertly used a piece of bread to gather up the food. It was amazing to watch how much they would manage to cram into one piece of bread.

In winter, hot *belila* was sold. This was a variety of

whole wheat or pearl barley which was boiled with water and milk – the Egyptian equivalent of porridge but much more elaborate. The seller put the hot *belila in* a bowl and added to it some sugar, fresh milk, raisins, a little butter, some orange blossom water, some desiccated coconut and a little cinnamon. In the Syrian Jewish community, it was offered to guests to celebrate a happy event, such as a baby's first tooth.

Another popular pudding made at home and sold in the streets was *mehalabeya*. It was made with milk and cornflour, to which cream and sugar were added. We often had it at home in winter. The street vendors waited outside the cinema for the crowd to come out after the performance, knowing they may be hungry and would be tempted to buy a bowl.

*Koshari i*s one of the national dishes of Egypt. It's a comforting bowl of simple pantry staples – spiced lentils and rice, combined with chickpeas and pasta, all smothered in a tomato sauce and topped with thin fried onion rings. The strangest thing is that I don't remember ever having it in Egypt, whether at home or outside. The first time I had this dish was a couple of years ago in Bristol, when an Egyptian friend made it for me.

My favourite dish was called *molokheya*. It's Egypt's most famous soup and the second national dish after *ful medames* and falafel. It derives its name from the leaf that gives it its distinctive dark green colour and glutinous texture. It's also known as Jew's Mallow, though no one can say where this name originates from. It looks similar to spinach, but tastes very different and its viscous consistency

214

is similar to okra when cooked. We often had it at home, served with rice and chicken, though the Egyptians preferred rabbit. My favourite way of eating it was putting the soup, the rice and the chicken all in the same bowl.

In Egypt, fresh *molokheya* leaves were chopped with a manual vegetable handler which had an arched blade attached to two vertical handles. The half moon blade was rocked backwards and forwards until the leaves were very finely cut. It took a long time to prepare and required patience. I once came across the fresh leaves in a vegetable stall in the Arab Quarter of the Old City in Jerusalem. Nowadays, we just buy it frozen from Middle Eastern supermarkets. It is not as nice, of course, but much easier to prepare.

Dukka, or *do'ah* as we called it, was another favourite. It's an old Egyptian speciality – a mixture of coriander seeds, sesame seeds and hazelnuts in a dry, crushed but not powdered form. It was often served at breakfast time, but at home we had it as an appetiser or a snack. Egyptians dipped a piece of bread in olive oil first, then sprinkled the *dukka* on top. It was also sold in the streets in small paper cones.

My favourite sweets were *kounafa, baklava or basbousa,* whether at home or outside. *Kounafa* is made with a shredded filo dough known as angel's hair. It has a thick layer of cream or nuts in the middle and is basted with a thick sugar syrup when it comes out of the oven. *Basbousa* is a mixture of semolina, butter, sugar and yoghurt, also basted with a sugar syrup. All these are now widely available in Turkish and Middle Eastern supermarkets, as are packets of filo pastry and *kounafa,* so they can be made at home.

This was not the case for many years when we came to England and I remember trying to make it with Weetabix. Needless to say, it didn't work.

In the 1950s, all the above dishes and desserts were not were known outside Egypt. Nowadays most people are familiar with humous, *babaganoush*, falafel, etc and baklava is often served as a dessert in restaurants. However, there is so much more to Egyptian cooking and I keep discovering dishes that I didn't even know about when we lived in Cairo. One of them is called *aish el saraya*, which means 'the bread of the palace'. The name itself is enticing and the dish lives up to expectations. It's a bread pudding made with milk, cream and nuts, as is another one delightfully named *Om Ali*. Then there is *bessara*, a fava bean and herbs dip which is rooted in Egyptian history and is said to date back to the pharaonic era.

A few words about our colourful language and expressions

My life straddled two worlds. There was the Egyptian one around me, with the flowery Arabic language, the popular songs, the colourful and noisy markets, the beauty of the Nile and the infinite Sahara desert. The muezzin called the faithful to prayer five times a day – at dawn, noon, mid-afternoon, sunset and nightfall. At these times, they stopped whatever they were doing and took out their prayer mat. This call was familiar and the background to our daily lives. I get emotional and filled with nostalgia if I ever hear it nowadays and it instantly takes me back to my childhood.

I didn't realise it at the time, but I am now aware that there was a world beyond the Cairo I was familiar with – the one which resembled Paris, with its wide avenues, modern cafes and fashionable department stores. There was a different world, with narrow meandering streets where the Arab population lived, mosques with minarets, public baths, modest shops with very small fronts and popular cafés spilling onto the streets. I wish I had been allowed to get to know it, but we were kept away.

My other world was the French influence and the language I spoke at school and with family and friends, at the Sporting Club and in department stores such as Magasins Circurel, the Salon Vert and Chemla. The names of all the streets were written in French, with the Arabic one underneath. We knew all the songs which were popular in France and the singers who were at the top of the Hit Parade. Egyptian culture had little influence on our life and we took no notice of the songs played in the streets.

I loved all the anecdotes and jokes about *Goha* and they were numerous. He is the folk hero of the Middle East, known in various countries as *Joha, Hodja, Mollah or Nasreddin* and loved by grown-ups and children alike. Whatever people call him, he appears as an innocent, even stupid fool but, time and time again, he turns out to be wise and outwits those who call him a fool. There is a moral to all the Goha *noktas* – the Arabic word for anecdotes.

Here is a short tale of Goha:

Goha was found by a friend, squatting by the edge of a lake with a spoon and a pot of yoghurt.

"What are you doing?" said the friend.

Goha stirred a spoonful of the thick yoghurt in the water and said: "I am turning the lake into yoghurt."

While French was the language used by my family and most other Egyptian Jews, we also spoke Arabic, but only with the servants and locals. Egyptians called a European gentleman *khawaga* and a young lady was *masmaselle*. A lady was *sett* and the biggest compliment you could pay her was to call her as *sett el settat* – literally translated, the lady of all ladies or the best of ladies. We often used this expression if we were talking about someone we admired. We knew all the colloquial insults from an early age – it was inevitable that we would learn them, being surrounded by Arab people.

The Arabic of the streets was very colourful, especially when it comes to insults. The one used right, left and centre, aloud or muttered under your breath was *ibn el kalb*, which means 'son of a dog'. Like every other language, the correct pronunciation was very important or you inadvertently ended up using a word which had an entirely different meaning. For instance, the word *hara* in arabic means street, whereas *khara* means crap. Arabic requires a guttural 'h' sound and *harah* has to be pronounced with a harsh emphatic 'h', otherwise you may end up with embarrassing results!

The French we spoke was correct, but sometimes rather unorthodox. We had special intonations and facial expressions and we also spoke with our hands, every word being punctuated by gestures. To an outsider unfamiliar with our culture, it may have looked like we were arguing, whereas we were just having a normal conversation. Everyone spoke loudly, so it didn't appear strange.

In our community, French and Arabic were intermingled, almost creating a new language which we called Franco-Egyptian, only comprehensible to us. We rolled our r's when we spoke, a little like the people of Marseilles. Our French was mixed with some Arab words and expressions and the result could be hilarious. To say that Thursday was laundry day, we would say that it was the day of the *ghassal*a (laundry lady in Arabic). When we cooked a dish of sweet potatoes, we called it a dish of *batata helwa* (the Arabic word).

Arabic is a flowery language and some expressions are unique and very expressive but cannot be translated, so we often intermingled them during a conversation. To thank the hostess for a meal, we said *yesalem ideki* which means God bless your hands and *sofra dayman* – may you always have a plentiful table. If someone's daughter has achieved something and you wanted to praise her to her parents you said *khamsa yaleha* meaning may the Five protect her, referring to Fatima's hand. Happy birthday was *kol sana wentu tayebin* – may you be in good health every year.

Some words were made up and no one knew their origin. We called nail varnish *éclat d'or* and for years I believed this was the right word, except that it's *vernis à ongles* and éclat d'or means burst of gold! I have no idea why we called it that. The correct word for straw (the kind you use to drink) is *paille* but we called it *chalumeau*. It was embarrassing for those who subsequently moved to France, as it left the locals bewildered.

The way we described going up and coming down

the stairs was strange. In French, only one word is used – *monter* means to go up and *descendre* means to come down. It's simple. However, we said *monter en haut* and *descendre en bas* which translated as 'going up upstairs' and 'coming down downstairs'. It sounds absurd, but it's quite amusing.

Even now, if I speak to my sister, my cousins or friends who were brought up in Egypt – and we speak mostly in English – we sometimes get stuck for a word and can only say it in Franco/Egyptian. Some Arabic expressions cannot be translated, so we carry on using them because we know exactly what is meant. For instance, you can describe someone as *dammou te'il* and *dammou khafif* which literally translated means his blood is heavy or his blood is thin! The real meaning is that a person is disagreeable or agreeable. One of my favourite expressions is *bokra fil meshmesh*. Literally translated, it means tomorrow when the apricots blossom. It conveys a Middle Eastern indolence, where tomorrow is another day and whatever one is waiting for may never happen.

There are still some phrases or words which I use automatically, forgetting that the person I am speaking with will probably not understand. For instance, if I want to compliment someone on a new event or achievement, I will sometimes say *mabrouk* – that was the word we always used in Egypt and it can be translated as *mazaltov*. It's a hard word to forget, especially as it's used throughout the Arab world. An expression which has now seeped into many cultures, including Israel, is *yalla*. It means 'let's get going', 'come along' or simply just 'get on with it'. It's great that one simple word can convey all that.

A few weeks ago, I was having a phone conversation in French with my cousin Esther in Paris. She wanted to describe one of her acquaintances and could not find the right expression. She hesitated and finally used the Arabic word *ho'na'*. I burst out laughing because I knew exactly what she meant. The word cannot be literally translated and conveys that a person is a mixture of silly, awkward and a bore. The strange thing is that my cousin was only five years old when she left Egypt.

Un aller sans retour (No return) – our exodus from Egypt

Our departure and life in Bridgend hostel, Stonehouse

Some Egyptian Jews suspected of Zionist sympathies or links to Israel suffered as a direct result of the Suez crisis. A policeman knocked on their door – most often in the middle of the night – and peremptorily ushered the suspect out of his flat and into a police car. He was then taken to a prison camp and often the family did not have any news for weeks. Sometimes the prisoners got on very well with the soldiers, sometimes not. In general, they were reasonably well treated. There was never a trial, so they did not know precisely what the charges were. In many cases, they were summarily escorted from the prison camp straight to the port of Alexandria, where they were reunited with their family. They then boarded a ship bound for Europe, never to return to Egypt.

In most cases, Jews were just issued with an expulsion order. Police officers came to the workplace or the home of the people who were being expelled and asked them to leave the country within a certain period of time. Soldiers with rifles knocked on our door one evening and delivered the fateful order. It was very frightening and a shock, even though we had been expecting this. I think my father had always hoped against hope that things would get better. How do you suddenly leave the country you were born in, everything you know and own, wondering if you will ever see your family again?

Although stateless, my father was allowed to travel with us. My parents were forced to sign a supposedly 'voluntary' form renouncing all claims, property and citizenship in Egypt. The declaration stated that they were 'donating' all their property to the Egyptian government. Upon leaving, my mother's passport and my father's laissez-passer were stamped with the words 'ONE WAY NO RETURN'. My father's 'laissez-passer' had the words *'Apatride'* (stateless) stamped in large letters across one of the pages. I came across this document while I was clearing up his things after he had passed away. It was a stark reminder of my father's status, or lack of it.

We were only allowed to take clothes with us – a suitcase of maximum 20 kilos for each of us and twenty Egyptian pounds in total for the whole family, worth just under twenty British pounds at the time. No other money, jewellery or anything of value. If we were searched at the airport, these would have been confiscated or worse. Some people managed to smuggle diamond rings and other jewellery by some ingenious means, but my father was too frightened to risk it.

Thus began a week of frantic buying. Our first trip was to Magasins Cicurel, the large department store. Unlike Egypt, winters were fierce in Europe and we were in December. It was therefore important to buy adequate woollen clothing. We knew very little about England and thought we were going to the North Pole. The problem was that you could not find warm clothing in the shops, as there was no need for it. Furthermore, many families were in the same predicament, so most stuff was sold out. We bought what we could find and my mother managed to get us woollen underwear and a winter coat each, as well as some jumpers. They turned out to be of little use in the English winter. We also bought Egyptian cotton sheets, towels and thick woollen blankets which we afterwards kept for years, even when they became threadbare.

We purchased sturdy brown suitcases, which we packed with personal effects. We probably suspected that most of the flimsy clothes we were taking would not be warm enough for England, but we had to fill up those cases. We dreaded the cold weather in Europe but still, we never imagined how cold it would actually be – we had never left Egypt and had only known hot weather. We were not allowed to take silverware or carpets, so any valuables were left behind.

The next thing was to decide who was going to leave. My mother's brother, Uncle Victor and his wife Nina decided they would come with us – my uncle also had a British passport and had received his expulsion papers. It was also agreed that my grandmother would accompany us. I don't know the reason behind this decision, probably because she was also a British subject. She was old, frail and totally bewildered by everything that was happening around her. Our goodbyes to the rest of the family were very tearful and emotional, as we did not know when we would see them again.

Although we were given two weeks to leave, there was no guarantee we would manage to do so within that time. There were thousands in the same predicament and travel agencies and airline companies were crowded with people anxious to procure whatever means of leaving available. Flights were fully booked and it was utter pandemonium – Nasser had also declared all Jews enemies of the State and, as such, they were subject to expulsion from Egypt, along with British and French citizens. There was the added fear of what could happen to us if we didn't manage to leave as ordered. Would we be considered to be in the country illegally and would we be thrown in prison? Fortunately, my father managed to get us tickets for a flight bound for England.

Thankfully, we left Egypt unharmed. We had eyed the servants nervously, wondering whether they would turn on us. They and all the local people around us remained very courteous and loyal to the end. They seemed sympathetic to our plight and were upset that we were leaving. On the morning of our departure, they all lined up to say goodbye. Everyone was crying and it was very emotional. The normal order had changed overnight and, as a result of recent events, the Egyptian people now had the upper hand. They could have turned on us, killed us in our beds and harmed us if they had wished to do so; the authorities would not have batted an eyelid. It was testimony to their integrity, their generosity and the good relations we had with them that none of these things happened to us or to anyone we knew.

The ride to the airport was sad and even the children understood the sheer magnitude of the moment. At the airport, we had to open all our suitcases for inspection. We knew there was nothing valuable inside them, but it was still a tense moment. Finally, we boarded and the plane took off. My parents must have felt overwhelmed or perhaps it was difficult to take in what was happening. There must have been so many mixed emotions – relief that we had left unharmed and were safe, anxiety about the future and sadness at being uprooted.

Our departure from Egypt had happened very quickly and had not been planned. It was traumatic but, compared to what happened to a few Egyptian Jews, it could have been worse. Although we had a good standard of living, we were not wealthy and my family did not own any land, buildings, business or shop. What we had left behind was not much – my father's car, furniture, carpets, silver and some money in the bank. Uncle Leon, who did not have to leave Egypt immediately, sorted all this out for my father and somehow managed to send him some money.

We left on 10 December 1956 on a KLM flight which stopped to refuel in Athens. We then flew to Sofia in Bulgaria and then on to Amsterdam, where we spent the night. The next morning we took a plane bound for England and landed in Heathrow on a cold and grey December morning. We were met by a government official, put on a bus and taken straightaway to what was to be our home for the next three months. We had no idea where we were going, but found out later it was Bridgend hostel in Stonehouse in Gloucestershire. It had been previously used during World War II, but not since then.

The hostel consisted of pre-fabricated rows of pavilions and each family had their own accommodation. Our rooms were in blocks of eight with two toilets, a bathroom and a kitchenette where you could make yourself a coffee or tea. We had one room for my parents and one room for us girls, with a wardrobe.

There was a big building at the end of the compound, where the dining room was situated. It was more like a canteen and this is where we had our breakfast, lunch and dinner. The meals were adequate, but we found it difficult, as it was food we did not know and were not used to. There was also a TV room with a television set – something we had never seen before – and a games room with table tennis. We did not mix with the other children in the hostel and rarely went to the main building. I think they mixed more; perhaps they had belonged to the same community in Egypt, but for some reason we stayed apart from all the activities.

Breakfast consisted of cornflakes or a cooked one. We had never had cereal before and it tasted strange, more like cardboard. The thought of having something cooked for breakfast was totally alien to us, so we didn't eat much. It was the same for lunch and dinner, the food was there but it was nothing like what we were used to. We couldn't stomach the pork sausages, baked beans or boiled cabbage that were on offer on a daily basis and we were hungry most of the time. Nor were we used to drinking tea or instant coffee – in Egypt, tea would have been for medicinal purposes like chamomile and the coffee had been *cafe au lait*, with lots of milk. In the end, my mother bought some dried pasta and a tube of tomato purée from a local shop, which she managed to prepare on a tiny cooker we had in the room.

We had arrived in England a couple of weeks before Christmas, so all the shops were decorated and looked festive. I saw my first Christmas tree and I remember looking at all the chocolate boxes displayed in the shop windows. They were the old fashioned colourful Cadburys tins, with a festive design on the front. I longed to buy one, but I knew it would not be fair asking my parents, as we were refugees and they had very little money.

The hostel was in the middle of nowhere, surrounded by fields and streams. It was a cold winter and it snowed a few days after our arrival. We were excited, as we had never seen snow before. However, the shoes we had were flimsy and totally inappropriate for the weather. We ventured outside the hostel for the first time and went to Cheltenham, the nearest large town, to buy some footwear. We saw a sign above a shop which said Boots and headed straight there – assuming by the name that they sold boots, but of course, it was Boots the Chemist. We did find something appropriate in the end and it sounds funny when relating this incident now, but at the time it was just another frustrating experience in a strange country.

We had learnt some English at school, but it turned out to be very inadequate. We could not speak a word – apart from my father who spoke good English, having worked for a British company for many years. We were a curiosity for the village children and they used to run in circles around us, taunting us and asking questions, such as did we live in tents and did we ride camels. They were not unkind, but they had never come across people like us and treated us like aliens.

We were sent to school, my younger sisters to the local primary and me to the secondary school. To get there, we had to go through muddy fields in the middle of winter. My younger sisters walked together, always hand in hand and I had to walk on my own, as my school was on a separate site. Nicole tells me that my little sister Claudine was so scared and stressed that she used to wet herself on the way or at school. My heart breaks when I think of it, my shy and vulnerable six year old sibling, who preferred to put herself through the daily ordeal of doing something which frightened her, rather than refuse to do it. She wasn't a mentally resilient child and I fear that this experience left her with some trauma.

I didn't fare better. I hated my school and felt completely lost. Cairo had been familiar and safe, and I had been used to the busy streets, the noise and the traffic. The hostel in Bridgend was not far from the school in nearby Stonehouse but, like my sisters, I had to walk through quiet fields and small lanes to get there. What's more, it was the middle of winter and I was not used to the freezing cold. Once at school, it was another struggle as I didn't understand a word of what was being said. No one befriended me or looked after me, neither teachers nor pupils, and I was left to my own devices. The worst experience was Physical Exercise.

I was expected to get undressed and run outside in the freezing cold with just a pair of shorts and a flimsy t-shirt, followed by a cold shower. I thought they were completely mad and I refused to go to school.

The Jewish families in the area were kind to us. One family who lived in nearby Cheltenham invited me to their house for Christmas and I expect they thought they were being nice. They had a huge Christmas tree – I had never seen one before and thought it was pretty, but could not understand why a Jewish family would have one. There was also a big dog, which I was very frightened of. I felt completely lost and, after only a few hours, asked to be taken back to my parents.

The hostel was full of refugees from Egypt like us. There were many Maltese families and other people we had never come across in Cairo. Under normal circumstances, we would not have had much in common with them, but these were different times. We had all experienced the trauma of having to leave Egypt very suddenly and the future was uncertain. We were also trying to cope with the cold weather and a different culture and language. My parents must have been scared and worried, but they never showed it in front of us.

I wonder how my poor grandmother felt – she was in alien surroundings, probably feeling cold most of the time and missing everything she knew and had been familiar to her. The language was an additional barrier, since she could only speak Arabic. I have a photo of her outside the pavilion and she looks sad. We probably failed her when she lived with us in the UK. I don't think I ever had a conversation with her beyond the usual civilities and perhaps the fact that she could only speak Arabic made things difficult. At any rate, children and teenagers often take their cue from adults and I wish my mother had encouraged me to make an effort.

I don't have bad memories of the three months spent in the hostel in Bridgend, though I don't have any positive ones either. I try to tell myself that, compared to what refugees have to go through nowadays, often just to reach the UK, we were not too badly off. We had left Egypt unharmed and had been looked after by the British Government from the moment of our arrival in the UK. We had a roof over our heads and regular meals, inedible though they were. We just didn't know what the next chapter held and missed our family and our life in Cairo.

I came across the Stonehouse Historical society recently and met a gentleman who remembered all about the hostel. As we live nearby in Bristol, we met him in Stonehouse, which was exactly as I remembered it – even the village shop and newsagent where I had stood all those years ago, looking longingly at the Cadburys chocolate boxes, was still there. He took us to where the hostel had once stood. It had been replaced by rows of bungalows, but the area looked the same and you still had the feeling of being in the middle of nowhere.

I felt very sad for a few days after this trip down memory lane. We are so busy with everyday mundane matters, we rarely give ourselves the time to stop and remember. What I was feeling was a huge sense of loss – for my parents and my sister Claudine, who were no longer with us, for the time that had gone by and for the young girl I had once been, bewildered perhaps, but still full of hope and dreams. The years had flown by and I would have given a lot to go back in time and be in that hostel with all my family. As the saying goes, you can't put the clock back, so all I had was nostalgia and memories.

The treatment of Anglo-Egyptian refugees by the British government

I have recently read a very interesting PhD thesis by De Aranjo, Alexandre GA on 'The Assets and liabilities of the refugees from Hungary and Egypt in France and in Britain, 1956-1960'. It explains many things and has changed my previous naive perception of the treatment of the Anglo-Egyptian refugees by the British government. The following chapter is essentially a resumé of what I have read.

I can no longer feel particularly grateful towards the British government with regard to our initial treatment. After all, it was mainly because of a political blunder by Anthony Eden, the Prime Minister at the time, that we suddenly found ourselves uprooted, living in a hostel in the middle of nowhere, in a strange country and in winter. It seems that the refugees from Egypt were considered to be liabilities by the British government for two reasons. Firstly, because they were associated with postcolonial immigration – the question of restricting this had been surveyed by the Cabinet since the arrival of the Empire Windrush in 1948 and the Anglo-Egyptians came at a time when the government was considering restricting immigration from the West Indies, India and Pakistan.

Secondly, most of the refugees were Jewish and the British government had a tradition of limiting Jewish immigration to Britain. In 1956, Anglo-Egyptian Jews were seen as another wave of Jewish refugees and associated with undesirable immigration. Moreover, they were composed of large families from a predominantly middle class background, which did not match the country's economic needs at the time. Because of their North African origin, some government officials associated them with 'southern races' and therefore saw them as a racial problem rather than an asset.

However, the unpopularity of the Suez crisis motivated the Government to give the impression that refugees from Egypt were treated as British nationals. The Home Office created the Anglo-Egyptian Resettlement Board, to manage the hostels and resettle the refugees in the most efficient way possible. These efforts were limited by views within the British administration who saw them as colonial immigrants, rather than British citizens. British immigration policy was framed by the concept of race and good race relations, rather than assimilation as in France.

Years later, I discovered how British bureaucracy still managed to discriminate against immigrants born outside the UK. I had applied for a job which I was keen on and was eliminated, without the chance of an interview – at the time, the position required the applicant to sign the Official Secret Acts and this could only be done by someone who was born in the United Kingdom. There were other instances when putting Cairo as my place of birth worked to my disadvantage.

My father's experience also proves the point. He had held a responsible job in Egypt, where he had been the Managing Director of a well known British company. Yet he was not treated with a lot of respect when he went to the company in London looking for a job. Initially, they offered him what amounted to Hobson's choice – emigrate again to the other side of the world, where he could have a similar position to the one in Cairo, or stay in London and start at the bottom. He opted for the latter but he had to suffer a lot of prejudice initially. It was only thanks to his capabilities and his patience that he was eventually promoted to Export Manager. It couldn't have been easy, but he never complained in front of us.

When we had arrived in London, although we had been met by an official – probably a member of the National Assistance Board or the Red Cross – we had been given no information as to our destination. In any case, the places refugees were sent to were so remote and isolated that they were usually unknown to them; we knew the main cities in England, but had certainly never heard of Stroud or Stonehouse, so the name would not have meant much to us. The refugees had no choice regarding the hostel they were sent to and the fact that most of them spoke very little or no English did not help.

The financial help given to refugees in hostels was not great. Those without means were accommodated on a free basis and given 12 shillings a week for an adult and 5 shillings a week for a child. Those who worked were charged for board and lodgings in such a way that they would be left with at least £2 a week. Some refugees found this very unfair and viewed the hostels as 'camps'. Many could not understand how they were supposed to leave them so quickly, when financial support was very low. After all, they had been reduced to a state of temporary destitution through no fault of their own.

In the face of much criticism, a scheme to help the refugees was quickly set up. A grant of £100,000 was made to the Anglo-Egyptian Aid Society for the relief and reception of British Nationals from Egypt. The AEAS was a charity which benefited from a good reputation, as it had previous experience in supporting and dealing with the British from Egypt.

The aims of all the hostels were the same – to put the refugees from Egypt into employment and private accommodation quickly so that they could re-settle, or to organise the re-emigration of those willing to go to another country. They worked with local authorities in order to check if housing and work were available. During my recent visit to Bridgend, I found out that many of those who had been at the hostel had never left the area, but had settled there and become part of the community.

The fact that the Egyptian refugees were described as British Nationals meant that there was a problem of perception of identity by the public and the press, who believed that they needed less help than the Hungarian refugees, who were foreigners. In the first couple of months after the Hungarian revolution, references to them oscillated between freedom fighters and victims of oppression. They were therefore not perceived as economic migrants. At a popular level, they reached a level of acceptability which the refugees from Egypt were not able to achieve.

This was partly due to the unpopularity of the Suez crisis in Britain and partly because they were not wanted by the British government. This was upsetting, as they felt that their treatment was far from what they should have received as British nationals. Their argument also was that, if Britain had never launched a military operation with France and Israel to regain control of the Suez Canal, the Anglo-Egyptians would still have had their assets and properties. There were only a limited numbers of ways for the refugees to leave the hostels and one of them was to find a job and private accommodation. Thankfully, my father managed to achieve this and we were able to leave the hostel relatively quickly.

Settling in London

We had spent three months in the hostel, waiting to hear when we could move to London. On our arrival in the UK my father had immediately contacted John Dickinson, the British company he had worked for in Cairo. Their Head Office was in the City of London. They initially offered my father the option to continue as Managing Director, but that could only be in Australia, Canada or South Africa.

Australia felt like the end of the world, Canada was also too far away and South Africa could eventually explode because of apartheid. He thought about Israel, as most of his family had settled there but decided against it. The

State of Israel had only been in existence for eight years and life was hard. He finally opted to work for the company's Head Office in London, but starting from the bottom in a low position.

When we left the hostel, we initially stayed in Earl's Court, where a lady called Sophie Kemkenian, who had been my father's Personal Assistant in Cairo, had a large house. They had had an excellent working relationship and had kept in touch, so she was happy to put us up. Earl's Court was a busy area and we enjoyed our first taste of London. We went for tea at Lyons Corner House in Marble Arch a few times and were very excited to discover Lyons sliced bread with the distinctive blue, red and green gingham wrappings for thin, medium and thick sliced bread.

The Anglo/Egyptian Resettlement Board moved us to a large flat in Kensington, where our rent was to be paid by the British Government for 18 months. It was situated in Palace Gate, one of the wealthier areas of London. We lived a few minutes' walk from Kensington Gardens and High Street Kensington and we instantly fell in love with the area. Most of the families who were in the hostel were also transferred to London – those who had families were given a flat and the couples without children had rooms at the Alexandra Hotel; this was also in Kensington, just off Gloucester Road and a few minutes' walk from where we lived. Uncle Victor and his wife Nina stayed there and we visited them regularly. My grandmother lived with us.

The flat was large and comfortable, but in need of repair. The ceiling in one of the bedrooms once collapsed, fortunately when no one was in the room. My father used to buy sweets, but as he did not want us to help ourselves, he hid them in a small cupboard in the dining room. Being rather greedy, I thought I would help myself anyway. I had the shock of my life when a small mouse jumped out when I opened the door. My father had the unenviable task of chasing and killing it and, needless to say, I never ventured to open that particular cupboard again.

It was hard trying to adapt to a new life and a culture which seemed alien at first. It must have been especially difficult for my mother. In Egypt, she had had servants do all the hard work and, as long as she managed the day-to-day running of the house, she had been free to go out and enjoy herself. We had had a servant to clean the house, someone to do the weekly washing and all the ironing was sent out. In England, she had the responsibility of all those tasks, plus looking after her elderly and frail mother. Yet to her credit, she never complained and tried to adapt as best as she could. Perhaps her difficult upbringing helped, as she certainly had not been spoilt as a child or a teenager.

The weather had improved greatly by the time we moved to London in April. This made a huge difference, as we were able to play tourists at weekends and enjoy what the capital had to offer. The fact that the flat was so centrally situated made it easy to explore – the Natural History Museum, the Science Museum and the Victoria & Albert were all within walking distance. We made the most of weekends and went somewhere different every time. As well as museums and parks, we visited the Tower of London, Hampton Court Palace, The National Gallery, etc.

My favourite park was St James's Park and my most

vivid memory is Duck Island, the nature reserve for the bird collection, situated at the end of the lake. When asked what ice cream I wanted, I always chose an Orange Maid ice lolly. We often went for walks in Kensington Gardens, as it was so to speak our local park. We tried the cinema but that was a waste of time. The very first film I saw in London was The Tea House of the August Moon with Marlon Brando and I didn't understand a single word.

The subject of the right school was a delicate one. After my negative experience in Bridgend, I had made it clear that I did not want to go to an English school. I now understand why I insisted on going to a French school in London – I was keen to carry on with my French education and, to a certain extent, ignore the fact that I was now living in England. Like most Egyptian Jews, I associated myself with the French culture; the difference between this and the British one was exacerbated by the fact that I did not speak English and was not in a hurry to learn.

The Lycée in South Kensington was the only French school in London and my parents managed to get a scholarship for me and Nicole – that was because we had attended the same school in Cairo. There were two sections, the French one, for those who wanted to study for the Baccalaureate and the English one, where the pupils studied French but would ultimately take the English GCE exams.

As I didn't speak English and was making no effort to learn it, it was decided that I would be placed in the French section, thus carrying on with what I had been studying in Cairo. Initially I was very happy, but gradually I became aware that things were not as simple as I had expected them to be. The school was private and the tuition fees expensive, so it was mostly attended by wealthy children whose fathers were high up in the embassies of their country or even ambassadors. The English students also came from wealthy families.

I was a refugee on a scholarship and was aware of it. The girls all wore stockings, which I envied and I had short socks because that was all we could afford. At lunch time and after school, they went to the numerous cafés in the area, whereas I went across the road to the Natural History Museum to eat my sandwich. My weekly pocket money was three pence, with which I regularly bought a Fry's chocolate and a honeycomb bar, as they were my favourites. I used to look forward to this all week; I would go up to my room and eat them while reading a Russian novel – I was very much into Dostoyevsky at the time.

Elvis Presley was popular, as were various rock and roll artists. The song Tequila was one of my favourites. There were lots of parties which I never went to; I was not invited and they were out of my league anyway. Once again, it felt like I was on the outside looking in, but unlike my experience in Egypt, I did not mind. Those children were rich and spoilt and I did not want to be in their company. The most exciting event during my four years at the school was a visit by General de Gaulle. We all assembled in the large playground to meet him and he was so tall he towered over everyone, including the headmaster.

I made a couple of friends and was happy in their company. One was called Helen and was a refugee from Yugoslavia who had come to England with her mother and brother. She was also on a scholarship and told me they were so poor they could only afford bread and margarine most of the time. My other friend was German. Her name was Karen and she once told me that there would eventually be a resurgence of Nazism in Germany – she didn't know I was Jewish and I should have said something.

I also befriended an Italian girl called Gigliola, whose father was someone important in the Italian embassy. She went home for lunch and there was always a car with a chauffeur waiting to pick her up. She often invited me and it was like stepping into another world – lunch was a proper sit down meal served by a waitress and the food tasted wonderful. I may have been a young refugee, but Gigliola was not snobbish and her friendship was genuine.

The Spanish and Portuguese Jewish community took the Egyptian Jews under their wing, but they were a little patronising. I think they were surprised and shocked that we were so secular and expected us to learn from them and start behaving like observant Jews. We had come to England carrying our Middle Eastern baggage and that was obvious from the way we behaved. I don't know quite how it happened but one lady, called Miss Levy, became the person every Egyptian Jewish family was anxious to please and terrified to offend. We were all frightened of her, my father included. It was considered an honour if she attended one of your parties and we had to come up to the standard she expected from us, as incurring her disapproval was not an option.

Miss Levy, along with other members of the Spanish and Portuguese synagogue, insisted that the children should attend the religion school on Sundays. I hated being told what to do and complied reluctantly, but I am glad I did as I learnt to read Hebrew. I thought I had forgotten it all as I had not read it for decades, but I was surprised at how quickly it all came back when I joined a synagogue in Bristol.

On Saturday mornings, we attended Shabbat services at the Spanish & Portuguese synagogue in Lauderdale Road. It's a beautiful synagogue and the people were friendly and welcoming. The Hakham, the Reverend Dr Solomon Gaon, had a strong voice which filled the synagogue and a choir of small boys with angelic voices added to the beauty of the service. I appreciated it, as I had been brought up as a traditional Sephardic Jew. Nowadays, I still miss the Sephardic liturgy, the particular way of chanting and the special intonations.

My favourite moment of the service was when everyone stood up to receive the priestly blessing. This called for any man who was a Cohen, a descendant of the ancient order of High Priests, to stand up and bless the congregation. Fathers covered the heads of their sons with the wings of their tallit, each generation blessing those below and being blessed by those above it. Watching from the women's gallery, I found this tradition particularly moving and inspiring. It's the essence of Judaism – le*dor vador,* from generation to generation.

My mother, who had been used to Middle Eastern cooking and ingredients, made the best of what she could find in London, sometimes with amusing results. She once bought flour to make a cake, well at least she thought that's what it was. We could not understand why the cake was flat and dense and had not risen until we had a look at the packet. It turned out that my mother had bought potato flour instead of flour. In spite of this, the cake tasted nice!

In 1950s London, you could not find the variety of foreign and Middle Eastern ingredients which are available nowadays. My father used to go to an Italian supermarket in Soho called Fratelli Camisa, to get pasta, cheeses and olives. Once a week my mother went to Portobello Road to do her shopping and I liked going with her if I was on holiday. We took the no. 49 bus, along High Street Kensington and onto Notting Hill. She went to the same supermarket and always bought some luncheon meat and pineapple jam. Sometimes we walked along the Portobello Road market, which was always busy. I loved the hustle and bustle.

Through mutual acquaintances I met a young girl my age who also came from Egypt. We became friends and I often used to go and stay with her at weekends. She lived nearby in Holland Park and I liked visiting because, unlike us, her family had a television set. We loved watching all the programmes popular at the time, such as Rawhide, Juke Box Jury and Six Five Special.

My mother and I sometimes went to the cinema on a Sunday afternoon and the Odeon in Kensington High Street always showed the latest films. We still didn't understand much of the dialogue, but I remember going to see Pal Joey with Frank Sinatra and the Inn of the Sixth Happiness starring Ingrid Bergman. My parents very quickly met couples from Egypt with whom they could socialise, and they took it in turns to host a card game on

Saturday evenings.

Sadly my grandmother was very unhappy living in London and, because she only spoke Arabic, none of us children had much interaction with her. My mother was having to do all the things she had not done in Egypt, such as cooking, cleaning, shopping and perhaps did not have too much time for my grandmother, who had to go into hospital a few times. This must have been terribly hard for her, surrounded by strangers and unable to speak English. It was clear that she missed Aunt Marie terribly and all she wanted was to be reunited with her. Eventually Marie and her family left Egypt and settled in Milan, so my grandmother was able to join them. I am glad that at least she had peace of mind for the last few years of her life.

For nearly two years after our arrival in London, I managed to continue to live in the bubble I had built around me. I spoke French at school, with the few friends I had outside and at home. I lived in Kensington, one of the nicest and most exclusive areas of London and behaved like a tourist every weekend, going to museums and places of interest. There were reasons for this behaviour – I had very suddenly been uprooted from the country I had loved and where I had grown up and, although protected by my parents, had been old enough to be somewhat traumatised. The three months spent in a hostel in the middle of nowhere, exposed to a new culture which I didn't understand and was alien to me, had not helped. One way of dealing with all this was to postpone the reality check for as long as possible. This finally came when I was forced to learn English for my GCE exams and we moved to North West London at around the same time.

After 18 months in the French section at the Lycée, it was decided that I should be moved to the English side. It made sense, as I was expected to take my O Levels at the end of that year. The problem was that I had made no effort so far and I was shocked when I looked at my set books for English literature, as I couldn't understand a single word.

I proceeded to look up every word of Shakespeare's Macbeth in the dictionary, certainly a long and laborious task. By the end, I knew every word of the play and my English was grammatically correct. Learning the language was relatively easy, what I found difficult were all the idiosyncrasies and the fact that I still kept thinking in French. For ages, I insisted on referring to hair in the plural as in French 'hair' is *les cheveux*. Then there was the fact that words like 'sponge' are pronounced differently, depending on whether you were referring to a type of cake or a kitchen sponge.

My maiden name was Chouchan and, whereas I had never had any problems in Egypt, I found out that English people had difficulties with the name. For one thing, they could not write it down – I spelt it slowly and carefully and they still got it wrong. Then there were those who thought they were being clever, so I was called Chou Chan, Shoe Shine, etc. It may have been funny for some, but I found it highly irritating and sometimes upsetting.

In order to supplement my weekly pocket money, which was very little, I started giving private French tuition. I regularly met with a very nice lady called Prue and we used to have an hour's conversation sitting in her car. She had a high powered job and just wanted to practise some French conversation. I also taught this to a couple of 10 year olds in their house. The reason why I liked going there was that, after the lesson, their grandmother served tea in the lounge. This was served from a teapot in beautiful china cups and there was always a delicious fruit cake. She was ladylike and courteous, and I enjoyed what I saw as a very civilised experience.

The time came when the British government was no longer going to be paying the rent on our flat in Kensington, so we had to move out. My parents could not afford any rented accommodation in the area and bought a house in Hendon, North West London. I was very upset and felt like they were taking us to the end of the world. Hendon is very much part of London now and very expensive, but in those days, it was practically at the end of the Northern Line and very suburban. I am essentially a city person and would happily live in Piccadilly Circus in London or Times Square in New York.

North West London and after

We left Kensington, moved to Hendon and began yet another chapter of our lives. The house my parents had bought was in a Jewish area and very well placed – ten minutes' walk to Hendon Central underground station and with a kosher butcher and bakery nearby. It had four bedrooms, a large kitchen/diner and a separate lounge and dining room. However, it was in a slight state of disrepair and the builder my father employed was very slow – it took him two years to complete the work and through all that time we felt we were living in the middle of a builder's yard. He was quite a character though and very likeable, not that this helped with the constant mess and dust.

The house was always cold and draughty and my father only allowed the heating to be on for four hours in the evening. Initially, we had no central heating and it was very cold in winter. We had an Aladdin heater which was switched on in the evenings, as well as electric fires with one or two bars. We sat as close to the electric fire as possible and always ended up with red blotches on our legs. My bedroom was even colder, as a window pane was missing and was covered with some cardboard. I sat as close to the electric fire as possible to get changed and, if my father came in the room and noticed it was on, he made me switch it off. Money was tight at the beginning, so he was anxious about running up high electricity bills.

There was a department store called Houndsditch in the City of London. It was very popular with refugees from Egypt, probably because they offered a discount. They sold furniture and electrical stuff and everything we bought came from there. You were always sure to bump into a fellow refugee while shopping – we recognised one another easily by our loud voices, our broken English and our mannerisms.

On Sunday evenings, we gathered round the TV set in the dining room to watch the popular programmes of the day – Sunday Night at the London Palladium and The Saint, the Black & White Minstrel Show – which seems so politically incorrect now – and later on The Avengers. My parents sat in the two armchairs and we sat on the floor, as near to the electric fire as possible in winter. TV viewing was much less complicated in those days – there were only two channels, the BBC and Southern Television, the forerunner of ITV.

One of our favourite shows was Dr Kildare, a medical drama television series which ran from September 1961 until August 1966 – this was long before series like the ER and Grey's Anatomy became popular and propelled actors like George Clooney to fame. Dr Kildare was an instant success and made a star of Richard Chamberlain, who played the title role. Raymond Massey starred also as his senior, Dr Leonard Gillespie. The series had a soap opera touch and none of the gory details you get now when you watch medical drama series. However, episodes frequently highlighted diseases or medical conditions which had not been widely discussed on television, such as drug addiction.

There was another medical drama series also very popular at the time. It was called Ben Casey and starred Vince Edwards as the main character, a young, intense and idealistic neurosurgeon in the fictional County General Hospital. He was tall and stocky and would have looked more in place in a boxing ring than in scrubs – the complete opposite of Richard Chamberlain, both in physique and the role they played, but we loved them both. Fortunately, they were shown on different channels and on different nights, so we did not have to choose.

Everything had to be watched live so it was normal for families to gather together in the evenings. In a sense, things were less complicated. We had a radio in what we called the morning room, which was in effect a kitchen/diner. Radio Luxembourg was always on or French stations like France Inter if my mother was listening. Sunday afternoons were sacred, as we always listened to Top of the Pops and to the countdown of the Top 10. We waited impatiently to find out which record had reached no 1 that week.

Popular music was very much part of our lives. There were so many bands, it was difficult to say which was our favourite. The obvious choice were The Beatles and The Rolling Stones, but also Gerry and the Pacemakers, the Searchers, the Animals, the Byrds, The Who and The Beach Boys. The tunes were catchy, the lyrics simple and you could sing along. My favourite songs, amongst many others, were Paint it Black by the Stones and Don't let me be misunderstood by The Animals. On Bank Holidays, Nicole and I, and sometimes Claudine, used to go to Hampstead Heath. We always had a small portable radio with us, to make sure that we didn't miss Top of the Pops at 3.00 pm. Alan Freeman was the DJ and he called his listeners 'pop pickers'. I remember these times with a great deal of nostalgia.

When Coronation Street started in 1960, my father took an instant dislike to it. I suppose he thought of Northerners as odd people from another country, who could not even speak English properly. He refused to watch it, which meant that I couldn't. That was one of the many disagreements we had over television programmes. Years later, we fell out over politics. He voted Conservative and I was always a staunch Labour supporter. When Margaret Thatcher became Prime Minister, he put her on a pedestal. She could do no wrong as far as he was concerned and we had heated arguments about it, especially during the Miners' Strike, when he called their leader, Arthur Scargill, 'the red devil'. The funny thing is, he was not joking and he really believed that Scargill was a bad man; he used to get very upset with me because I was supportive of the strike and the miners' plight.

My mother cooked the same meal every different night of the week. We had pasta on Mondays, fish on Wednesdays and liver on Thursdays. The Shabbat meal was chicken soup, followed by shoulder of lamb with potatoes. The lamb was very fatty and had to be eaten quickly. Dessert was fresh fruit and my mother baked a cake once a week, usually a fruit one or a chocolate marble cake. She didn't have a huge repertoire, but what she made was always very good. We had an apple tree in the garden which produced plenty of fruit every year, so she regularly made apple jam, as well as her *compote de pommes,* stewed apples. This was our dessert practically every evening and, in fact, it was pointless asking what we were having, as it would be inevitably be *compote.* It was made with water and very little sugar, so apart from being repetitive, it was rather insipid.

One of the first things my father had told us when we had arrived in England was that we should learn to behave as the British do and forget all about Egypt. Perhaps he was remembering the words of the Jewish philosopher and scholar Maimonides, who warned that a person should beware not to cast his thoughts backwards, for his eyes are placed on the front of his head. My father kept true to this. Neither he nor my mother ever mentioned Egypt and it was as if that part of their life had never existed. However, the contradiction was that they only socialised with Egyptian Jews. They may have talked about Egypt with their friends or perhaps they did not feel the need, but they never broached the subject with us. There were quite a few families in London and very soon my parents formed their own group of friends.

London in the 1960s had very few delicatessens, so my father continued his regular visits to Fratelli Camisa in Soho, which he had first discovered when we lived in Kensington. This was one of the first Italian delis in London and soon became famous as the place to go to buy authentic Italian produce. It was still in the same place until 2013 and I paid a visit a couple of times when in Central London, more as a pilgrimage and in memory of my father. It was a small shop, crammed with goodies and the wonderful aroma of cheese and salami greeted you as soon as you opened the door. It is still operating, though it's now an online business. He also discovered a Greek shop in Moscow Road in Bayswater, called the Athenian. He loved going there and I am glad that it still exists after all these years, as it's another place to visit if I want to remember him.

My father also found a coffee shop in South Molton Street, just off Bond Street, where you could get your coffee beans ground any way you liked. It was one of the few places where asking for the beans to be Turkish ground was understood. It has long gone, probably replaced by one of the many outlets selling overpriced merchandise to tourists. My mother had bought a *kanaka* with her from Egypt – the special long-handled pot with a pouring lip designed specifically to make Turkish coffee and my father was thus able to have a small cup of his favourite drink every evening after dinner.

My parents managed to transfer some of their social life from Egypt to London. They played cards every Saturday evening – they were invited to friends' houses or, when their turn came, they hosted a game. There were one or two card tables set out for the ladies in the living room and the same for the men in the dining room. The evenings when they hosted were called 'receptions' and were quite a formal affair. My mother made bridge sandwiches with different fillings, savoury pastries and at least two or three cakes, which on those occasions were more special and elaborate than our everyday ones. The ladies had to outdo each other – so what started as serving just one cake became two, then someone made three, until it got out of hand. They would then agree to go back to just one cake, but could not keep this up for long.

I used to hide upstairs in my room when it was my parents' turn to host, whereas Nicole loved those evenings. She was the perfect daughter, helping my mother to serve tea and food, and chatting happily with everyone. In contrast, I sneaked into the kitchen when I was sure there was no one around, so that I could help myself to the leftovers. It sounds a little immature now, but I lacked confidence and hiding away seemed the easiest option.

The drawback was that waiting for the coast to be clear could take ages and then there was no guarantee I wouldn't bump into one of the guests who had got up to use the downstairs toilet, which was situated near the morning room. My favourite dessert was called a Mont Blanc, which my mother made with meringues shells, whipped cream and chestnut purée, all artistically arranged. However, the dessert was very popular with all the guests, so most of the time and much to my disappointment, there would be very little left by the time I came downstairs to help myself.

As well as Saturday evenings, my mother played cards with her friends once a week on a Wednesday afternoon. That was the only time when she went out and socialised. The rest of the week she spent at home, shopping, cleaning and cooking. She never learnt to speak English properly, so it remained very basic and we always spoke French with her. With my father, it was a mixture of French and English, depending on the subject matter.

Both my parents were on the whole parsimonious, especially my mother. I think it must have been as a result of her upbringing. She could never resist a bargain, so she bought more of what she actually needed, simply because it was on special offer. She refused to throw away any food and kept even a spoonful of a leftover, carefully putting it away in the fridge. I used to find it slightly annoying, but now I believe that there is something to be said for not wasting food. We have gone to the other extreme and think nothing of throwing away vast amounts, mostly because we overbought in the first place.

My father was also careful about spending. Now and then he splashed out on a few treats, but on the whole he always seemed to be worried about spending too much. His bugbears were the phone and heating bills, so he kept a tight rein on our calls and how electricity was consumed. I don't think he was worried that he would not be able to pay the bills, he just saw certain things as a waste of money.

Perhaps my parents had been different while they had lived in Egypt. They had had a good social life and been able to go out most evenings, so they must have been happy to spend money. This lifestyle disappeared overnight and they became refugees in a foreign country, which must have had a huge effect on them. I have adopted the reverse philosophy – if no one knows what the future holds and things can change suddenly, then it's better to spend what extra money you have, though wisely of course.

My mother spent a lot of her time cleaning the house – it was old, so it was not an easy job. Nevertheless, she regularly washed all the doors and windows and there were many, as the house was big and the windows were the old fashioned ones with panes. They must have been difficult to clean, especially as you needed to climb on a small ladder. I couldn't understand why she insisted on doing this thankless task so often, as it seemed an utter waste of time and energy.

My fathered suffered a coronary thrombosis one Saturday night, after one of those receptions. It was just a coincidence but, as he was complaining of pains in his stomach during the night, we initially thought it was indigestion. I thought it better not to go to work in the morning and we called the GP, who diagnosed a thrombosis and called the ambulance. My mother panicked and did not know what to do, so I went in the ambulance with my father and did all that was required. We were understandably very worried and, although I kept my calm throughout and did all the necessary, I found myself shaking uncontrollably in the evening. Thankfully, my father made a slow, but very good recovery.

The general consensus was that the thrombosis had been caused by stress. He had found out a couple of months earlier that he could no longer work in the John Dickinson office in the City of London. Instead, the company transferred most of their staff to their site in Hemel Hempstead in Hertfordshire. This meant that he had to catch a bus very early in the morning – instead of the convenience of catching the Tube where trains were frequent, the bus only came once every hour and he was always late, as was his habit. He either missed it or caught it by the skin of his teeth and this meant a constant daily stress, which proved to be detrimental to his health.

If I had been afraid before of doing anything that could upset my father, I was even more so after his illness. I was convinced that, if I did, I could be the cause of another thrombosis or a heart attack. So, the 60s passed me by, as had the late 50s. I never wore a mini skirt, but that was probably because I was too self-conscious. My life was ordinary and that was just how my parents expected it to be. I had very few opportunities to rebel anyway and things would have been very different had I gone to university instead of opting for a secretarial course. At the very least, I would have had the opportunity to meet some like-minded people.

For a lot of young people, the 60s were exciting and full of hope. The music and the clothes were different, and they were experimenting with all sorts of things. Whenever I hear people talk about what they got up to in the 60s, I regret that I allowed myself to remain such a conformist. No parties, no colourful clothes and certainly no drugs, not even a joint. The area where we lived was considered suburbia and far away from the excitement of the Kings Road. My most exciting purchase was a gold shift dress which I had bought from a chain store called C&A and wore as often as I could. C&A had two big branches in Oxford Street and was known was for selling affordable, conventional, middle of the range clothes – a far cry from Biba in High Street Kensington and the shops in Carnaby Street.

Once I left school, I stopped going to synagogue every Saturday morning. As soon as I eventually started earning some money, I enjoyed going to Oxford Street and looking round the shops. This became a weekly pilgrimage – Oxford Street first, then Golders Green, where I walked around more shops. In the evening, I went with a couple of friends to a club called La Cage d'Or in Finchley Road. It was frequented mostly by Moroccan Jews and Israelis. On Sunday evenings, it was usually the dreaded Jewish dances. I didn't like the snotty Ashkenazi boys and always tried to find an excuse to avoid going. My parents insisted, so it was a relief when sometimes the weather was so bad it gave me an excuse to give it a miss.

I tried joining a few Jewish social clubs. One of them was called The Arcadians and they met once a week somewhere in the West End. I went out of duty more than anything else. I never enjoyed it, partly because I lacked confidence and partly because I was bored. A few young girls who also originally came from Egypt and were the same age as me joined this club. They seemed to do well, so perhaps they were more adaptable.

I went on holiday to Tunisia one summer and was very pleased to come across an audio cassette (that was pre-CD days) of a French singer who had been very popular in Egypt in the 50s. His name was Dario Moreno and one of his songs which I loved, was called Me Que Me Que. The song had been popular in Egypt for months and everyone had known the refrain. When I returned to London, the first thing I did was to show my father the cassette. I was very excited – it was a rare find and very much linked to our memories. My father's reply was that he had never heard of the singer! That was highly unlikely and of course he knew who it was. Aside from the disappointment at his behaviour,

I wonder why he was so adamant; it felt as though he wanted to wipe out anything and everything to do with Egypt and our life there.

Once on a visit to my aunt Sophie in Paris, I tried to find out more about our lives in Egypt and what she remembered. I expected her to start telling me all about the good memories. Instead, she was very dismissive and did not have a good word to say either about Egypt or the Egyptians. Yet to my knowledge neither she nor any member of my family were ever treated badly or imprisoned. Perhaps she was just angry that we had been forced to leave and that was all she chose to remember. Neither she nor my father's family had been particularly comfortable with Arabic, though they spoke it fluently. This was not the case with my mother's family, since my grandmother only spoke Arabic.

After we moved to our house in North London, family members were able to come and stay with us. Aunt Marie often came in the summer with her two children, Rony and Daniele. She always complained that the house was too cold, even in June. One year, they brought with them a portable record player and two records – Ciao ciao bambina by Domenico Modugno and Diana by Paul Anka – all gifts from our uncle Clement. We played them non-stop. The very first record I ever bought was an Extended Play by Elvis Presley with Teddy Bear and Hard Headed Woman on it.

I enjoyed Aunt Sophie and Uncle Leon's visits, as I was very fond of them. My father always got very excited beforehand and bought lots of special treats. We took them to see all the main attractions in London. Sometimes, when my aunt and my father were alone together, they suddenly lapsed into Ladino during their conversation and then reverted back to French. The same thing happened when Sophie chatted on the phone with her sister Suzanne in Israel.

My father loved his family, but for years Sophie was the only one he saw on a regular basis, although he corresponded with the rest of the family in Israel. However, he never mentioned them or talked about them to us. Whenever he received one of their letters, he just read it and put it away. He did not inform us when my aunt Esther passed away or Uncle Solomon. It was my mother who casually mentioned it weeks later. Had he been more talkative, we would have known a little more about our family in Israel and even kept in contact. Years later, when he finally summoned the courage to get on a plane – he had been too scared until then – he visited his family regularly and stayed for a month. He was very generous and always took gifts for everyone with him, which my cousins still remember.

In 1960 a singer called Bob Azzam released a song called Mustafa, in France. He had also originally lived in Egypt and the song was a mixture of colloquial Arabic and French. Although it was a very catchy tune, the lyrics made absolutely no sense at all, yet all Egyptian Jews loved it and it also became an international hit. To this day, everyone who comes from the Middle East knows the song Mustafa. If I ever want to cheer myself up, all I have to do is find it on YouTube and play it.

Dalida was another singer who had been brought up in Egypt. She had achieved some fame while still living there –

some acting roles in local films and the title of Miss Egypt. She settled in France, where she became very popular. She sang mainly in French, but also in Italian. Years later, after she had died, I discovered that she had also recorded songs in Arabic. They were beautiful nostalgic songs.

I had continued my studies at the French Lycée in Kensington, which meant a daily commute on the London Underground. After I took my A Levels, I had been planning to go to the University of London to study for a degree in French and Italian. However, I changed my mind at the last minute. By then, my best friend was working and earning a reasonable salary. This meant that she could buy nice clothes and a few treats. I had had enough of the weekly allowance of a few pence and the prospect of three more years with very little spending money was daunting. The decision not to go to university was a big mistake and I can only blame myself for that. It would have opened my mind to many things, given me a degree of confidence, and the opportunity to meet new people and make different friends.

I was able to make up for this years later when, at the age of 40, I went back to university as a mature student and this time chose law for my degree course. I loved law right from the beginning and enjoyed every minute of those three years. The icing on the cake was getting a First Class Honours.

When I left the French Lycée; I took a secretarial course and learnt shorthand and typing, which was what most girls did after leaving school. Once I had decided not to go to university, this was the only option. The course was boring, but I met a group of foreign students and socialised with them outside college. They were all there to learn English and there were many nationalities within the group. I had been living in England for a few years, but I still sought the company of foreign people, whose culture was generally more akin to mine.

I found a job as soon as I left college. It was for a small company in Moorgate, in the City of London. There were only three people in the firm, the two bosses and a general clerk who was very kind and took me under his wing. I left after one year to work for the Reuters News Agency. I thought it would be exciting, but my boss took a dislike to me and was nasty all the time. He ordered me about, talked down to me and even shouted. His behaviour would never be tolerated now and he was either anti-Semitic or didn't like the fact that I was a refugee from Egypt; perhaps it was a combination of both. I worked there for three months and have no idea why I put up with it for that long; in the end, he sacked me unceremoniously. Nowadays he would have to answer to a tribunal, but it wasn't the case then. I was relieved anyway and quite glad that the decision had been made for me.

I found another job straightway. In London in the 1960s, secretarial jobs were plentiful and you could change jobs easily. I found a position in a Swedish company called Ekman & Co in Blackfriars; they imported paper pulp from Sweden. I was very happy and worked there for three years, until I left to spend some time in Milan. My colleagues were fun and we all got on very well. I learnt to appreciate Swedish people when they came to visit the London branch – they are one of the most courteous and considerate people I have met. The two managers were easy going and approachable. They had a predilection for liquid lunches, which in those days was the norm, but that never impacted on their behaviour. Sadly, the younger manager died when he crashed his car on his way home late one evening, probably the worse for drink. I was in Milan at the time and did not find out about it until much later.

One of the advantages of working for this company was that they gave us luncheon vouchers. These were a perk which some companies offered to their employees, who used them to buy lunch at any of the places which accepted them. Most restaurants did and my colleagues had a sit-down meal every lunchtime. I joined them sometimes, but mostly I bought a sandwich and used the remaining balance to buy something for dinner – which strictly speaking I should not have done, seeing as these vouchers were meant to cover lunch and nothing else.

The office was only a few minutes' walk from the Thames and I often took my sandwich and ate it while watching the river. Other times, I walked to Fleet Street, St Paul's Cathedral or Leather Market. I loved the fact that all these places were within walking distance from my office, and I got to know the City of London well. At that time, there were very few clothes shops in the City; they were all situated in the West End around Oxford Street and most young girls preferred to work in that area, so that they could go shopping at lunchtime. I much preferred the more sedate atmosphere of the City. At Christmas, the whole office went for a drink in a local pub and I always ordered a snowball, which is a classic Christmas cocktail – a mixture of advocaat and fizzy lemonade, with a cocktail cherry on top. We were given some chocolates as a present, they were expensive ones and very special. I have nothing but good memories of my time with the company.

When I was 20, I decided that I wanted to learn how to drive. I was working and could afford the cost of driving lessons. My father discouraged me, saying that I would be a bad driver as I would not be able to concentrate. Foolishly, I listened to him and gave up the idea. My sister Nicole, on the other hand, did not discuss the matter, took driving lessons at 24 and passed first time.

Because of the way my life subsequently unfolded, the opportunity to learn how to drive was gone. Eventually, I went to live in Milan for what turned out to be three years and after that, my first marriage was so turbulent that learning how to drive was the last thing on my mind. After the divorce, I simply could not afford it and when I finally could, it was too late. I was in my 40s, so still young enough to learn, but by then I had lost the confidence of youth. I got very nervous and anxious before every lesson and was convinced that any car coming in the opposite direction would crash into us. I tried again unsuccessfully a couple of years later and in the end had to give up.

I have always regretted not being able to drive and see it as the wrong decision, made under my father's influence and perhaps not in my best interest. I think he was sometimes subjective in his advice and it's possible that he did not want me to learn how to drive because he would have worried whenever I went out in a car. Perhaps it was easier to discourage me, or he may have been protective and believed he was doing the right thing.

We went on holiday to Italy every summer. My uncle Clement lived in Milan and was very attached to Aunt Marie. He was still a bachelor and had done well for himself. He rented a villa for the month of August in an Italian resort, large enough for us and Marie and her family. The place was called Forte dei Marmi and was very exclusive – it still is. It was a couple of hours' train journey from Milan, near the resort of Viareggio on the Mediterranean. I used to look forward to this holiday all year. Before I had a full-time job, I did temporary work in June and July to save up for this and also went on a very strict diet so that I would look good in a bikini.

We travelled by train from London Victoria to Milan. The journey took over 24 hours and we had to change in Milan for the train to Forte dei Marmi. I bought all sorts of goodies for the journey and always some jam tarts. The big highlight was the ferry crossing from Dover to Calais and my special treat was having a gin and orange. We had sleeping compartments on the train and by the time we woke up in the morning, we were travelling through Switzerland and could admire the beauty of the Alps from the train window. The train was full of Italians who worked in England in menial jobs and returned to their homes in Calabria and Carrara for the summer. They were very friendly, but they liked their salami and red wine and by the following morning the smell of these was overpowering.

We usually had a couple of hours' wait between trains. Milan has a beautiful train station and I fell in love with the city without even going outside. I thoroughly enjoyed the three weeks spent in the resort. We went to the beach first thing in the morning and stayed there until lunchtime, often going for a walk along the front, so we could show off our figures in our bikinis. My father had his own routine. He liked getting up early in the morning and going to the market to buy fresh fruit and vegetables for the day; that was something he had never done in Cairo, but he enjoyed walking around an Italian market, which was far less chaotic and more civilised than an Egyptian one. My mother and aunt then cooked whatever he had brought back with him. They were experienced cooks, so the preparation did not take long and by 11.00 am they were ready to join us at the beach. Lunch was mostly vegetables and pasta with a sauce. Dinner was always something light, various cheeses and cold meats, olives and fresh bread.

In the evenings, it was time for what the Italians call la *passeggiata*, which is walking and people watching. We always had an ice cream and the nightly dilemma was which one of the many flavours to choose from. There was an exclusive nightclub in the resort called La Capannina di Franceschi. It was an exclusive night club, so not everyone could afford to go there, as drinks were very expensive. They had an orchestra with a popular singer and it was the place to go and be seen – I think we managed it twice in six years.

We carried on going to Forte dei Marmi for our summer holidays for six years. In the very first year, I met someone called Bruno. He was a local boy and always went round with a group of friends. We liked each other from the first time we met and spent most evenings together – nothing was ever arranged in advance, we inevitably bumped into each other at some point in the evening, as the centre of the resort was very small. At the end of the holiday, we just said good-bye and never arranged to correspond. The next summer I always bumped into him again and we carried on from where we had left off. It was a very strange relationship, but one that suited us. I hated going back to London at the end of the three weeks because it was such an anti-climax. I then spent many evenings listening to all the Italian songs which had been popular that summer and wouldn't stop crying. Nicole remembers all this with some amusement.

I went back to Forte dei Marmi in 2002. I had expected it to be very different, because most places change nowadays. Much to my surprise and delight, it hadn't. It was still as exclusive as I remembered it, probably even more so. All the shops sold designer goods and even the weekly market was expensive. It brought back many good memories and a lot of nostalgia.

We were expected to clean our own room on Sunday mornings. I had my own bedroom and my sisters shared one. Their room was always very warm because the boiler was there. Nicole liked playing music while cleaning her bedroom. Most often it was a long playing record by Charles Aznavour which I found depressing, as all the songs were sad and spoke of lost love and lost opportunities. I was never upbeat on a Sunday morning anyway.

My father continued to be very strict, at least with me. I was always a little scared of him and the thought of rebelling like my sister did not occur to me – I was just frightened in case I upset him. He had had his coronary thrombosis when I was 21 and, although he had recovered fully, I was always worried in case I triggered something off. This didn't mean that we didn't fall out – I once spent six months without talking to him, which made things very awkward for everyone. However, on the whole I was always careful to toe the line, especially as he was often impatient and quick to flare up.

I don't know how, why or when, but at some point I must have subconsciously decided that I was responsible for my father's health. It was emotional blackmail, but one which was self-inflicted. Whatever the reason, it always stopped me from confronting him or expressing how I really felt. Nicole was fortunate in that she was not plagued by those imaginary fears and more or less did as she pleased, within reason. Claudine was always treated like the baby of the family.

In a sense I was a rebel who did not have the courage to rebel. I was very stubborn though and on occasions, if I got an idea into my head, I stuck to it. I suddenly decided that I no longer wanted to have my evening meal with the family as I had always done, and chose to eat later. By then, I was working and could afford to buy a few treats with the luncheon vouchers provided by the company. I sometimes fried onions late, which annoyed my parents greatly; they would not let the matter drop and there were constant arguments about it.

I took everything to heart and often overreacted, but that was due to anxiety and a constant fear of the unknown, rather than the desire to draw attention to myself. My opinion did not seem to count for much, at any rate that is how I felt at the time. I still remember one incident which upset me a lot. It was a Saturday morning and Nicole and I were sitting in the morning room. My mother had gone shopping and as soon as she came into the room, she went straight over to Nicole to show her what she had bought and asked for her opinion. I turned to my mother and asked her if I was invisible and why she did not seem interested in what I thought. She mumbled some apology, but she was clearly embarrassed.

I think my mother preferred my sisters, but that was probably because she was more comfortable with them. Claudine always remained the baby of the family, but what was difficult was watching Nicole manage to do what she wanted and still be praised. I was not allowed to stay out after midnight and was cross-examined by my father on my return; going out with someone who was not Jewish would have been unthinkable. My parents must have been bothered by the fact that Nicole was going out at the time with someone younger who was not Jewish and staying out late. I think they tried talking to her, but she did not take any notice, which is probably the attitude I should have adopted.

Gradually, the atmosphere at home became more tense. My parents continued to insist that I should comply with their expectations. I refused, though I did not challenge them openly. There were constant arguments and questions – why did I want to have dinner on my own after everyone else, why did I not want to go to Jewish dances, etc. In those days, it was unusual for a young unmarried Jewish girl to leave home and live on her own. It would have looked bad in the eyes of friends and acquaintances.

In 1966, it was finally agreed that we all needed a break and the solution was to go and spend three months in Milan, Italy, where Aunt Marie lived. I had been in my job for a while and liked it, but it was more important to have a break, so I reluctantly gave my notice. My aunt had a small two-bedroom apartment right in the city centre. With her husband Zaki and her two children, the flat was already crammed – Rony was 12 and Daniele 11. Still, we managed, and I was happy to put up with the lack of comfort because my life in Milan seemed more exciting. The three months eventually stretched to over two years.

I was very happy in Italy, at least initially. I had studied Italian at A Level and, as my two cousins spoke Italian at home, I soon learnt to speak it fluently. I found a job with a Jewish Egyptian man who dealt in import/export. He was very kind, but not a good businessman and most months he did not manage to pay my salary on time. The position suited me though, as I was the only one in the office and he was never in – he just needed someone to answer the phone and take messages.

The office was not very far from where my aunt lived, and I used to get there by tram. This reminded me a little of the Cairo trams, though it was not as crammed or uncomfortable. Nevertheless, no one ever queued, which was disconcerting to begin with. I was used to London, where forming an orderly queue was second nature and I did not appreciate everyone scrambling to get on when the tram arrived. I went back home at lunchtime and returned to the office at 3.00 pm. This was still the custom for all offices and shops in Italy.

I liked Milan and felt relaxed, even though I was far from independent. I had simply exchanged my parents' control over me with that of my aunt's. I did not realise it at the time, as she was far more diplomatic than my father. Nevertheless, she did have a huge influence on me and I always took her advice, which was not always the right one or in my best interest. I had an Italian boyfriend for a short while but broke up with him, as of course it was unthinkable that I could marry someone who wasn't Jewish. The irony is that both my cousins have non-Jewish partners.

Uncle Clement was still single when I arrived in Milan. I had half expected him to take me under his wing, as he was well off, had his own business and knew a lot of people. This didn't happen, in fact it was the last thing on his mind. He took me out only once, and that was at Aunt Marie's insistence. We went to the cinema, to see The Ten Commandments, by Cecil B DeMille. He owned a small company which sold pharmaceutical products. My aunt asked him to find me a job within the company, but he was very reluctant. I worked there for a couple of days, stuck behind a desk doing very little. It was embarrassing so I left and thankfully found a job which I enjoyed.

I had always thought that my uncle was not particularly interested in me and this feeling was certainly reinforced when I lived in Milan. I was reluctant to admit it, thinking that perhaps it was my imagination, but it was obvious and even embarrassing sometimes. He was asked to 'introduce' me to a suitable Jewish boy, as he had many contacts. He finally did so, to someone much older than me, very unattractive and unsuitable. That was the one and only time when he made a semblance of an effort and I would not have wanted to repeat the experience. I have understood since then that the reason why he was indifferent towards me was simply because I did not display the adulation and admiration he was used to receiving from the rest of his family, especially Nicole. I was totally the opposite and he probably found this irritating.

By my mid-twenties, I had got used to constantly being told that I was wrong or overreacting and I did not think to challenge it. I had a mind of my own and a good logical brain with regard to practical things but, to a certain extent, I was influenced by my mother and Aunt Marie with regard to emotional matters. I had no other point of reference and didn't discuss things in any detail with friends. My friendships were usually ones of convenience and lacked any depth or trust. However, given my mother's temperament, it was inevitable that we would clash. I was as emotional and pessimistic as she was pragmatic. It didn't take much for me to create a storm in a teacup, so perhaps it was not surprising that I was not taken too seriously, even when it mattered.

I was rather naive and assumed that you had to trust your family implicitly, because whatever they did or said was always in your best interest. When I lived in Milan, I did not find it strange when my father asked me to continue giving him a part of my salary, as I had done when I lived at home. So, every month, I wrote a cheque and gave it to Clement, who put it in a Swiss bank account in my father's name. It never occurred to me to question the fairness of this, even though back home both my sisters were working and contributing and my father must have earned a reasonable salary.

Similarly, I gave my aunt some money every month, which was fair, since I was living with her. However, I continued to do the same when I eventually moved to a bedsitter. She had told me that she was keeping that money to give me when I married, but that did not happen. I haven't thought about this for years, but it was a rather unusual arrangement – I was not earning very much, and part of my salary went to my father, part to my aunt and eventually part towards the rent for my bedsitter. No wonder I didn't have any money left.

I was not particularly bothered about this at the time, probably because money has never been my priority and I was always trying to please. Although I was still living under the watchful eye of my family and strongly influenced by them, I was happy in Milan. My aunt's flat was near the city centre, which was very convenient. You could go and see a film at 10.00 pm and have a drink in a bar at midnight. It was exciting, especially compared to North West London. I made friends with a few girls who had also lived in Egypt and we went out every weekend.

There was a social club where Egyptian Jews met every Saturday evening – the adults to play cards, the younger ones to socialise and perhaps meet a suitable husband or wife. I always hoped that I would meet someone and get married in Milan, but that didn't happen. Instead, I met a South African Jewish man who came for business once a year. He wanted to get married but was highly unsuitable – not only was he divorced and had four children, but he saw nothing wrong with apartheid. My father regularly sent me letters begging me not to go to South Africa and warning me that there would be a bloodbath there eventually.

This relationship came to nothing and it became obvious that I was not going to meet a suitable Jewish boy in Milan. The few I knew had got engaged or married. By then, I had overstayed my welcome at my aunt's and had moved to a room in a house with an Italian family. I still went to my aunt's every evening, but had to go back to my bedsit, where I felt lonely; I had no TV or radio to pass the time and only silence around me.

Out of the blue, an Egyptian Jewish man I had met years before phoned me at my aunt's house and asked if he could come to see me Milan. His name was Raphael. We had been formally introduced a few years before but, after going out a few times, had decided that it wasn't going to work and called it a day. I am not clear why he had decided to phone me, as it was unlikely that it would work out any better the second time.

Nevertheless, strongly encouraged by my aunt, I agreed to meet him if he came to Milan. I was nearly 25 by then and her opinion was that I had to get married as soon as possible, otherwise I would be left on the shelf. Once again, I believed what she was saying and assumed that she was right. She gave me all sorts of platitudes such as 'every saucepan has its lid' and it all sounds quite ridiculous now, but at the time I believed what she said. Perhaps she meant well with all her advice, but I also suspect she had had enough of me by then and wanted me to go back to England. I convinced myself that I was doing the right thing, packed all my stuff and returned to London.

There is no doubt that my family had a huge influence on me when I was young. Their approval mattered a lot and it never occurred to me to go against what was expected. Jewish girls were supposed to marry someone of the same faith, anything else was frowned upon. My father would have been very upset and disappointed if I had brought home a non-Jewish guy and the myth I was sold all along was that, as long as I married someone from a 'nice family', I would live happily ever after. My mother went further and maintained that it didn't matter if things were not quite right before the marriage, the important thing was to get married and you could 'change' your husband later on.

The added pressure was the suggestion that, if you were not married by the age of 25, you were likely to be left on the shelf. It is not surprising that, with all the brainwashing from an early age, I made the wrong choice and was totally unprepared for marriage. I had huge doubts during my engagement, but believed my mother when she assured me that things would be fine afterwards, especially as my husband-to-be was Jewish and he had been brought up in Egypt. It is highly likely that, as unprepared as I was, I would have got divorced anyway, no matter whom I had married. We got engaged and were married within three months. We wanted to do this before Passover, otherwise because of Jewish law, we would have had to wait three months, until after the festival of Shavuot. I don't know what the rush was on my part – probably the fact that all my friends were getting married or engaged.

Uncle Clement had promised me a generous sum of money as a wedding present. True to his word, he sent a cheque a few weeks after my engagement. My father insisted that I should sign this over to him and I duly complied. He promised to buy us some lounge and dining furniture with the money, though I am sure I would have been capable of choosing my own. I liked the G Plan brand, which was popular at the time, but my father said it was too expensive, so I found myself limited to the budget he had set.

He refused to tell Raphael, my husband-to-be, that the money was actually a gift from my uncle, so Raphael was all the time under the impression that it was my father who was generous. It did not occur to me to put him right and I really wish I had, because it all came to a head a couple of days before the wedding. My uncle had travelled from Milan to attend the wedding and was offended that Raphael had not bothered to thank him for his wedding present. Of course, that was not possible, since he did not know anything about it! They were both understandably angry when the truth came out – my uncle because his gift has not been acknowledged and Raphael because he felt he had been misled. I was blamed as well and all I wanted was the whole sorry subject to go away.

The matter was never discussed again, but there had been a breach of trust and it affected our future before we had even started our married life. Deep down, I was hurt by the way my father had behaved, but I would not, or could not admit it. Instead, I went on the defensive. I had been brought up to believe that parents were always right and you never challenged their behaviour, as everything they did was out of love for their children and to think any other way would have been a betrayal.

I buried the whole story somewhere in my subconscious and never talked about it again. I did not ask my father why he had thought it necessary to do what he did, and I probably would not have got a straight answer. To give him the benefit of the doubt, perhaps he was acting with the best of intentions. He didn't trust the man I was about to marry, that much I know. In fact, he had suggested to postpone the wedding for three months, just to make sure I was doing the right thing, but I refused. Perhaps he thought that the money my uncle had given would not be put to good use and he could look after it better. However, he should have acknowledged that the money was a gift and given a thought to the consequences of keeping silent.

The marriage was doomed from the beginning. Perhaps we would have worked it out eventually, but we both involved our families in every single detail of our lives right from the start and there were clashes of culture and expectations. I had naively thought that the fact that we were both Jewish and had lived in Egypt was enough common ground, but it turned out to be the exact opposite. I had lived in a more liberal society in Cairo, where a woman was not expected to be a subservient wife and was allowed to have a mind of her own. In contrast, Raphael had grown up in Port Said, totally integrated within the Arab community, where ideas were much more old fashioned. Their mentality had remained similar to that of their Arab neighbours of old, oblivious to some social changes, in particular the status of women.

Furthermore, my father was a snob – I don't know why; after all, he came from a modest family, though he had done reasonably well for himself. He thought my in-laws were provincial, especially as they only spoke Arabic. He was always very polite and courteous with them, but the feeling of superiority was there. My husband remarked on that, but I denied it categorically, again acting out of misguided loyalty to my parents. There were clashes and misunderstandings right from the start and I often felt like a ping pong ball being hurled between the two camps.

The marriage lasted seven years, but I spent more time at my parents' than in the marital home. I made the mistake of constantly asking my parents for advice, probably because I was overwhelmed by the whole situation. I had been brought up to believe that you get married and lived happily ever after, yet there I was, constantly in the middle of a battleground. Everyone was eager to tell me what they would do in my place and every sentence started with 'if I were you'. The problem with people who say this is that they later go ahead and do precisely what they had told you not to do.

I was delighted to fall pregnant and thought that may be the end of our problems and a new beginning, as perhaps a child would bring us closer together. That didn't happen and I had post-natal depression. Unfortunately, this was neither diagnosed nor recognised. I used to disappear for a whole day and wander the streets aimlessly, leaving Ilana, my young baby daughter, with my husband. I was crying all the time for no reason. My family thought I was just being difficult and could not understand why I was behaving that way.

We decided to emigrate to Israel and I was pregnant

again with my second child Daniel. I had agreed to the move because my husband had been relentless about it for a while and it seemed easier to give in. The marital home was sold and I was supposed to stay at my parents' for a couple of weeks until our departure, while he went to his parents'. It later transpired that he had never intended to move to Israel, but had deliberately sold the house, which was in his name, because he had wrongly thought that I was going to divorce him. That had never been my intention at the time. The two weeks stretched to two and a half years.

It was very hard living at my parents' and I was not happy. I shared a bedroom with my daughter and baby son. My parents clearly did not want me there and had never expected to have their married daughter, a young toddler and a baby living with them indefinitely. The atmosphere was often tense and my father could be harsh at times. I felt an utter failure, especially as all my friends were married and seemingly happy; I hadn't managed that and didn't even have a home of my own. The one thing I looked forward to was going to my uncle Victor and my aunt Nina's every Sunday afternoon.

I would like to pay a special tribute to Aunt Nina. She and my uncle Victor were very close, as they had no children. She came from a relatively wealthy family and had never had to lift a finger while in Egypt. My mother and her family always underestimated her and were dismissive of her. She proved them wrong when we came to England and adapted well, in spite of all the hardships. When Uncle Victor passed away suddenly, she was devastated but managed to build a new life, all the time feeling lonely. She was always dignified, never complained and was a lady in the true sense of the word. Her wisdom meant that I could always rely on her to give me good advice. She died tragically in a hit and run accident and, together with my aunt Sophie, is the family member I still miss most.

When she died, my cousin Doris, Nicole and I spent a couple of Sundays clearing her house. We gave everything to charity, but for some reason I kept an oil painting which appealed to me, probably because it depicts a Paris street at night. I am so glad I did – the painting now has pride of place in our lounge and, every time I look at it, I am reminded of my dear uncle and aunt.

I was eventually reunited with my husband. By then, his mother had died and he was staying with his father and brother in a small flat in Temple Fortune in North West London, not far from my parents. The flat was very small, and living with my in-laws was another unmitigated disaster. After a while, we moved to a rented house in Bushey in Hertfordshire. My husband had made it a condition of moving that I cut off all contact with my parents. I complied, but I found it increasingly difficult as I did not know anyone in the area and missed my family.

I did some home typing, starting late in the evening after the children had gone to bed and working until the early hours of the morning, so I was physically exhausted. I took too many pills once and ended up in hospital. It was treated as attempted suicide, but the gesture was merely a cry for help and only intended to attract my husband's attention. It made no difference, but fortunately, the doctor who examined me recognised that I was at the end of my tether. He insisted that I join a therapy group at the psychiatric unit of Watford General hospital.

My husband left suddenly, and I found out that he had not been paying the rent for months, which meant that we were going to be evicted. We were homeless and going back to my parents was of course out of the question. All this was taking place around Christmas time. On Christmas Eve, there was a knock on the door – it was the Salvation Army, who wanted to know if I needed food and a turkey. I didn't, as I was spending Christmas with my parents, but I was very touched by their gesture and their kindness. I have supported their organisation ever since.

The Council stepped in and rehoused us. It was a small house where an old lady had lived for years and it had been badly neglected. Someone said that it would need a lot of elbow grease to get it looking decent and, still not familiar with some English expressions, I asked where I could buy elbow grease! With the help and support of people I had met at the psychiatric unit, staff as well as patients, we painted the house and made it look acceptable. The Salvation Army stepped in again and donated beds, blankets and furniture.

The group therapy helped, but there were many other things going on. The divorce was acrimonious and my husband fought for custody of the children. He was not successful, but all the stress of the previous years took its toll. I left the group therapy too soon, in spite of being advised not to. I could not cope with what was going on in there – two friends had died after taking an overdose, another one was killed while driving her bike and someone who had been very supportive committed suicide. I was very affected by all this and decided to stop going. The therapist in my group begged me not to leave, saying that I was not ready and had never explored the relationship with my mother. I refused to listen and at the time still thought that this was not a problem.

To complicate things, I had wrongly befriended another patient in my therapy group. To all intents and purposes, this lady seemed fairly balanced, but she had her own agenda and deliberately caused me a lot of harm. She pretended that she could read the future and predicted that something I wished for dearly was going to happen. It seems incredible now, but I was quite disturbed at the time and I believed her, even when the evidence was before me and I knew that she was not making sense. I carried on trusting her, all the time getting more and more desperate. Had I been my normal self or rational, I would have seen through all the nonsense. Eventually, I saw the light and confronted her. She admitted that she had made everything up, as she had thought that I would not be her friend otherwise. The sad thing is that in the end she lost my friendship, whilst doing a great deal of harm.

Somewhere along the line I had a breakdown. At the time, I did not realise this was happening. I started to behave strangely – taking far too many tranquillisers, going off the rails or simply sitting in the armchair for hours unable to move. I was going through the motions, mostly in a blur and unfortunately my children suffered a great deal as a result. It's a miracle that I didn't set the house on fire, as I was smoking and sometimes dozing off with a cigarette in my hand. I find it difficult and painful to remember this period of my life. The children went to their father every other weekend and he looked after them well, regularly taking them out to the cinema or for a meal, something I never did. My family were supportive in their own way – Ilana stayed with Nicole, and Daniel with my parents, when they were not with their father.

The house we had initially been given by the council was down for demolition within a few months of us moving in. We were allocated a ground floor flat not too far away and after a year we were moved again, this time to a brand new house on a council estate. It was a lovely house, and all the neighbours were friendly.

I recovered from my breakdown, though it took a while. The dead end hopeless relationships I got involved in did not help. Eventually, I summoned up the courage to start studying for an A Level in Law. I enjoyed the course and the tutor suggested I should continue and go to university to get a Law degree. At first I dismissed the idea as ludicrous, but came round to it slowly. I prepared myself for a year beforehand, saving as much as I could by cleaning private houses every day. I had to decide between University of London and Middlesex University and opted for the latter, as the Law campus was in Hendon, not far from where my parents lived, which was very convenient. I enjoyed the three years of my degree, as I met new people and challenged my mind. I was a mature student, so my fellow students were much younger than me, but that didn't matter, as they were very friendly.

In spite of achieving academic success, I really wish I had not spent three years studying. Although I was very interested in all aspects of the law, one of my reasons for going to university as a mature student was to prove something, to myself first, but also to my family. My divorce and subsequent breakdown had made me feel like a massive failure and it was probably how my family saw me. However, because I don't know how to do things in half measures, all I did for three years was study, neglecting my children once again.

They were still very young – Ilana was 13 and Daniel 10. They paid the price for my overly ambitious need to prove something. During the week, I went to the campus every day and spent all afternoon in the library. The journey home was long and I didn't get back until early evening. Weekends were spent studying, starting at 6.30 am and finishing around 7.00 pm. During that time, the children were required to be quiet – they could not watch television, as I was in the living room, nor could they play the radio or make any noise, as I found that too distracting. It seems incredible now that I could have expected this from young children for three long years.

The question I ask myself now is whether this law degree was worth the sacrifice. To restore some of my self-confidence, the answer is yes, but for everything else the answer is an emphatic no. This should have been my chance to rebuild my relationship with my children, after neglecting them for so long during my breakdown. It would have been far better if I had looked for a job and spent quality time with them at weekends.

In any case, apart from the momentary glory of getting a First Class degree, it did not really change my life and I did not manage to get a job in the field of law; a degree on its own was not enough and I did not want to continue with my law studies. I was exhausted, needed to start earning money, and at 43, the thought of spending a further two years studying to be a solicitor was daunting. I settled for a job in a Life Assurance company dealing with pensions, but never settled there. I was a Customer Service assistant and the job itself was as boring as it sounds. However, I don't like change and generally avoid it if possible, so I stayed with the company for seven years, until we were all made redundant and our branch was closed down.

The women in the company had decided to resent me even before I joined and had lots of preconceived ideas about me. They had been told that I had a law degree and they immediately assumed that I would feel superior to them and behave accordingly. Nothing was further from my mind. However, the cultural differences between us were obvious right from the beginning, notably, the one between my multi-cultural upbringing and theirs, which was very insular. The furthest they had been outside England was to Spain or the Balearic Islands. They hated the fact that I was better educated and spoke several languages. The way they dealt with it was to constantly make fun of me – what I wore, what I said, who I went out with. To an outsider, it would have been seen as harmless banter, but it was bullying and it was constant. The way the office was laid out did not help; my tormentors were six women and they all sat together along one long table. I sat on my own at the opposite side of the office, with my assistant. One woman in particular thought it was okay to constantly make fun of me and the others followed her lead. I should have left, but by then I had bought my house and the mortgage had to be paid.

My next job was a great improvement. The company conducted research projects for life assurance companies in the UK and all over Europe. I had an opportunity to use my French and went to Paris regularly to take notes for committee meetings. I was the General Manager's Personal Assistant and we got on very well. My main responsibility was to organise an important annual meeting attended by the Chief Executives of all the main life assurance companies in the UK and in Europe. The meeting took place in a different European city every year and was always held in a 5-star hotel. I enjoyed travelling to places and staying in fabulous hotels.

I remember one particular hotel in Oslo. I had breakfast in my room and every morning, among other stuff, there was a huge plate of smoked salmon and scrambled eggs on the trolley, enough to feed four people. I ate what I could, but could not bear to throw away the rest, so it went in the fridge. I did that day after day and finally had throw the whole lot away before leaving. We had reindeer one evening, which was considered a delicacy, but it was tough and tasteless. Lisbon and Madrid also hold good memories, as both times, we stayed at a Ritz hotel. Wherever the annual meeting was held, I always arranged to arrive a couple of days early and stay over after the meeting was finished, so I managed to explore a few European capitals.

These meetings were a huge challenge to organise and, apart from the logistics, you had to make sure that you did not offend any of the delegates in any way, even unintentionally – they were all Chief Executives of large insurance company and expected to be treated with huge deference. The biggest logistic nightmare was something called the Gala Dinner. That was the highlight of the meeting, where important guest speakers gave motivational talks. The delegates were seated at tables of 12 and, since they insisted on sitting only with delegates from their country, there was no question of mixing the nationalities. The problem arose when there were 13 or 14 from the same country and you had to decide how and where to place the extra people. The wrong choice could have grave consequences and there were constant changes as people registered at the last minute and others dropped out. Nevertheless, I loved the challenge and always experienced a sense of anti-climax when the meeting was over.

Return to Cairo, a trip down memory lane

I went back to Egypt for the first time in 1994. The holiday was a seven-day Nile cruise starting in Luxor and ending in Aswan, with a two-day break in Cairo. As soon as we got on the boat, I dropped my guard with regard to food. I believed that I could eat whatever I liked because I had grown up in Egypt and therefore, unlike my fellow passengers, I had some immunity. I bought some fresh dates in a market in Aswan and washed them with tap water in the cabin – that was polluted Nile water and I was sick for the rest of the trip.

The holiday triggered a lot of memories and it was a difficult trip, as I was constantly torn between trying to find the world I had known and remembered, and the reality of a new and different Egypt. When we had left Cairo, it had been a beautiful and relatively quiet city, once known as the Paris of the Middle East. I had returned to find a very different one – the elegance had disappeared, gone forever and the wide boulevards which I remembered from my childhood had been replaced by overcrowded streets, chaotic traffic and the incessant honking of cars.

I was sad to admit that the Egypt I had known no longer existed. Everywhere was crowded, the numerous shops sold cheap gear, all the signs were in Arabic and the air was so polluted that all you could see from the balcony of our hotel was a haze. Gone forever was the Cairo of my childhood. Instead, there were modern 20-storey buildings and elevated highways. There were still feluccas on the Nile, but also many speedboats.

We stayed at the Hilton hotel in downtown Cairo and had a room on the sixth floor with a balcony. The view of Cairo from the balcony was great – at least, it would have been if it had not been permanently spoilt by a haze, due to all the pollution in the city. The hotel was situated in a busy elevated highway. To get to the shopping area in central Cairo, you had to cross four roads, each busier than the other. There did not seem to be any traffic lights, or if there were any it must have been just for show, as no driver respected them. To cross each road, you had to take your life in your hands. It was scary and I decided that the safest way to cross was to do so by remaining behind an old lady and following her.

This worked up to a point, until a young man came over and offered to help us cross. I assumed he was being kind, but suddenly he pulled me by the hand, calling me 'sister' and urged us to follow him. We ended up in a very small shop nearby and it became clear that he wanted to sell us some cheap perfume; he was obviously adept at luring tourists who looked lost by offering to help them. We did not feel threatened, just inconvenienced and we hastily ran out of the shop when he went to fetch some stock!

The next stop was Groppi, the tearoom I had loved so much as a child. It was still there and the neon sign looked the same, but that is as far as it went. Inside, the sophistication that had been Groppi had disappeared completely. There was a very limited choice of pastries and drinks, and a couple of counters with a few sad-looking chocolates. The staff were unprofessional, the tables and floor uncleared and the decor was drab. I asked for a coffee with milk, but they could not provide this, only lemon. There were no reminders of Groppi's past glory, only evidence of mismanagement and indifference.

When I had lived in Cairo, it had been common for Egyptian women to appear in public unveiled and in Western clothes. What I was seeing from the window of our taxi were young women in Islamic dress. Gone were the colourful, western style dresses their mothers and grandmothers had worn; instead, they were wearing mainly long or ankle length skirts, long sleeved blouses and a headscarf.

We took a ride outside downtown Cairo to the Meadi district. This had once been an area where well-to-do Europeans had lived and was now practically unrecognisable. It had become a middle class neighbourhood with small villas with gardens. I have an Egyptian friend who knows many people living in Cairo. She tells me that they are all moving to the Meadi and Zamalek districts; they have young families and Cairo itself has become so chaotic and polluted that no one wants to live there if they can help it.

It was a shock to see soldiers with bayonets standing at the entrance door of all the tourist sites. I had felt rather uneasy when we had visited the tombs in the Valley of the

Kings during our Nile cruise, especially when we had gone down inside one of them. It was an essential part of our cultural itinerary but, in this vast open area, you could not help but fear the possibility of a terrorist attack. When I had lived in Egypt, you could just walk through to the Pyramids and the Sphinx. This was no longer so, they were fenced off, you had to pay an entrance fee and there was security everywhere.

At the time of the 1952 revolution, Cairo's population was around two million people. It has since then exploded, and it is estimated that between 14 and 20 million people now call the capital their home. The city I was seeing during my visit had changed beyond recognition. It had expanded from all sides. Everywhere was built up and it was pointless trying to recognise the wide boulevards and streets I had known. They were now overrun with shops spilling into the pavements and I was surprised to see how many of those sold shoes and how cheap everything was. I could have bought five pairs of leather shoes for the price of one in the UK.

The names of the streets had changed. The elegant Fuad Street was now chaotic and was called 26th July Street. Midan Ismail where Uncle Mayer had lived had become Midan El Tahrir and Midan Soliman Pacha was now Talaat Harb. The imposing statue of the soldier on horseback had been removed and replaced by a statue of the banker Tallat Harb. I tried to imagine the streets beyond and the one where we used to live, all the time feeling sad and nostalgic.

We spent three days in the capital and, after a while, I began to relax. The charm of Cairo started to work and

I didn't even mind the noisy and dirty streets. The longer I stayed, the more I felt at home. I was excited and, in some way, experiencing a second childhood. I became more confident walking through traffic and enjoyed the conversations that were taking place around me. I ate *molokheya* and *ful medames*, drank pure mango juice and bought baklava and *kounafa* from the pastry shops. I was in Egypt and Cairo was still, as it will always be, the city where I was born and had spent my formative years.

I was surprised that I could still understand what was being said when Arabic was spoken. I had grown up hearing Arabic around me and I was used to the colloquial language spoken in the streets. My dilemma was whether I should let on that this was the case. On the one hand I was tempted, as it would have established an instant connection. On the other, I was a little wary as it was clear that I was not Egyptian and I would probably have to give details of when we had left and why. The other person might guess that I was Jewish and I wasn't sure if that was safe. I have since read about the experiences of Egyptian Jews returning to Egypt and how most of them have been welcomed with open arms, but that would not necessarily have been the case in 1994. Besides, there was a certain advantage in being able to understand what was being said without letting on, especially if you are a tourist.

During my visit, I wanted to try and find the block of flats where we had lived. Once at Soliman Pasha Square in the heart of the city, I was amazed that, without an address or any idea of where I was heading, I started walking and almost as if blindfolded arrived at the street where we had lived, which was called Rue Cherifen at the time. I stopped at the corner of the street and looked up – there was the apartment building, exactly as I remembered it. I just stood there and started crying.

There was a travel agency next to the block of flats and someone came out and asked if I was okay. When I explained that I had lived there many years ago, the gentleman insisted on taking me inside his shop and offering me a coffee; that was the kindness of Egyptians which I remembered well. He offered to take me up to the flat where we had lived but I refused, not wanting to disturb the residents. I have regretted it ever since.

My search for the Maimonides synagogue, also known as the Rav Moshe synagogue, proved less fruitful. I was also eager to see if I could find any vestige of the long-gone Jewish community which had once lived in Haret El Yahoud, the Jewish quarter. I knew it was in the Muski neighbourhood but, when we finally found it, I realised that the area had been turned into a market. The synagogue was tiny and at the back of the market. It was covered in garbage and graffiti, and the windows were broken. This was where one of the most famous Jewish thinkers had worshipped, yet the site felt anything but holy or historic. Since then, the Egyptian government has financed a $2 million, 18 months restoration project which was finished in March 2010. Along with the tomb of Maimonides, the synagogue contains many treasures, one of which is a Bible which was allegedly written by Maimonides himself.

The Egyptian Museum of Antiquities – the Cairo Museum – is one of the first places tourists visit when in

Cairo. It is located in the city centre in Tahrir Square and its holdings include some of the finest antiquities discovered in Egypt, including royal mummies and the treasure of Tutankhamun. Incredibly, we were never taken there when we had lived in Cairo, but thankfully, I managed to find the time for a visit. There was so much stuff, it was quite overwhelming, but the most striking displays were the numerous boats designed to transport the souls of the dead Ancient Egyptians to the other world.

We also went to the Khan Khalili market. Even for a seasoned ex-Egyptian like me, which is how I like to identify myself, it was an overwhelming experience. The market was so packed you could hardly move. Music blared everywhere, a different tune from every shop, thus creating something of a cacophony. The winding streets were packed with storefronts selling anything and everything that would appeal to tourists. The most attractive were the polished wooden boxes and the small tables intricately inlaid with geometric patterns in mother-of-pearl and bone. Other shops sold carpets, rugs and copper pots. Men in *galabeyas* (caftans) were sipping cups of Turkish coffee in an outdoor cafe, intently hunched over a backgammon board or smoking a shisha – that was a familiar sight which I remembered well.

The Cairo Citadel was built by Saladin and is famous for the amazing panoramic outlook you get from the upper esplanade. I am very glad that I managed a quick visit during our stay and it was well worth it; the view of Cairo spread before us was amazing and you could see all the landmarks, the Nile and all the minarets poking up to the sky. The interior of Saladin's mosque was magical with its sparkling lights.

Many positive changes have taken place since my visit. Of the 80,000 strong Jewish community who lived in Egypt, only four Jews remain in Cairo as of April 2020. In spite of this, the Ministry of Antiquities has insisted on taking on the restoration of the 12 synagogues. According to Magda Haroun, the present Head of the Cairo Jewish Community, these will be designated 'Historical Monuments of Ancient Egypt'. She is reassured that the Egyptian government has enshrined in their constitution that the synagogues and documents are protected by the Ministry of Antiquities, in case of a change of government and the possible arrival of an Islamist one.

Cairo's Bassatine cemetery is believed to be the second oldest in the world, only surpassed by the cemetery at the Mount of Olives in Jerusalem; it dates back to the 9th century and lies in the southeast of Cairo. Although the diversity of tombs of all different periods of Egypt's history is remarkable, very little from the cemetery remains. Following the abrupt decline of Egypt's Jewish community in the mid-20th century, the cemetery entered a process of degradation and suffered substantial damage. This was due mainly to the negligence of the authorities, but also to the settlement of squatters and the theft of most of the graves' marble slabs.

The efforts to keep and restore the site only really started with the Drop of Milk organisation in 2017. In September 2020, a small but significant restoration project was completed. In addition to the government recently taking action to document and protect the country's Jewish heritage, the Bassatine cemetery can increase the world's understanding of this.

The main temple in Cairo,The Ismailieh synagogue, has recently been renovated. It is now called Shar Hashamayim and is open for services and visits. Most of the Torah scrolls left behind cannot be taken out of Egypt, as the government considers them to be 'Egyptian relics'. I would love to revisit the synagogue and it would be an emotional experience, as the memories would come flooding back; this is where we worshipped and where my parents and all my family members were married.

Thanks mainly to the efforts of the current Egyptian President Abdel Fattah el-Sissi, the Eliahou Hanabi synagogue in Alexandria has been restored to its former magnificence. Maimonides is said to have worshipped there, though the building is not the actual one where he prayed. The synagogue was apparently burned by Napoloeon's troops in 1798 and rebuilt in the 1850s by an Italian architect in a Classical style, with a tall Carrara marble colonnade. Mohamed Ali is said to have contributed financially towards its rebuilding, as did Sir Moses Montefiore and other benefactors.

The weekend of 16 February 2020 marked the largest Jewish prayer gathering in Egypt for decades. From across the diaspora, some 180 Jews of Egyptian origin flew to the land of their fathers for a Shabbat dedicated to marking the newly restored 14th century synagogue. I can only imagine how emotional it must have been for all those guests to sit where their fathers and grandfathers had worshipped and to step back in time.

The Ben Ezra synagogue in Fustat in old Cairo has also been renovated. It is now a historical monument and one of the most visited Jewish sites in Cairo. According to local folklore, the synagogue is located on the site where the baby Moses was found. It is said that several of the biblical prophets have lingered there – Jeremiah was buried beneath the temple's stone foundation.

This is also the synagogue where, in the 19th century, its Geniza, or storeroom, was found to contain a treasure of forgotten, stored away Hebrew, Aramaic and Judeo Arabic secular and sacred manuscripts. It is known as The Cairo Genizah and is a collection of the 400,000 fragments and documents which were found in the storeroom of the synagogue. They had lain undiscovered for many decades, in fulfilment of a rabbinic prohibition against the destruction of sacred texts. Documents, worn out Jewish books and other writings had continuously been placed in the genizah since the Middle Ages, awaiting burial.

With the approval of the then Chief Rabbi of Cairo, the majority of the hundreds and thousands of document fragments were removed and taken to Cambridge University. Known as the Taylor-Schechter Genizah, it is a treasure trove of priceless Jewish manuscripts, containing examples of practically every kind of written text produced by the Jewish communities of Cairo, Damascus, Jerusalem and elsewhere over a period of more than 1000 years.

The Egyptian President has promised to build new synagogues if Jews return to Egypt and has also pledged to fully restore the ninth century Bassatine cemetery, which is the oldest Jewish cemetery in the world. Tempting as this offer is, I doubt that any Jews will return to live in Egypt. My parents' generation, which was the most affected by our forced exodus, has now gone. People from my generation are too old to uproot themselves again and the younger ones would not be interested; they are fully integrated in whatever country they live in and see Egypt as some exotic faraway place where their parents lived once upon a time.

In January 2011, the eyes of the world were focused on Tahrir Square in Cairo. I looked at the Egyptians, young and old, men and women, seeking to oust the old order and calling for freedom and democracy. They were challenging authoritarianism and hoping to make their country a more tolerant one. The world sympathised with them and urged them on. So did I of course, but for me, the demonstrations had a special meaning. I felt emotional, as those people were probably the children and grandchildren of the generation I had known. Watching them, I hoped that Egypt would finally manage to free itself from the shackles of its dictators and become what it had been promised for a long time: a democracy. The jury is still out on this, but there is hope. Secular forces have reasserted themselves and Egypt may ultimately be able to progress socially and economically. Perhaps, in time, it will also remember its Jewish community, because we certainly have not forgotten the country where we grew up.

In 2014, a documentary was released in the US called 'Jews of Egypt, Erasure and Exodus: The forgotten history of the Jews of Egypt'. The film concentrates on the period of time between the creation of Israel in 1948 and the Suez crisis of 1956 – seen by some as the transition between the cosmopolitan Egypt of old and the modern Egypt of the 21st century, characterised by intolerance. The director of the film, Amir Ramses, states that the popular 'association of Arab Jews with Israeli policy is what caused the situation we are currently living in'. Street interviews at the beginning of the film show that a few years before the 2011 Egyptian revolution, many Egyptians did not know about Egyptian Jews and the few that did rejected them as Zionists. It is sad that there are millions who forgot that a thriving Jewish community once existed in their country. On a more positive note, Amir Ramses states that, since the revolution of 2011, groups of enlightened Egyptians have begun to embrace the diversity of their national identity.

The final chapter

My father retired when he was 65. Many women get
very anxious at the prospect of their daily routine
suddenly changing with a husband at home every day. My
mother took it in her stride, as she did everything else, and
adapted to my father's timetable, rather than the other way
round. He used to have breakfast late, around 10.00 am
and she had to wait until the breakfast table was cleared
before she could start with her chores. Lunch could be
any time between 1.00 and 3.00 pm, depending when my
father had been. He liked going out every day, mainly to
the supermarkets in Golders Green and he often took the
underground to go to the fruit and vegetable market in
Soho or to Fratelli Camisa, his favourite Italian delicatessen.
He always seemed to find somewhere to go or something
to do and, although he had no hobbies, he was happy in
his retirement.

My mother displayed endless patience when it came
to my father. He was a very bad timekeeper and was always
late for everything. If they were going out anywhere, she
was always ready on time and he kept her waiting forever.
She had even devised a little subterfuge, whereby she would
lie and bring forward the time they were supposed to leave

the house, in the hope that this would ensure that they left on time, but it made no difference. Going on holiday was the worst, as he left it so late, there was always a real risk they would miss the train or the plane. To this day, I have not managed to work out the reason for my father's behaviour, all I know is that it made him and my mother unnecessarily stressed.

I have very good memories of regular visits to Aunt Sophie and Uncle Leon in Paris and when the children grew up and eventually left home, I was able to visit them twice a year. It was very straightforward to get to Paris on the Eurostar and, although my aunt lived on the outskirts of Paris, the RER made it very easy to get to her house. We had a routine which suited me well. In the morning, my uncle gave me a lift to the station and I spent the day wandering around Paris. I knew my way round well and loved the city, so I thoroughly enjoyed the opportunity to explore it further, always stopping once or twice at a patisserie.

In the evening, after dinner, I had long chats with my aunt. My only regret is that I never asked her anything about the family. That was a missed opportunity and I could have found out so much more. Unfortunately, my aunt was bipolar; that meant that she had three months when she was hyperactive and bubbly, then suddenly overnight she plunged into a deep depression and took to her bed. It was a difficult situation for my uncle to manage and of course, I could only visit when she was well. Uncle Leon had a great sense of humour and was very witty, as well as wise. He was famous for his one-liners, which he delivered matter of fact and with a straight face. I often found myself sitting on the Eurostar back to London, smiling as I remembered something funny he had said the evening before.

When they had first arrived in Paris and before they moved to the suburbs, my aunt and uncle had lived in a tiny two-bedroom flat in the centre of Paris. There was no bathroom and the toilet was in the hallway. It must have been very uncomfortable and a far cry from the life she had known in Cairo, but my aunt never complained. Instead, she spent most of her time cleaning the small flat and trying to make it as presentable as possible.

She was another example of the courage and perseverance of the Jewish community after they left Egypt – most of them adapted remarkably well to their new lives, even though there were many hardships and challenges. The flat may have been small and uncomfortable, but my aunt was always happy to have regular visits from the family and welcomed us with open arms. We all loved the fact that it was ideally placed and within walking distance of many attractions. Everything was on the doorstep and my father especially enjoyed his visits. My uncle was very amused by one particular incident concerning me. Apparently, I had left my toothbrush behind once and wrote to him asking him to send it to me. He used to tease me about it, and it was indeed a silly request, but I was quite young at the time.

I retired at 60 and met Mike, my second husband, a few years later on a singles holiday to Cuba. By then, I had given up hope of meeting anyone – I had had a seven year relationship which had ended badly and had been on a few blind dates which had always been disappointing, for one reason or another. Mike lived in Bristol, I in Hertfordshire, but selling my house and moving to Bristol was an easy decision. Looking back, it was a risk but it did not feel that way; it felt right and we got married a few months after. I am thankful that, after a bad marriage and a few disastrous relationships, I have finally met the right person.

As you get older, you have more time to reflect on the past and see things in a more detached way. I realise now that, contrary to what I thought at the time, my mother was the strong one in her marriage. One word to describe her is phlegmatic. She managed to brush things aside whenever confronted in the belief that, if she denied something, it had not happened; for instance, she always refused to admit that she had actively encouraged me to marry my first husband. She had many friends bur never confided in any of them, as she felt that there was no need to share what was going on in her life with anyone. She was very hard working and just wanted to make the best of everything.

I think she never forgot her difficult upbringing, as she was always reluctant to spend money, even on herself. When she got older, we all tried to encourage her to have a treat now and then, such as a new dress or meeting with a friend outside for a coffee. She would agree with us, but in the end never do it. Instead, even when she lived on her own and didn't eat much, she regularly went to the local greengrocer and bought lots of vegetables and fruit that had seen better days, simply because they were going cheap. The greengrocer was called Carmel and the young owner knew my mother well.

Both my parents were hoarders but in a different way. With my mother, it was special offers. She bought more than needed of something because it was on special offer and then never get round to using it. When we cleared her flat after she had passed away, we found jams and cornflakes packets that were ten years out of date. Some of the jam jars still had the 'gollywog' logo, which had become politically incorrect many years before.

As my father had worked for John Dickinson, the paper merchants and stationers, he had regularly brought home all sorts of stationery, writing pads, wads of paper and envelopes. He had kept them in the loft, along with a variety of other items. When we cleared it after he died, we found reams of paper and other stationery items, none of them of any use, as they were totally discoloured with age. Much to my surprise, I also found out that my father had kept every single birthday card he had received from us over the years. They were all in the sideboard in the dining room and every single card still contained the money we had given him as his present. This upset me, as I felt that he should have enjoyed spending this money.

There must have been some superstition attached to his reluctance to spend that money. If asked, he would not have admitted to that and given some vague reason. Similarly, he refused to make a will. We kept entreating him to do so, but he kept putting it off and again, that was probably due to some superstition. However, as it turned out, we needn't have worried; after he died, we found out that he had made sure everything he owned was in joint names, so it was all straightforward and we didn't have to sort out his finances.

After my father passed away, I visited my mother every Saturday and chatted with her on the phone every day. The conversation was mostly general and about mundane things. I am glad that I was able to do so, as I know she enjoyed our conversations and my visits meant a lot to her. In any case, I could not have done it any other way – Jewish Egyptians believed that it was the duty of the children to take care of elderly parents in one way or another. My mother had a very close relationship with Claudine, who always remained the baby of the family. My sister was devastated when my mother passed away and never quite got over her loss. I was a little more philosophical, probably because I had grieved a lot when my father had died a few years earlier.

He died of a major heart attack. I had seen him on the previous Saturday and he was fine. The following Thursday, I received a phone call at the office from Nicole, telling me that he had passed away and I remember screaming. Some colleagues took me to my parents' house, and everything happened very quickly after that. My mother had prepared the breakfast table as she did every morning, waiting for my father to come downstairs. It was strange seeing it all still laid out, with his glasses still on the table. Everything felt surreal and we were all on auto pilot for the rest of that day.

The funeral took place the next morning, as required by Jewish law. Everything was a blur, but I will never forget the shock when the rabbi tore a piece of the shirt I was wearing – this was in accordance with the Jewish funeral custom of kriah (the Hebrew word for tearing) when a rabbi tears a small piece of the garment of immediate family members. I should have expected that but in my grief, I had forgotten it was coming.

We sat shiva for the required seven days and it was

important for us to do so. We were grateful for the visitors who came to offer their condolences and help us through our first days of shock and grief. They brought food and kind words, and we exchanged memories of my father. I remember in particular my cousin Doris bringing some smoked salmon and cream cheese; it was very welcome and we needed to eat, in spite of our grief.

There was a minyan for prayers every night. I was very emotional and I remember one incident which upset me a lot. My mother decided to share out a few personal items which had been important to my father. I had had no idea that she was going to do this, as I had been upstairs at the time, sorting through some of my father's paperwork. When I came downstairs, I found out that she had given my father's prayer book and tallit (prayer shawl) to Nicole and my father's ring with the blue pearl to Claudine. I was offered his key ring, which meant a lot less. I went into the dining room, closed the door and cried my eyes out.

Perhaps I needed a reason to cry and perhaps it didn't matter what I had to remember my father by, so long as I had something; nevertheless, at that particular moment I was hurt. At the end of the week of shiva, I went out and felt completely dazed and lost. It was the 22nd December and people were rushing around excitedly, doing their last minute shopping before Christmas. It made me feel even more sad and forlorn. The next six months were hard. I went back to work after Christmas and normal life seemed to resume. I coped well during the week but every Sunday I shut myself away in the kitchen and cried my eyes out.

After my divorce, I had cut myself off from everything

Jewish. In my mind, I had tried to conform to what had been expected of me by marrying someone of the same faith. It hadn't worked out and somehow I managed to blame my religion for this. I refused to attend any Seders at my parents' house, did not celebrate Rosh Hashanah or Yom Kippur and did not observe Pesach. I was angry that I had bought the fairy tale of happy ever after and felt a failure because my marriage hadn't worked out.

Jewish festivals are essentially about family, so avoiding them was the less painful option. I was aware that this was hurting my father, but I didn't care. It was more important to protect myself. Also, by then most of the festivals were celebrated at Nicole's house – she had a big house and a large dining table which could sit many people, and she was also a very good cook. Eventually, when I got my life back together, I was able to participate again. I am glad that, in the last years of his life, my father celebrated many festivals with my children and me.

My mother's death was fairly quick. I had been speaking to her on the phone one Monday and noticed a change in her during the conversation – suddenly, she sounded vague and disoriented. I alerted Nicole who lived nearby and it turned out my mother had suffered a brain haemorrhage. She was still semi-conscious when I got to the hospital and she managed to squeeze my hand, but she suffered a second stroke soon after. I stayed with her for the night, and Claudine and I were there when she died.

I have never doubted that my father loved me. However, he was overprotective and was convinced that he was always right – his way was the only way, at least with me. So, when he gave me advice during my first marriage, I didn't think to question it, I just followed it. He was bound to be right and I was the one making the mistakes. When I succeeded in getting a Law degree, I thought that he may see me in a different light and perhaps he did. Nevertheless, I was surprised to find out, quite by chance, that he used to visit Nicole regularly every Sunday morning. It wasn't just a social visit, as apparently he discussed his problems with her and asked for her advice. This went on for years, but I didn't know about it, though Daniel knew, as he used to stay with my parents some weekends. Nicole assures me that one of the reasons was that she lived nearer to him and he could get to her by underground. I wish he was still around so I could ask him why he felt that he could not come to visit me, at least once in a while. Another question that will never get an answer.

It is still difficult to understand why my father wanted to control me. I think his need stemmed from his own anxieties and insecurities. Sometimes, he insisted on knowing things which appeared totally unnecessary. For instance, he always asked as many details as possible if I went abroad on holiday and this continued long after I married and divorced. I had to give him the flight details and hotel phone numbers, as there were no mobile phones then. It was frustrating, but I didn't mind humouring him. It seemed an easy way to keep him happy and in one instance it turned out to be useful. I was on holiday in Tel Aviv when a bomb exploded at 10.00 am on a bus in Dizinghoff Street, right in the city centre. I was staying very near there, in fact I had been returning from the market when the bomb exploded, but fortunately I had been walking along a parallel street. My father heard the news, understandably panicked and phoned me at the hotel. It was fortunate that he had the number and I was able to reassure him instantly.

I am like my father in this respect, although it does not work in my case. When my children got older, they refused to give me details of their trips if they went away, and saw the request as controlling and unnecessary. What they didn't understand was that it had nothing to do with control, it was just a way of managing my own anxieties. All I was looking for was the reassurance that, if anything happened or I needed to get in contact, I could do so.

Claudine sadly passed away in 2016 at the age of 66. She was my younger sister and I had always felt protective towards her. The pain of her loss has dulled a little, but I miss her every day and I still have to pinch myself when my guard is down, and I remember that she is no longer here. I have put the pain away 'in a box' so to speak and I dare not open it too often. She was a gentle soul who didn't expect anything from anyone and would not have harmed a fly. She was always on the outside looking in and was often taken advantage of in the workplace, probably because people knew that she would not speak up or retaliate.

I have one memory of her as a child which I find very poignant. She was only about eight years old when we moved to our house in Hendon. My mother used to go out every Wednesday to play cards and Claudine would come back from school and just stand at the window of the living room waiting for her to return. She always remained the baby of the family and had a very close relationship with my mother, who was my sister's only friend. Claudine always went to her for advice and they talked for ages. This may sound strange, but my sister never felt the need to have friends and, like my mother, did not trust close friendships.

As well as feeling the sadness of her loss, I live with the regret my sister died alone and under very difficult circumstances. She had finally got married in her late thirties, to a man seven years her junior. He did not want children, so they didn't have any. They were happy for many years – there is that consolation at least – but things went downhill when she took early retirement. Her husband changed overnight, had affairs and constantly bullied her. Despite all that, she wanted to hang on to the marriage and agreed to sell their bungalow in North London and move to Yorkshire with him, believing his promise that all would be well again and he would look after her.

By then she had been diagnosed with terminal cancer, perhaps brought on by all the stress. As soon as they moved to West Yorkshire, her husband changed again and did not support her in any way, shape or form. More than that, he bullied her constantly and every day thought of new ways to upset her. I will never understand how someone can harbour so much hatred and resentment towards another human being, especially when that person is dying. We had to watch helplessly from afar, unable to do anything apart from visiting her when we could. To this day I think of her whenever I make *borekas*, the small Sephardic pastries. She loved them filled with cheese and I always took some with me; even towards the very end, she managed to have a bite.

I did not go up to Yorkshire to see her when she was

finally taken to hospital, when I knew she only had a couple of days left. I was a coward and the excuse I gave myself was that I wanted to remember her as she was the last time I had seen her, only a week before – she had still been in her bungalow then, had given me a hug and said goodbye normally, as if we were going to see each other again very soon. We both knew that it was the last time and I remember getting in the car in a daze. She died alone and this will always haunt me, as I should have been there to hold her hand; she may have lost consciousness by then, but I think at some level she would have known I was sitting next to her. A very kind nurse was with her until the end, but that does not exonerate me.

Until the pandemic, I had been volunteering for charities which help refugees and asylum seekers. Through this work, I met many lovely ladies from various parts of the Middle East and Africa. I found out that I have a natural affinity with Muslim people, partly because of my life in Egypt and partly because Judaism and Islam have a lot in common. We have many shared values and priorities, and I recognise in them the generosity and sense of hospitality I remember from my childhood. I have a lot of admiration for these ladies – they have been through emotional trauma, or at the very least financial difficulties, but they are always positive and smiling. They have a strong work ethic and are prepared to work hard to give their children a good life.

A couple of years ago, I decided that I wanted to learn Arabic again. I knew a few words but, with time, I had forgotten all the vocabulary. I tried to get a private tutor but didn't get very far. An Egyptian friend suggested that

I should just watch Arabic series on YouTube and assured me that it was the best way to familiarise myself with the language. I didn't believe her initially, but it turns out she was right. After over two years of watching many series – I have lost count of how many – my Arabic has come back and I can now understand most of what is being said. At the beginning, I was making a note of every word, now I just listen. I make sure that I watch one hour of Arabic TV a day, not only to continue learning, but also because it's my way of connecting with Egypt.

A couple of years ago, I decided that I wanted to go back to Cairo and, on the spur of the moment, booked us a couple of flights for the following spring. I also provisionally reserved some hotels. There was a big outcry when I told my family, as they thought it was dangerous for a Jewish person to go to Egypt. I wasn't too worried about this and was more bothered about the fact that arriving at Cairo airport as an independent traveller was supposedly a chaotic experience.

Nevertheless, I carried on with my plans and contacted a private guide who seemed very experienced. He asked me to send him an itinerary of the places I wanted to see during my visit. I did so and included the Shar Hashamayim synagogue in Cairo and the Eliahu Hanavi in Alexandria. The guide replied immediately by email saying that he was very sorry, but he had made a mistake and could not make those dates after all. It was clear that the reason was because he had realised that I am Jewish. I was very disappointed and immediately cancelled our trip. I regret it now, as I am sure not all Egyptians feel the way he does.

I can now acknowledge that, though they loved me, my parents were not good at parenting. They did their best, but that was not necessarily always right. They were the result of their own upbringing and what they thought they did out of love, was often misguided. I can accept this and it does not mean that I love them or miss them any less. I also have tremendous respect for them. The comfortable lifestyle they had known in Egypt was taken away from them almost overnight. They were in their 40s by then and had to start all over again, with very little money and the responsibility of three young children, yet they never complained or expressed regrets for the life they had left behind. Instead, they took the little they had initially and made the best of it. Theirs is the story of many refugees who, against all the odds, have succeeded and given back so much to the country which has welcomed them.

I have made many mistakes which can never be put right. I feel very sad that my children suffered because of this and I wish I could put the clock back. As the saying goes, hindsight is a wonderful thing, but there comes a point in your life when you have to accept your mistakes and learn to live with them. I hope I reach that point one day.

The past is never gone. It's always there and catches up with us when we least expect it. It's what defines us and makes us who we are today. The older I get, the more I realise that growing up in Egypt has been one of the strong influences in my life. My Jewish Egyptian upbringing has often had a bearing on the way I think and behave. It has not always been easy to grapple with different cultures, but I would not have had it any other way.

Friends have suggested that putting down my memories on paper would be cathartic. That was never my intention in the first place – mostly, I wanted to write about my childhood in Cairo and what I remember of it. I also wanted to talk about the wonderful country that Egypt was and still is. The scope gradually widened, and I found myself talking about many other things and thinking about what was and what might have been. The past has made me who I am today, but it's not always easy to accept what has happened or the consequences of one's actions.

Judaism teaches us to remember and to recount the history of our people from generation to generation. This is to remind us of our rich, complicated and often painful heritage and to make sure it's never forgotten. The Passover Seder is such a time of remembrance and recounts the exodus of the Jews from Egypt. In my story, I have attempted to recount my own exodus, as a part of history and for the next generation.

Bibliography

Aciman André. *Out of Egypt,* The Harvill Press 1997

Atira, Nayra. *Zikrayat: Eight Jewish women remember Egypt,* The American University in Cairo Press 2020

Bar-Av (Bentata) Avraham. *17 Sheikh Hamza Street: A Middle Eastern historical fiction,* Avraham Bar-Av (Bentata) 2015

Bigio, Alain. *From Ismaeleya to Higienopolis, The story of an Egyptian Jew,* Alain Bigio, 2nd edition 2014

Carasso, Luciène. *Growing Up in Jewish Alexandria, The story of a Sephardic family's exodus from Egypt,* Interactive International Inc. 2014

Cicurel, Ronald. *Mémoires du Caire, Souvenirs d'enfance d'un grand-père juif d'Egypte,* Editions Sarina, 1st edition 2018

Cohen, Stella. *Stella's Sephardic Table,* The Gerald and Marc Hoberman Collection 2012

Cooper, Artemis. *Cairo in the War 1939-1945,* John Murray (Publishers) 2013

Dammond, Liliane S. *The lost world of the Egyptian Jews,* iUniverse 2007

De Aranjo, Alexandre GA (2013). *Assets and liabilities: refugees from Hungary and* Egypt *in France and in Britain,1956-1960,* PhD thesis, University of Nottingham

Hinaekian, Peggy. *The Girl from Cairo: A Memoir,* Xlibris US 2020

Julius, Lyn. *The Suez crisis and the Jews of Egypt,* Fathom 2017

Lagnado, Lucette. *The Man in the White Sharkskin suit, My family's exodus from old Cairo to the New World,* HarperCollins 2007

Naggar, Jean. *Sipping from the Nile: My Exodus from Egypt,* Lake Union Publishing 2012

Pardo, Albert. *L'Egypte que j'ai connue,* Nahar Misraim, 2ème edition 2004

Roden, Claudia. *The Book of Jewish Food,* Viking 1997

Sardas, Jacques. *Without return, Memoirs of an Egyptian Jew, 1930-1957,* The American University in Cairo Press 2020

Printed in Great Britain
by Amazon